City Gate, Open Up

Bei Dao, wearing his father's sheepskin coat, 1970

City Gate, Open Up

BEI DAO

Translated from the Chinese by Jeffrey Yang

A NEW DIRECTIONS PAPERBOOK ORIGINAL

Manufactured in the United States of America
New Directions Books are printed on acid-free paper
First published as New Directions Paperbook 1371 in 2017
Design by Eileen Baumgartner

Library of Congress Cataloging-in-Publication Data
Bei Dao, 1949– author. | Yang, Jeffrey, translator.
City Gate, Open Up / Bei Dao ; translated by Jeffrey Yang.
Other titles: Cheng men kai. English
Description: New York: New Directions, 2017.
Identifiers: LCCN 2016039663 | ISBN 9780811226431 (alk. paper)
Subjects: LCSH: Bei Dao, 1949– | Poets, Chinese—20th century—Biography.
Classification: LCC PL2892.E525 Z46 2017 | DDC 895.11/52 [B]—dc23

10 9 8 7 6 5 4 3 2 1

New Directions Books are published for James Laughlin
by New Directions Publishing Corporation
80 Eighth Avenue, New York 10011
ndbooks.com

For Tiantian and Dodo

City gate, city gate how tall are you?
Three hundred and sixty feet tall!
What sort of lock is that on you?
A giant iron-diamond lock!
City gate, city gate will you open up or not?

—FROM A NURSERY RHYME

Contents

My Beijing

TOWARD THE END of 2001, my father fell seriously ill and I returned to a Beijing that had been cut off from me for nearly thirteen years. Nothing could have prepared me—it was unthinkable—Beijing had completely changed: Everything was difficult to recognize, nothing familiar. I was a foreigner in my own hometown.

I was born in Beijing and spent half my life there—the momentous years of childhood and adolescence. My experiences of growing up are intimately linked with Beijing. And they've vanished as the city that once was has also vanished.

It was during my return that the impulse to write this book ignited: I would use the written word to rebuild another city, rebuild my Beijing; I would use my Beijing to refute the Beijing of today. In my city, time flows backward, spring revives dead trees, vanished smells waft back with sounds and beams of light, demolished temples are restored with courtyard residences, along hutong streets, tiled roof rows rise in waves toward a low, low horizon line, pigeon-tail whistles echo through the deep blue sky, children appreciate the seasons' transformations, residents are sustained by an inner compass. Welcoming the drifting travelers of the four seas, welcoming the homeless solitary souls, welcoming all inquisitive guests, I open my city gate.

This long-consuming task of rebuilding and reconstruction—I feel it's almost impossible to achieve. Memory—selective, ambiguous, exclusive—can subsist even in a state of prolonged hibernation. Yet writing awakens the process of remembering: Within memory's labyrinth, one passage leads into another passage, one gate opens up to face another gate.

Childhood and adolescence are of enormous significance in one's life; it can even be said that those pivotal years shape or decide nearly everything else that happens after, often long after. Looking back into the wellspring of one's early years is akin to a kind of prehistoric excavation, accompanied by whatever happiness and sorrow are discovered. If escape and return are the two ends of a road, walking even farther means drawing closer to childhood; and it's precisely this primary force that pushes me toward the edge of the sea and sky.

I would like to give a special thanks to Cao Yifan—neighbor, friend, classmate—who not only plays a central role in this book but whose astonishing memory filled in and corrected a large number of crucial details. And of course I must thank Li Tuo and Gan Qi, two "fussy readers" who embolden me to write like I'm always treading on thin ice.

BEI DAO

JUNE 25, 2010, HONG KONG

City Gate, Open Up

Light and Shadow

1

IRETURNED TO THE city of my birth at the end of 2001, after a long, unforeseen parting of thirteen years. As the plane descended, the myriad lights of the houses and buildings rushed into the portholes, whirling and spinning. I suffered a momentary shock: Beijing looked like a huge, glittering soccer stadium. It was a cold, midwinter night. After going through customs, I found three strangers with a raised sign that read "Mr. Zhao Zhenkai" waiting for me. Though of different height and size, they weirdly resembled one another against the glow of the arc lights, as if shadows from some other world. The welcoming ceremony was brief and silent; not until we were all seated in a sleek black sedan did they begin to speak, though it was difficult to distinguish between courtesies and threats, as the lights rushing by outside like the tide kept me distracted.

When I was a child, nights in Beijing were dark, pitch-dark, a darkness a hundredfold darker than today. So, for instance,

Uncle Zheng Fanglong lived next door to my family in a two-room residence with only three fluorescent lights: eight watts in the sitting room, three watts in the bedroom, and a shared three-watt bulb that hung from a small window between the kitchen and bathroom. In other words, whenever the whole family celebrated New Year's or decided to live it up on any ordinary day, they never used more than fourteen watts total—those brilliant, bulb-lined full-length mirrors weren't in fashion yet.

Perhaps this is an extreme example for Sanbulao ("Three Never Old") Hutong No. 1, but for the rest of Beijing I fear the situation was even worse. My classmates often lived with their family in a single room with one light, and were commonly forced to observe "blackouts"—but once the light-string was pulled.... *What about homework?... Quit your lip-flapping, there's always tomorrow....*

The lightbulbs were ordinarily bare, uncovered, a dim, yellow softness; a shade made a mysterious halo, projecting a single spotlight upward, and washed out the numerous subtleties of darkness. Back then girls didn't wear makeup, or even dress up, though they were strikingly beautiful, which certainly had something to do with the quality of the light. The spread of fluorescent lights turned into a disaster, painfully dazzling the eyes while blotting out the skies as they enveloped the earth without impediment or pause. As the nighttime illumination on a chicken farm pushes hens to lay more eggs, fluorescent lights create the illusion of daylight, except human beings cannot lay eggs and so they become more agitated—heart vexed, thoughts confused. What's unfortunate is that kind of feminine beauty can't exist anymore—applying makeup on those ashen, worn-out faces is useless. And yet the people who suffer the most under fluorescent lights must be children. With nowhere to hide in that space erased of subtlety and imagination, they prematurely step into the savageness of a public square.

Our physics teacher once said that when one enters the dark, visual acuity expands twenty-thousand-fold for a brief moment. So darkness allows one to see things as clearly as a flame. Capturing fire originally signified humankind's first evolutionary milestone, but surpassing this milestone only produced an open-eyed blindness. To think that the male human beast once possessed the keen vision of a wolf, its swiftly adapting focus: *woosh ... see the flame ... woosh ... see the flock of sheep ... woosh ... see the matchless beauty of the she-wolf.*

In those days there were plenty of "four-eyes"—besides lighting conditions, it must have had something to do with study habits. Students would argue vigorously about why, then, in the unlit darkness of the countryside, there were so few "four-eyes"? Although the school provided night study rooms (i.e., a space with sufficient lighting), it couldn't prevent the round-the-clock overachievers and hard-core intellectuals, like my good friend Cao Yifan, from some light reading—nestling into his quilt with Dream of the Red Chamber and flashlight in hand, he long ago joined the ranks of "four-eyes."

Back then streetlamps in Beijing were scarce; many hutong alleys and lanes didn't have a single one, and even if there were any, each one would be separated by thirty to fifty meters of darkness and only illuminated the small area immediately below it. Adults often exploited the story of the beggar to frighten us. The forehead-tapping beggar used a certain enchanting drug to abduct children. The tale itself became an enchanting drug, bewildering countless children, the teller always conveying the fuzziest of details: For one thing, what exactly did the head-tapping trick entail to instantly stupefy a child into mechanically following the villain away? Didn't Taiwan unleash this kind of advanced weaponry years before? While we couldn't be sure if such a crime actually occurred, oil and vinegar spiced up the oral legend, which stretched through hutong history into my childhood.

For the night traveler, streetlamps are needed more for steeling nerves than for illumination. The night traveler rides her bicycle, whistles a faint melody, *ding-ding* rings her bell. If every streetlamp is out, or some scamp has shattered them with his slingshot, she panics, cursing eight generations of ancestors.

Given the scarcity of streetlamps, one required another light source to ride at night. Toward the end of the 1950s, some bicyclists still used paper lanterns, as depicted in Hou Baolin's masterful piece of comic *xiangsheng* crosstalk *Night Traveler*. Most used a kind of square flashlight that could be strapped onto the handlebars. The next grade up for such equipage involved a dynamo-powered light that generated electricity at the spinning hub through pedaling; if the bicycle's speed became uneven, the light flashed on and off, becoming a visible part of Beijing's nightscape.

At the end of the 1950s, modern streetlights appeared along Chang'an Avenue, the thoroughfare of Eternal Peace. Walking the expansive avenue as dusk settled and the lights flickered on filled one with pride—mind clear, eyes ablaze—as if devouring communism with a glance. In stark contrast, the lights in hutong neighborhoods stayed extremely dim. Once you strayed from that broad, open road, you'd be lost again in Beijing's endless hutong maze.

When I was a child I'd play the shadows game with my little brother and sister—intercepting the light with hands over-lapped and fingers intertwined to cast animals of all kinds onto the walls, weak or ferocious, from the chase to the fight. No one chose to be a rabbit, the weak meat for the strong; behind the succession of shadows lurked a will to power, the shawdowteers believing they were masters of the ten thousand manifestations.

For children, darkness is for hide-and-seek. Retreat from the realm of light into countless hiding places, deep into the nooks and corners. When we moved into Three Never Old Hutong No. 1, there was still a rock garden in the courtyard—strange, otherworldly forms of Taihu stone terrified people at night; whatever shapes one described they became. The courtyard was the perfect place to play hide-and-seek. Both sides trembled with fear—who could be sure one wouldn't encounter the ghost of the famous former resident, the voyager Zheng He, or one of his handmaidens? Hearing the high-pitched, trilling calls— "Saw you a long time ago, *yalayala!* Don't play dumb, come out come out!"—pierced our quivering hearts. And then, our bodies tingling with goose bumps, a shrill scream right behind us.

Darkness is also for telling stories, particularly ghost stories. Adults tell them to children, children retell them to each other. In a country that doesn't believe in God, to manipulate ghosts to frighten children as well as oneself reinforces Confucian or-thodoxy. Chairman Mao made appeals for don't-be-afraid-of-ghosts stories to be told in school, at once confounding the people. For one, the bold are few in this world; for another, to not fear ghosts requires a troubling complication: One must first accept the existence of ghosts to prove one shouldn't be afraid of them.

During the Cultural Revolution we'd make revolution by day and tell ghost stories by night, as if ghosts and revolution didn't contradict each other at all. In my first year at Beijing Middle No. 4 (also known as BHSF, or Beijing High School Four), I lived in the dormitory. More often than not, once the lights were switched off for the night, one student would start to vocalize some spooky music. At the decisive moment, inevitably another one would smoothly push over the guardrail of a bed or toss a metal washbasin to the ground. After such a special-effects assault, the self-professed bold ones could never withstand this test of fear.

As fluorescent lights became more common after 1970, Beijing suddenly turned bright and ghosts no longer manifested themselves. Fortunately, though, the power frequently went out. Once it did, houses here and there would glow with candles, as if remembering and mourning a lost childhood.

2

Waking up, ceiling bright with the reflected light of a heavy snowfall. Warm air from the heater stirs the curtains as the window frame blurs with the light pouring in, making it seem as if a train is slowly, ever so gently, moving forward, taking me to a faraway place. I linger in bed until my parents rush me out.

A heavy snow turns the city into a mirage, as if gazing into one face of a looking glass. In a flash the glass will smash and shatter, mud splashing everywhere. On the road to school wrapped in a padded cotton coat, I grab a handful of wet snow, roll it into a ball, and throw it at the old pagoda tree by the hutong gate. Alas, it misses its target. I burst into the classroom as the school bell rings. Once again, it is as if the windows of the room are those of a train leaving the platform, gradually accelerating. In the gloominess, the teacher's silhouette turns, chalk dust flies up, the numerals on the blackboard seem to fade. The teacher raises her pointer at me and shouts, "*Hai!* Yes, YOU—are you deaf?"

As soon as the end-of-school bell rang, spring arrived. The eaves once white with snow now seeped liquid black, the sky curved down, endless branch tips were tinted green, bees buzzed in the sunlight, a steady hum, the shadows of girls dashed around like kites whose strings no one could catch, fluff from willow trees fluttered down, irritating people. I started to write, first plagiarizing Liu Baiyu's *Red Agate Essays,* then Wei Wei's *Who Are the Most Beloved People?* Liu Baiyu wrote of watching the sunrise from a plane above Moscow. This passage I evidently couldn't plagiarize. I was puzzled: Why Moscow? I strolled over to Houhai Lake to watch the sunset. What exactly is that red agate over yonder? The setting sun looked like a two-fen piece of fruit candy. Swallows flew back and forth across the lake; the Western Hills folded up and down in layers. The waves glittered and a foul stench rose up from the foam.

On a windless day, a cloud paused, motionless, casting its shadow upon a playground. Some muscular upperclassmen swung themselves mechanically on some parallel bars, their shadows like a metronome. Beneath a horizontal bar, I positioned my feet, took a breath, and prepared to stretch upward. Grip fixed, the plan was to do six consecutive reps to pass. After two, spirit and strength already depleted, my legs kicked out and my forehead just reached the iron bar. It felt like I had exhausted all my energy to climb into the sky for a peek at that white cloud, so freely gathering without a care in the world.

The summer sun cut the streets into two halves. Shade made it as cool as water, as I passed like a fish through the crowd. I abruptly changed tactics and walked to the side of scorching sun, alone but proud, stepping on my own shadow, face dripping with sweat, my whole body soon drenched. When I reached my destination, I treated myself to a popsicle.

I enjoy wandering the streets aimlessly, without a thought or care. At the heart of the grown-up world, there exists a kind of subconscious security. Just don't look up, and everything one sees is below chest-level—no need to suffer if you're ugly, no need to be distracted by the pleasures angers sorrows joys of the world. When enveloped by a thronging crowd, sky a dark screen, tightly squeezed without a trace of wind, one must struggle and strive to break free from the siege. One benefit of being young is having a unique point of view: a deformed face reflected in a nickel-plated doorknob, the stream of human figures mirrored in glass display windows, countless feet trampling cigarette butts, a candy wrapper rises and falls along a sidewalk curb, sunlight on the spokes of bicycle wheels, the taillights of a trolleybus blinking on and off....

I like rainy days, the way the boundary between light and shadow fade, a harmony of milk and water, like the color palette of a dilettante painter. Birds and clouds descend to lightning-rod heights, empty crows' nests sway in the branches of tall trees, bright-colored umbrellas meet by chance like drifting duckweed, raindrops make tracks on glass, handwriting on bulletin boards smudge their convictions, the reflected light in puddles scatter beneath my feet.

Yifan and I would often walk over to Dongan Market. In

the 1960s, Dongan Market was renovated into a shopping mall, its name changed from East Peace to Dongfeng East Wind Market, its former ambiance wholly destroyed. Before, all the small vendors displayed their wares in charming disorder, whatever you wanted you could find. In my memory, that place is a maze of lights: a cross-luster of electric lamps, gas lamps, kerosene lamps, and candles all melding into a bewitching haze. Beneath such illumination, the faces of the vendors and customers appeared utterly mysterious. If one could but fix that moment onto a scroll it could represent the perfect scene of daily life at the time. Once in a while, a thread of sunlight leaked inside, barely shifting—that most ancient hour hand.

3

Every child naturally harbors many illusions. The play of light and shadow, the space of imagination, even the body's physiology and biochemistry shape these illusions. As children grow up, most of their illusions are forgotten—time, society, customs, systems of knowledge together forge this forgetting as one enters adulthood.

The three years between the ages of ten and thirteen were difficult for me—that breaking point of the advancing body and mind as puberty begins. Daily existence meant deprivation. In a photograph from that time I look like a starving African boy with eyes glazed in a fixed stare and the trace of a sly, strange smile at the corners of my mouth.

I must have been in the throes of a consummate illusion. Before my eyes I saw grotesquely shaped trees, brilliant flowers about to drop petals, smoke suspended in midair, water flowing backward, crooked houses, stairs rolling out, clouds turning into monsters, inscrutable shadows, stars so big and bright.... When I finally encountered van Gogh's starry sky I felt no surprise. For me, such visions were the normal result of a deprived existence.

I'd walk the streets with eyes glazed over, straight ahead no turns, talking to myself. In class, especially, immersed in my imaginary world, I could barely hear a word that came out of the teacher's mouth. The teacher would ask a question, my reply would be nonsense. During parent-teacher conference, she transferred all her worries to my mother and father. Being a doctor, my mother didn't make a to-do over nothing. But I was put under close surveillance.

Waking up in the middle of the night, I watch my shoes shuffle along and make a circle before returning to their original place. An enormous ship suddenly rushes in through the window, a stranger's face appears in the glass, a forest lit from behind erupts in flames....

One evening I returned home alone and found a white cloud motionless above the gate of Three Never Old Hutong No. 1. Not huge, slightly curved in the canopy shape of a large umbrella, the cloud hovered incredibly low, even a little lower than our four-story home. Some years later I learned about UFOs and enlightenment struck. Beneath that cloud it was as if I had been put under an enchanting spell—mind a confusion of tangled threads, body completely rigid. Time seemed to have stopped. I finally took a step forward, and quick as a wing flap ran into the house.

Smells

1

WHEN I THINK about Beijing, the first thing that recurs in my mind are smells, smells that change with the changing seasons. In this respect, the human species reminds me of our canine friends. Why else do those elderly Chinese emigrants, upon returning to the motherland after so many years, look blankly around, slack-jawed, taking in a whiff to the east and a sniff to the west, desperately trying to find those precise Beijing scents in their memories.

The smell of winter white cabbage. When the year reaches the nineteenth solar term marking the start of winter, a temporary vegetable stand appears outside the entrance of every grocery shop—white cabbage is heaped into a hillock, long lines form from dawn to dusk. Each family buys at least a few hundred catties (nearly four hundred pounds), piling them onto a flatbed tricycle, or child's bicycle, whatever means to peddle them home, neighbors helping one another with transport, particularly those solitary elders who have difficulty getting around. The cabbage is first peeled open and sun dried, then stacked below the hallway window by the balcony doorway and covered with a grass curtain or old cotton quilt. Through desolate winter winds and snow, the cabbage desiccates, withering away like a mummy, and pungent waves of mold scent emanate forth, calling attention to its hidden existence.

The smell of coal smoke. All the neighborhood furnaces burning coal cakes and honeycomb briquettes for cooking and heating look like chain smokers with their flue pipes sticking out the window, puffing out clouds, spitting fog. Coal tar oozes from the pipes and drips to the ground, forming sticky lumps of black ice. On windy days, a strong gust swiftly swivels the elbow of a furnace pipe—reversing the thick smoke and causing family members to choke in tears and snot, coughing uncontrollably. Better to not bring up that sinister coal air: It catches you off guard, kills you off gently, softly.

The smell of dust. Take a shade of iron gray and add a hint of ocher: the essence of Beijing's winter color. Dust is the commander in chief of all odors, making one's mouth parched, tongue dry, throat a smoky soreness, mood foul. It borrows the northwestern winds and grows even more terrible, an army of ten thousand soldiers and horses, *concealing sky and swallowing earth*, invading rooms through cracks around doors and windows, no place to hide, no place to flee. In those days if you didn't wear a dust mask, venturing outside meant getting a mouthful of grit.

It's understandable that Beijing residents survive with little patience, caught in a swirling snowstorm that suddenly shrouds the whole city. In the middle of the storm drifts a cloud of peppermint scent; its presence, upon stepping outside, so strong in that first gulp of air—a cool, refreshing softness. With shouts and hoots, children rush outdoors, tossing away dust masks, flinging down gloves, white breath puffing out while throwing snowballs and piling up snowmen. Where the mud on the road dirties the ice, the children slide, squat down as inertia takes over, tumbling flat on their backs into the "old man flops into a quilt" position.

My home wasn't very far from Houhai Lake. Children often went there for the "wild ice," bringing their handmade skates, sleds, and skis, crowds of kids howling and screaming, powder spraying up in bursts, wind blowing it into faces, tongues licking it like grains of sugar, a sweetness born from nothingness. Workers chipped pieces of ice off the lake with an iron hook, then took the wood-plank path to the shore and on to the icehouse at the north side of Li Guang Bridge. When no one was looking, my classmates and I would sneak into the icehouse— a dim murky chilliness, a fishy watery smell mixed with the scent of dried grass. Chunks of ice were stacked on a multilevel wooden frame, each level of ice separated by a bed of straw, and then covered on top with another layer of straw, wooden planks, and dirt. Come summer the ice would be used to keep produce and other perishables fresh. I imagined myself as a fish frozen to the bone inside there.

Winters lasted forever, people grew anxious and irritable, children gazed restlessly toward spring. Then May Fourth arrived and the willow trees along the banks of the Houhai suddenly turned green, their branches velvety, issuing forth a subtle pungent scent. The melting lake ice resounded with sharp rupturing cracks, snow water dripped down the eaves, the lumps of frozen coal tar flowed away like ink. Our cotton-padded shoes changed shape, turned flat as a toad with a grinning mouth, and smelled like salty fish.

Nearly every year the narcissus my mother bought would silently bloom around the time of Spring Festival, its fragrance billowing out sub rosa, brightening up the oppressive air inside. Outside, the apricot trees bloomed earliest, swiftly followed by pear, lilac, peach blossoms, wind sweeping along the flowery bouquet, a fragrance so intense it made people dizzy, luring them to sleep. An oft-repeated saying during my childhood days went: "Spring brings sleep, autumn exhaustion, summer's for napping, don't wake for three months in winter"—apparently, no one knew enough about hay fever back then to complicate the spin.

By the time the pagoda trees bloom it's summer. Pagoda trees have a northern temperament, their beauty evoking a kind of fierce, unrestrained wildness. By contrast, their pale yellow blossoms flower with an ordinary banality—a passing wind and the petals fall like raindrops. The fragrance of their blossoms, though quite faint, can travel great distances like the notes of a xiao flute. But their scent arrives with the haunting "ghosts of the hanged." Inchworms suspended in midair by invisible threads rise and fall, blocking off walkways. To pass through the "ghosts of the hanged" phalanx is like passing through the gates of hell—once they dangle from face and neck, it's nearly impossible to get rid of them; the body breaks out with goose bumps, screams difficult to suppress.

Summer marked the year's happiest season, largely because

of summer vacation. We regularly went to the Chinese Association for Promoting Democracy (CAPD, or Min Jin, "people's progress") at the Drum Tower to watch TV and play Ping-Pong, or to the sports facility in the Shichahai district to swim. As we swam, we'd bob up and down in the smells of formalin, bleaching powder, urine, bob up and down between the boisterous din of people, with a moment's serenity underwater.

Torrential rains seemed to burst forth from an inner pressure. When the heat reached an unendurable critical point, thunder and lightning recurred with earth-shattering intensity, and the agitations of puberty could find a certain measure of release. Once the rain stopped, children rushed into the street gutters, trampled through the water, shouting and singing: "It's raining *lah*, it's bubbling *lah*, the old turtle's wearing a straw hat *lah*....!"

I'm not sure why autumn is often associated with sadness, though it might have something to do with the start of school: freedom surrendered. Yes, autumn has come to symbolize the mechanical rhythms of the school system, its systematic order. Chalk dust flies into the air as words and numerals on the blackboard materialize, then fade away. Above the foul stench of the reeking feet and the rude language of boys floats the overpowering essence emanating from the bodies of girls, wisp upon wisp, causing bewilderment and confusion.

Autumn rains fall in bursts, leaves turn and whirl away, damp, then soaked, the bitter aroma of strong tea, over-steeped, gives way to the aroma of fermenting mold. Which, in mutual correspondence, is soon succeeded by the aroma of stored winter white cabbage.

2

Considering the senses, besides the olfactory, the gustatory is naturally involved, too. Taste's memory being even more innate, and thus more enduring.

The taste of cod-liver oil awakens my earliest childhood dream: Deep behind the doors and portholes of a paper-boat cutting, lamplight glows, bearing a fishy odor. That lamplight must be interlinked with my early experiences with cod-liver oil. Before my parents' solemn faces, I took it regularly, as if it were medicine, swallowing it down with an instinctive vigilance.

When cod-liver oil passes through an eyedropper to fall on the tip of the tongue, a sharp chill quickly fans out, filling the mouth with its flavor. This oil extracted from codfish brought the loneliness of the ocean's abyss to me. Eventually I learned that the theory of evolution supports this experience: Our ancestors can be traced back to fish. As I grew a little older, the loneliness amplified into the inner roar of puberty. Then the eyedropper turned into a capsule and cod-liver oil turned into a kind of candy for me—the antipathy disappeared. I'd first bite open the capsule, wait for the fish oil to leak out, and then delicately chew the gel, which had the texture of Cowhide Sesame Candy.

The taste of White Rabbit Milk Candy—surely the King of Candy, foremost for its semitransparent rice-paper wrapper that dissolves on the tongue, triggering delight's anticipation. White Rabbit Milk is extremely potent: They say that seven pieces equals one glass of milk, and so all malnourished children thirst for it. Sadly, it went through some difficult times when it became known as "high-class candy," a perfidious jingle spreading through the ether: "High-class sweets, high-class candy, high-class old man clambers onto the chamber pot"—this "high-class" saying clearly had nothing to do with the common folk. Some years later in Paris, a French friend of mine reunited me with the White Rabbit, offering me a piece; my heart skipped a beat, deep emotions stirred within me, and from then on I would always carry a few pieces with me, as I joined the ranks of "high-class old men."

During that torturous period as my body matured and transformed, I secretly started to eat anything in our house, from the chlorella algae in the fishbowl to the viscous lecithin doled out by my parents, from calcium tablets to dried wolfberry, from mustard tubers to soybean paste, from dried shrimp to scallions … my parents tried to *fortify the walls and raze the fields,* but couldn't hinder my appetite that expanded with each passing day. Whatever I ate, I devoured with monosodium glutamate. Much later in life, after settling for a period in America, whenever I dined at a Chinese restaurant with foreigners, they usually said, "Please, no MSG"—each time this happened, with their words ringing in my ears, my heart would become so motherfucking vexed.

I took a pinch of MSG from a jar and sprinkled it into the hollow of my palm, licked it with the very tip of my tongue, firing off the taste-bud nerve clusters, impulses shooting through the brain layers and triggering an electrifying buzz—as if savoring the vast ocean refined and purified, that sensory sensation called "umami"! I gradually increased the dosage, the high continuing to rise, until the umami taste completely faded. Finally, I just dumped the half-filled jar of MSG into my mouth, causing the signals in my cerebral cortex to misfire or short-circuit, leading to dizziness and nausea; I collapsed headfirst onto my bed. I suppose this must have been similar to a drug trip.

"Who spilled all the MSG?" Father and Mother complained.

Right outside the walls of the playground at my primary school stood a peddler who always tried to lure innocent souls with his hawking shouts. Like a magician, he would conjure all sorts of candy and snacks from his knapsack. From a classmate's recommendation, I fell in love with cinnamon bark. Cinnamon bark, commonly used in herbal remedies, comes from the inner bark of the cassia tree, its spicy flavor suffused with a delicious sweetness. Two fen could purchase several pieces, which lasted longer than candy. I'd wrap the bark up in a handkerchief and, during class from time to time, sneak in a lick. Truthfully, besides the taste of cinnamon bark, the rest of my education in those days made no lasting impression on me.

One night, Guan Tielin and I were walking home from school when we happened upon a peddler carrying his wares with a shoulder pole, singing out: "Stinky tofu, fermented tofu …" I had never tried stinky tofu before and, egged on by Guan Tielin, I spent three fen on a piece, took one bite, gagged, and threw the rest onto a roof. When I got home, Qian Ayi ("Auntie Qian") shouted out that something stank, as she sniffed to the east, sniffed to the west, determined to track down the source. I rushed into the bathroom to brush my teeth and gargle, then slipped into the kitchen and scooped two spoonfuls of sugar into my mouth, pasting it shut. But Qian Ayi's nose still twitched like a police dog's as she continued to search and search every which way.

3

One summer morning, Yifan and I set off from Sanbulao Hutong No. 1 and headed for the CAPD at the Drum Tower Square Brickyard, 98 Xin'anli Lane—that political party a testament to the organized labor of my parents' generation. As usual during summer vacation, we'd go there to play Ping-Pong, passing a wild pear tree along the way from which we'd pick some of the little sour pomes.

Leaving Sanbulao via Denei ("Inner Virtue") Street—my primary school across the way in Hongshan Hutong—the small sundry store on the northeast corner emitted its invisible signals and the conditioned reflex in my brain switched on its red light, causing a secretion of saliva in my mouth; walking to school, I'd often waste two fen on candy there, pressing the pieces into the bland corn-cone buns to dress up breakfast.

Continue along Denei Street south a hundred or more steps, across the next intersection, and arrive at Liuhai Hutong market. Outside, the vegetable stand overflowed with seasonal tomatoes, four catties for one mao; salted beltfish, one cattie for three mao eight, attracted a swarm of flies impossible to swat away. Yifan and I wanted to buy two juicy tomatoes, so we pooled all the coins in our pockets, gulped down our drool, and rushed off with our booty.

Heading east toward Liuhai Hutong, then turning north onto Pine Tree Street, just past a large, new hutong, we stopped at the public toilet off the roadside there, the salty stench of piss in the pit pools assailing our nostrils so that we couldn't even open our eyes; it was as if we were training to hold our breath underwater, and only after fleeing far away could we take a deep, deep breath, the fragrance of flowers seeping into our hearts and spleens, a field full of blooming pagoda trees. It had rained the night before; a small puddle of water reflected the sky, light, tree shadows.

Turning north onto Willow Shade Street the neighborhood changed into stately mansions and spacious courtyards—rumor had it that the official residence of Marshal Xu Xiangqian, one of the founders of the People's Liberation Army, could be found at the northern end, enclosed behind tall walls. Beneath the shady trees we bought red-bean pops, two for five fen, saving us one fen. But these ready-made red-bean pops were soft and droopy, at the cusp of melting into nothingness; thus powerless to savor the delicious icy red-bean bits at a leisurely pace we inhaled them in two bites, craning our necks, bending back, faces to the sky, stomachs rumbling.

Emerging from Willow Shade Street to Houhai, a bright expanse suddenly opened out. Houhai Lake is one of the three lakes in Shichahai, a neighborhood that dates back seven hundred years to the Yuan dynasty when Beijing was known as Dadu, or the Great Capital. The northern terminus of the Grand Canal ended here, the area once a flourishing commercial district, as colorful as a brocade. Around each bend enormous pagoda trees spread upward, and beneath them, concealed in the shade, people play what's called xiangqi, "the figures game," or Chinese chess. Some strapping lads dig for clams in the lake, each taking a deep breath before leaping into the water and diving down, feet sticking out, treading open air, their laughter infective. Clams pile up on shore, the largest ones as big as a pot lid. They give off the strangest fishy smell, as if issuing humanity a final warning.

We followed the path south around Houhai, banging willow branches against the iron railing that ran along the lake. The wide expanse of the water abruptly narrowed and a stone bridge linked the two sides of the shore, none other than the famous Silver Ingot Bridge. From the bridge, the view across the lake of the western hills is renowned as one of the old Yanjing capital's Eight Landscapes of scenic beauty. Beside the bridge stands Ji's Mongolian Barbecue, an establishment more than a hundred years old whose name has been raised to the heavens and whose very existence presents an excruciating test for my impatient nerves: the smell of roast mutton, the smell of charring coal, the smell of myriad spices commingling in the breeze, stirring our stomachs, reminding us that lunchtime approached.

Like a wisp of smoke, we slipped along Slanted Tobacco Pipe Street and reached the bustling Di'anmen Avenue, Drum Tower to the north, crossed the road and walked south, passing the Gate of Earthly Peace Shopping Mall, where we read this pasted announcement: "Handouts for Leftover Sweets (an assortment of leftover sweets for sale)"; we churned into a whirlwind and hurried in, and then the whirlwind went hurrying out, "leftover treats" actually referring to "those looking for love"—too bad our coupons and coins were so limited.

Continuing on Di'anmen Avenue, we turned left into Brick Factory Hutong, where they used to make bricks for the imperial palace, then skipped along Xin'anli Lane and arrived at our destination. A sign reading CHINA ASSOCIATION FOR PROMOTING DEMOCRACY NATIONAL COMMITTEE hung in the air, imposing and grand, and yet however one looked at it, it looked like a reactionary slogan.

Yifan and I first charged into the Ping-Pong room and battled out three games, then, stomachs rumbling like a windlass, we decided to go pick some sour pears to ease our hunger. The pear tree wasn't tall and grew in a corner where two walls met—three to five little dusty gray pomes drooped down from the highest branches. After climbing onto Yifan's shoulders I shimmied up the middle of the tree and headed for the tallest branches. Just as I spied a pear and reached for it, the back of my hand felt a sharp jab—a "foreign stabber" had ambushed me, one of those spiky slug-moth caterpillars.

I climbed down from the tree and sucked the stinging red wound, though I felt no relief, the stinging refusing to ease. I fished out a few little pears from my pocket, wiped one on my pants, and took a bite, the taste as sour and as tart as could be, my mouth swelling with a hard-to-swallow mush. The lunch-room bell rings out—a savory whiff of pork cabbage stew wafts over.

Sounds

1

ROUND AGE SIX or seven I composed a musical invention: to the sounds of car horns I hummed a tune in counterpoint. Together these two sounds defined the metropolis for me. As dream became reality, the proliferating noises of the metropolis (particularly the sounds of drills and jackhammers) tormented me to madness; after many long nights of fleeting sleep, I ultimately concluded that to the children of our agricultural empire, the so-called metropolis, the great city, has had little relation to their verbal creativity.

Beijing at the turn of 1960 still seemed like a large village; early in the morning, one could even hear a rooster crow. It lived nearby with the Gong family on a small plot of land in their enclosed courtyard where, besides squash and bean vines, one could find a chicken coop; the proud, solitary rooster would herald the dawn each day, waking me up, its crows projecting like a singer's vocal exercises, listeners following it with hearts in their mouths, climbing the scale up into the clouds until it unexpectedly stopped, leaving them suspended in midair. The Gong family also raised a lone turkey, the guttural *ge ge ge* calls echoed out from within the swaying flesh hanging from its neck, making the animal seem like an asthmatic old geezer. In fact, the turkey was strong and robust, and as tame as it was docile, letting all of us kids take turns riding on its back, strutting forward with head held high.

I flip over, wanting to return to my dragon sleep, sparrows flap-flapping on the roof tiles, *ji ji zha zha* chattering away, the hollow echoes of pecking on the iron drainpipes. Among the flock, one chirps out the shrillest, its wings fluttering with intense vigor. Winter—the boiler-room workers begin to add more coal for heat, hot water circulates through the heating pipes, *hua hua hua* burbles along with the *si si* sibilants of the ventilation to a sudden clash of warm and cold air that *pi pa!* bursts with a clang. It felt like being caught in an enormous digestive excretion system.

The movement of people below, a confusion of footsteps clearly distinguishable: male heavy, female lighter, street workers chaotic, office workers steady, sluggish elders pause, children as a rule vary—some prance and skip about, some drag their feet on the dirt, shoes worn down. The rush of bicycles magnifies the early-morning silence: spokes whistle in the wind, tires fly with dust and stones, chains *keng keng keng* rub against their guards, bells ring out, a deafening gong splits the air.

I flip over again, still listening into the distance—a horse snorts, iron hooves slip on the asphalt; the cart driver shouts out rebukes, his whip slashes through the air, the shaft of the cart jolts and creaks. The No. 14 bus sails by, motor rumbling, *tu tu tu* spurting out clouds of exhaust, pneumatic doors open and close with a hiss, the ticket collector lazily announces, "This is Liu Hai-er Hutong...."

Around 7:25, the head teacher, Mr. Li, passes through Three Never Old Hutong. Tall and thin, upright as a pencil, eyes never askance, meteoric strides forging ahead, the *tuo tuo* echo of his black leather shoes. With a soft clearing of his throat and a quick turn of his head, he hawks up a loogie. The instant I hear Mr. Li's footsteps and his phlegm-hawking I hop out of bed in a flurry.

2

Whether sick or just pretending to be sick, I'd linger in bed. Around 8:30, Xiao Li the mailman would arrive on his bicycle to deliver the newspaper and mail. He squeezed the brakes and hopped off, popping the kickstand with his foot, and languorously yelled, "X Y Z registered mail, come stamp your chop."

The sun comes up and the hawking cries of the street peddlers rise and fall in endless waves, faint threads drifting away. The uniqueness of Beijing's hawking cries certainly has been shaped by the depths and breadths, the curves and bends, of the hutongs—for the daily news of commerce to spread door to door, the singsong cries must be stretched and pulled along the lengths and widths of more than seven twists and eight turns. Beijingers talk in quick, equivocal garbles, and the cries serve as a corrective for the local dialect: each tone slowly lengthens, each word fully valued, like candied hawthorn fruit pierced together in a line, flowing out crisp and melodious in patterned rhymes. Excessive lung power is crucial, the power to propel and exchange air without changing the sound, keep steady, then shift to a higher octave, halt without dropping, and extend the rhyme. In his essay "Sounds of the City," the popular early twentieth-century novelist Zhang Henshui wrote, "I, too, have walked the quays from the south to the north, listening to the cries of the street peddlers, and no other place can surpass such songs as those in Beiping. Beiping's hawking cries, so intricate and yet harmonious, no matter day or night, freezing or sweltering, move listeners to their very core."

Rags I'll buy, old rags worn, shoes worn, socks I'll buy.... This ragman's use of anastrophe demonstrates the self-confidence of society's lowest rung; it is a self-confidence that in a flash can be transformed into the self-poise of an empire: *A-bombs I'll buy....*

Then there's the unmatchable talent that Beijing natives have for clever, silver-tongued chatter. For instance, the cry of the pantao peach seller: "Not the ones pricked by First Lady, nor the ones embroidered by Second Lady, these are Third Lady's stroll through the garden lightly padded on flat-capped peaches....!"

Stinky bean curd, fermented bean curd, Wang Zhihe's timeless stinky bean curd.... Advertising lingo simple and clear, brand and stock list in perfect order. There is a local saying: "Yell what you sell"—this ancient way of doing business discloses the plain, unassuming side of Beijing natives, to cheat neither elder nor child, at most a little boast, which is of course the basic function of advertising: "Ice-cold watermelon, crisp flesh-firm pulp—" "Radishes sweeter than pears, if spicy hot money's returned—" "Sipping honey persimmons, big as a lion's head—"

The hawking cries are often sung with instrumental accompaniment, for example: To sell fried sesame-dough twists use a woodblock *bangzi*; for a monkey performance use a *daluo* gong; to collect rags use a little drum; to sell iced plum juice use two little copper bowls, one on top of the other held in one hand, fingers clink them *chuan chuan chuan*, while crying out, "Icy cold cups …!" And then there's the street barbers with their "tuning fork," banging it with an iron plate, the humming metal making you dazed, momentarily restrained, and no matter if your hair's short or long, they shave your head bald as a gourd, then talk later. "Sharpen your scissors, hone your cleaver," the knife sharpener hollers while swinging the "iron head," five sheets of galvanized iron strung together, *hua la hua la* clatter racket.

From down below emerges the most moving of hawking cries: "Popsicles, three fen for one, five fen for the other …" The ones for three fen were hawthorn-fruit and red-bean pops; the five fen ones milk pops. With only two fen in my pocket, I figured I could haggle with the old lady peddler for a defective one or half a hawthorn-fruit pop.

After listening to Hou Baolin's comic *xiangsheng* crosstalk *Service Manners* on the radio, Yifan and I leap into Liuhai Hutong's sundry shop and begin to imitate a sketch, singing, "Buy sell sell buy, harmonious air breeds more wealth, stand at the counter with a beaming smile, don't drift off, don't space out, how can you not get rich if you buy and sell like this…." With the song unfinished, we get cut off and chased back out.

3

More than anything else, mosquitoes craved being a part of our lives. Mosquitoes—swipe at one, swipe at another—resistance proves futile. Some tried to use fans, incense coils, or DDVP to keep them at bay—all to no avail. Summer nights filled with the steady drone of mosquitoes. Their strange, swerving buzz contains a metallic bite, a hidden bitterness mixed with menace, that magnified ten thousandfold would approximate the scream of a guided missile pursuing its target. A variety of repellents cropped up at the decisive moment, but the mosquitoes quickly adapted, to the point that they seemed like drug addicts, immortals floating high in the clouds and mist, emitting an intoxicating murmur. A cartoon once appeared in the *Beijing Evening News*: Four mosquito coils smoldered at the foot of a bed on which a man lay dead from smoke inhalation, while a single mosquito nonchalantly pierced the tip of his nose.

I wielded a flyswatter in front of the corner shop at Luo'er Hutong and, using a rotting fish head as a lure, swatted flies down. With bamboo tongs I pinched a few of the dead bodies and dropped them into a glass bottle, counted then counted again, only about two-thirds through finishing my assignment, a school-wide regulation that forced every student to kill at least fifty flies each day. A swarm of the insects descended and dove, flying low like Japanese kamikaze fighters, straight into the fish head, not hesitating to smash their bodies to smithereens.

Summers belonged to the crickets and cicadas. The Swedish poet Tomas Tranströmer once wrote in a poem: "the frenzied sewing-machine pedaling of crickets." And this is exactly how one of these little tailors sewed up the days and nights of my childhood, letting my dream-soul wander. In the hundred-flower depths around Huguo Temple I bought a cricket, placed it in a clay jar, and used a piece of hemp straw to tease open its jaws, whereupon the cricket rubbed its wings and released a sonorous chirp, thinking its moment of triumph had come. One day the clay jar wasn't covered tightly and the cricket disappeared. I rushed about in a frantic search, tossing and flipping things over to no avail—the cricket had found some hidden nook in our home and pedaled its sewing machine with a relentless urgency.

Around early July, after the Minor Heat of the eleventh solar term, cicada nymphs emerge from the earth, their cries filling the air: *zhi liao zhi liao zhi liao!* Golden cicadas, scientific name *Tibicen linnei,* commonly known as the annual cicada. Jean-Henri Fabre wrote in his study of insects *Souvenirs Ento-mologique*s: "Not content with carrying an instrument called the cymbal in a cavity behind his wings, the cicada increases its power by means of a sounding board under his chest. Indeed, there is one kind of cicada who sacrifices a great deal in order to give full play to his musical tastes. He carries such an enor-mous sounding board that there is hardly any room left for his vital organs, which are squeezed into a tiny corner."* In fact, cicadas are pure noisemakers. They overturn heaven and earth with their ruckus, spreading chaos through Beijing, the inten-sity of their calls growing with the heat, distressing hearts and disrupting thoughts. With other children in our building, we'd venture forth to glue-stick the bugs. First, we'd mix flour and

---

* From *Fabre's Book of Insects, retold from Alexander Texeira de Mattos' translation of Fabre's "Souvenirs Entomologiques" by Mrs. Rodolph Stawell* (Mineola, NY: Dover Publications, 1998).—Tr.

water to make a glutinous paste, then mold this mixture onto the end of a bamboo stick, and, with the instrument in hand, carefully climb up to the fork of a large tree. One by one we'd cover cicadas with the glue, their bodies quivering, to clamor no more.

By the Mid-Autumn Festival, cicadas withdraw from the stage and katydids take their place in the limelight. The peddlers who sell katydids on the streets today have no need to hawk their wares—the insects' calls serve as the most persuasive advertisement. Compared to the call of the cicada, a katydid's sounds ten times sweeter to the ear. Katydids are also pleasant to look at, like extraterrestrials—blue face, pink abdomen, purple wings. Kept in a bamboo cage—heart content, thoughts calm—it will live a perfectly happy life and sing to the skies until the Great Snow of the twenty-first solar term.

4

After joining the Young Pioneers of China, the highest rank I could ever attain terminated at leader of a small squad (one-bar armband), a source of deep humiliation for me as even my younger brother became captain of a squadron (two bars). By a stroke of good fortune, however, I was chosen to be a drummer, and so could run wild with joy. This elation was obviously connected to my deep love of the Soviet film *Fate of the Drummer Boy*. The father of Seriozha Batashov, the drummer boy, is an engineer who is arrested and imprisoned for losing some top-secret documents. A spy pretending to be an old Red Army soldier swoops onto the scene. Batashov ultimately discovers the soldier's true identity and fights the enemy to the end....

I played one of those small military-band drums, leather strap slung diagonally across the body, each hand grasping a drumstick, white gloves white shirt white slacks, along with a red scarf—me: the drummer boy Zhao Zhenkai, how glorious his name. Drumming looks easy; only a drummer really knows how difficult it is to play, the complex rhythmic changes tapped out with the crisp, ringing dexterity of a galloping steed. My problem is that I lacked coordination, *tending to this and losing sight of that*, my hands like two lame donkeys turning a millstone. Guided by the spirit of Pavel Korchagin in Nikolai Ostrovsky's *How the Steel Was Tempered*, I sweated tirelessly to learn the basics, usually without drumsticks, just using pencils or my fingers; I became possessed, tapping on desks on doors on windows on dustpans, even on public buses—*dongdong daladala dong*—and after about three weeks of practicing, the two lame donkeys finally parted from the millstone, though they still limped and stumbled along.

Accompanying the drumbeats, I followed Pavel Korchagin in raising my class consciousness. I discovered streets teeming with suspicious individuals, our residential complex a virtual spy headquarters. With a drummer's arrogance, I never greeted anyone who seemed a potential enemy. One day while walking on Huoguosi Snack Street I saw the "rightist" Big Brother Pang glancing back and forth with a flustered expression, and knew he must be meeting a secret agent from Taiwan. I hid behind a tree, followed him down an alley. As he climbed the stairs, I observed that his back pocket bulged with, no doubt, a pistol....

A week remained until the procession ceremony and I practiced to the bitter end, drumming even in my dreams. The two lame donkeys finally became one, trotting along, though still far from a galloping horse.

On the day of the ceremony, as I stood ready and waiting, instrument weighing me down, I suddenly heard a drum tap, then another—listening again, it was actually my beating heart. At the signal, the three other drummers and I started to tap out a rhythm and walk forward, onto the stage. But on the steps up to the platform, my little drum began to slip and loosen, and with a crash fell to the ground, causing the whole audience to erupt with laughter. With humiliating haste, I picked up the drum and began to beat it furiously with my fist, leading the other little drums astray, into total disarray. And so the fate of one drummer came to an end.

5

A small textile factory operated across from Three Never Old Hutong No. 1, nothing out of the ordinary with their goings on. But when I was eleven I can recall a big-character poster pasted up on a wall inside the factory that exposed Director Shua's immoral behavior. I wandered over with a few other kids from our building to see the tittering crowds. At the time there were still many words I couldn't recognize to read, and even if recognized, couldn't understand. For instance, the word "breast" is composed of two characters *ru* (乳) and *fang* (房), the latter meaning "room," and so seeing *ru fang* on that poster made me wonder: Exactly where is this secret room concealed on the human body?

In the mid-1960s, during the Grasp Revolution and Promote

Production initiative, textile factories began to expand, their new buildings squeezed into streets along with piles of sediment that formed detours for walkers and bicyclists. All the opened skylight windows of the factories seemed like a hundred loudspeakers directing propaganda at us. At home on sweltering summer days, once the windows of the textile factory by us were opened one needed to shout to talk. Every Friday the factory closed, the quiet oddly disconcerting as if something were amiss, sleep proved difficult, and each household longed for the factory to open again immediately. As if the racket of the spinning machines wasn't enough, the factory's two loudspeaker systems played a constant stream of high-pitched revolutionary slogans.

Yifan started to learn Japanese, teaching himself as he translated Japanese reference material. He told me that noise is measured in decibels against an international safe standard, and that the noise of the textile factory exceeded the standard by ninety to hundred decibels, easily causing hearing loss and even eventual deafness with continuous exposure. Yifan wrote a letter of complaint, but to whom could he send it? To involve yourself with such unpleasantness disturbed the Great Path of the Revolution. Fortunately, the first victims of hearing loss ended up being the old grannies of the Little Feet Neighborhood Patrol; each of them became slightly deaf, hardly able to hear a thing above the turbulent noise—and so we sang at the top of our lungs, recited poems, debated heatedly. The noise turned into our protective shield.

One night, in the early days of the so-called cultural revolution, a classmate and I cycled by Ping'anli ("Peaceful Safety") Lane. Night deepened into stillness, and as if out of nowhere, ten or more donkeys suddenly appeared with a peasant in the lead, herding them westward. My friend told me that a drove of donkeys passed along here every day, entering the city in the middle of the night, through the red gate in the east, and on to their destination, the zoo. I froze, then asked him what exactly for. He laughed and said that they were being sent to the slaughter, the next day's fodder for the tigers, leopards, wolves. A long time after this incident, I tossed and turned late into the night, listening for the disordered clip-clop-clip-clop of those donkey hooves on the pavement. They must have sensed their coming doom, just like that drummer boy, falling into step, embracing the will to die.

Toys and Games

THOSE TOYS, SO time-worn and faded in memory's ravines that they seem to have preceded my birth, lurked in ambush on the path of my adolescence.

The first toy to appear, a tin motorboat—lighting a little oil lamp inside its cabin converted heat energy into a propulsive force and *tu tu tu* the tin boat puffed around the curve of the tub. It was also equipped with a miniature dynamo; one crank of the wheel and a small light lit up, flickering on and off. In truth, it really became my father's toy, fulfilling his own, long-unfulfilled childhood wish.

After the dynamo motorboat, a glass car coruscates in the light, waiting in the line to my adolescence. It actually was a glass jar blown into the shape of a car that originally held a bounty of colorful jelly beans, dappled and bright; on the back of the vehicle a spare tire functioned as a cap. That car represents the tangible thirst left over from a sweetness long dissolved, glass being so easily broken after all.

I see a son's love for weapons as my own, male karma passed down from generation to generation. In Hemingway's *A Farewell to Arms*, the word "arms" takes on a double meaning: weapons as well as a woman's embrace, referring to the male protagonist's struggle, namely, parting from weapons of war as well as parting from maternal love—his loss involves the relation between the maternal bond and masculine approbation.

The first weapon that was passed to me: a Soviet-style rotary submachine gun—wind its handle and it rattled away *ga la ga la ga la*. In an old photograph, I'm holding the submachine gun strapped across my shoulder, head raised, chest out, glaring straight ahead. At some point my uncle Biao Jiu (maternal cousin's father), a sailor in the navy, gave me a precious gift: a revolver. Made out of cast iron, the gun felt the perfect weight; leather holster slung across my body, the gunslinger looked like a round commissar. My self-centeredness knew no bounds back then. Even more miraculous, pulling the trigger of the gun advanced a roll of paper caps that ignited under each snap of the hammer, striking fear and terror into hearts and minds. These military gifts have a kind of ceremonial significance, backing up a cycle of violence through the ages, to the moment an accident happens.

That day, on an outing to Beihai Park with my family, we stopped for tea at a restaurant near the Five Dragon Pavilions. While the grown-ups chatted, I strapped on my revolver and embarked on a reconnaissance mission, leading the charge, seeking a place to bivouac. Coming into a small grove of trees, I brushed past another little boy. He eyed the gun strapped to me and spit out a profanity; hatred like a magnet pulled us close together. Before I could draw out my weapon, a dagger appeared in the form of a screwdriver aimed at my chest. He didn't care if he was younger and smaller than me. From his ragged clothes, scabby face, blackened neck, I could see he dwelled on the lowest rung of society.

The standoff lasted a minute or two at most, yet it seemed to last forever, time progressing at the pace of a heartbeat. Being so close together I could see the murderous intent in his eyes, my chest pounding like a hammer. Finally, I retreated a step, turned, and walked away, behind me the wild *hee hee hee* impish laughter of the victor. Leaving the grove of trees and returning to the happy family chatter, I felt an incomparable sense of injustice and choked back tears. I knew that in order to be a real man, I, alone, needed to swallow the bitter-tasting pill of defeat. And so the round commissar shed his shell and returned to the plowed fields, the revolver tossed aside, forgotten.

My fifth uncle's family on my mother's side had four beloved daughters, each one as beautiful as the next; but as they had no sons I was looked upon as a treasure, and, given this lack of male progeny, my parents proposed an exchange with the daughters that involved them borrowing me on a regular basis. So during winter and summer breaks I would go to Fifth Uncle's for a short stay. Living among girls, I felt different from them—no wonder Jia Baoyu of the *Red Chamber* turned out the way he did. When you enter a village follow its customs, and so I participated in all the girls' games and activities: weaving purses, jumping elastic rope, playing hopscotch and throw the bag, while the local boys jeered and wisecracked. Then, as we started to play house, make-believe transformed into reality as I gradually fell secretly in love with my older cousin Mei.

My uncle's family lived in the Hepingli district, in the residential housing for the National Measurements Officewalk—in those days, you stepped out and into open fields. In the summer, my sister-cousins would take me to pick fingernail flowers (scientific name Balsaminaceae); we'd mash the peach-colored petals into juice and paint our nails, layer upon layer deepening the shade. It felt quite stimulating at first, and I even showed off my nails to other people.

We often played "snatch the bones," a variation of the Mongolian game shagai. Take the anklebones of a sheep's hind legs, dye each of the four sides a different color, and divide them into four to eight bones per group. As you toss up a small cloth beanbag or a Ping-Pong ball, with the same hand flip over the sheep bones and arrange them in a certain combination before catching the bag or ball, not letting it fall. "Snatch" here is a very imagistic verb, evoking the nimble use of the five fingers to seize and arrange each sheep bone into its proper position. I, however, lacking agility and coordination, caused my cousins to roll back and forth with laughter.

After vacation, I returned to the world of boys. I never mentioned playing girls' games to my buddies. I lived in these two separate worlds until I experienced a sudden sexual awakening early one spring morning. In the throes of my secret love for cousin Mei awoke an awareness of incestuous relations, the chasm between the two worlds impossible to leap across.

We lived near Huguo Temple. A temple fair took place on the grounds every ten days, twice a month, food stalls, zoetropes, street operas, folktale tellers, martial arts performers, anything one could ever want could be found there—for kids, the place to be after school. The back gate of Huguo Temple faced a small street called Hundred Flowers Abyss where the cricket sellers gathered. Most of the crickets were kept in woven bamboo thermos holders, with gauze used as the bottom of each cage. Those contained the inferior crickets, two or three fen for one, while the royalty lived alone in separate quarters, in a clay or porcelain jar, their loud chirping muffled but still heard. The fiercest and most robust species of cricket, commonly known as the Coffin, had a triangular head and usually sold for around 120 RMB: for us, naturally, an astronomical amount.

Beside the cricket market a number of old men sat along a wall, first fighting among themselves before letting loose two crickets to fight, whereupon we'd circle around to watch. The two heroes engaged in combat, teeth bared bodies entwined, never dividing never parting, until the defeated fell and fled, the victor's wings vibrating *ming ming ming*. The trainer used his "probe" to draw the defeated out, and after three consecutive losses, would retire him.

Yifan and I fabricated an iron-wire trap, dumped out a salt container from my place, and, though it was said the probe was made from the whiskers of yellow weasels, we turned to our native habitat and found a kind of *Humulus japonicus* wild grass, split it in half, inverted it and pulled it apart, exposing its fine, slender villi for our probe. Preparations in order, we sent out some feelers that caused us to break out in a cold sweat: Apparently, of all the realms under heaven, our brave heroes liked to hide outside the city walls in the desolate wilderness of the cemeteries. As if warriors going to battle, we walked for many *li*, ears raised, through brush and bramble thickets, flipping over old bricks and debris. Then at last we heard the chirping of crickets. After exhaling with relief, we discovered the hopelessness of trying to pinpoint the exact location of the source; it was as if the chirping came from all around us, the *qu qu qu* of the open wilderness; we were trapped by the crickets' encircling siege, the songs of Chu coming toward us from the four directions. We returned home empty-handed, muscles aching, energy depleted, *qu qu qu* echoing in our dreams.

Boys' games often involve an element of gambling, as with "fan the triangle." Pile up empty cigarette packs into a triangle and compete by trying to fan your own triangle to knock down your opponent's, so your triangle not only must fall accurately but must also carry sufficient force. Typically, given my poor coordination skills, an opponent toppled my triangle. Before the game could start, though, positive identification needed to be checked, for only worthy cigarette brands qualified for competition. During the Difficult Three Year Period of the Great Famine, my uncle Da Gufu, the husband of my father's elder sister who was a senior engineer and enjoyed special remunerations, gave my father his monthly allotment of two complementary boxes of premium Chunghwa and Peony cigarettes, as he didn't smoke. With eyes full of angst, I paced behind my father as he billowed out mist and clouds of smoke, dying for him to finish puffing his two boxes. I became a direct beneficiary of his privilege. Despite my dire technique, a brand-name triangle in hand felt just like holding a winning hand, *drawing the bow without releasing it*; fortunately, there weren't many such brands that could qualify for competition—no battle, no victory, no loss.

Whenever I pass a golf course I'm reminded of playing marbles, these two sports sharing not a few things in common, and yet if you care to peer more closely at the differences, marbles is by far the superior game. First, marbles adapts to local conditions—just dig five little holes and preserve energy as well as the environment, while golf simply increases the number of holes across a greater expanse, forcing one to *let loose the mounts to raid the land*, and construct sand traps, plant trees, meticulously tend and protect the poisoned grass where no sheep can graze and no dog can urinate. Second, marbles is economical—a handful of little glass spheres and nothing sets the heart racing more, while golf expenditures require drivers, woods, irons, putters plus a club membership fee, as well as hiring someone else to carry your clubs—all of it adding up to pure money-spending anguish. Third, playing marbles is carefree and easy—just lower your head, stick out your butt, circle about five small holes wearing just shorts and a T-shirt, or even go shirtless, unfettered and unhindered; but playing golf is mostly about sticking out your chest, sucking in your gut, kitty stepping or duck waddling, and pretending to be relaxed—take a deep breath, then another even deeper breath, and through enormous exertions emerge from this ocean of a contest for another breath.

Considering competitive games in general, marbles is particularly complex and unpredictable as you not only must shoot your own ball into each of the five holes in turn but also need to attack and defend the path forward. Perhaps the most important tactic in the game is winning your opponent's marble. Like winning a lover's heart, it is the most soul-stirring moment. Because of an unresolved impediment of dexterity, I rarely experienced this soul-stirring moment myself. My style of playing marbles could be called "zit squeezing"—weak pinch with zero accuracy. One need only observe a master smash a marble with a flick of forefinger or thumb, one-eyed aim straight as a plumb line, precise, unyielding, consistent, *ding dong! clack-clack,* five to four, and so on, sweeping across the land.

I've found boys in particular go bananas for toys that spin, like the "whipping top, " also known as a "whipping traitor," a name that arose, it seems, during the war with Japan. Tops were a typical DIY craft: take a shovel and saw off part of its handle, then use a knife to whittle it into a conical shape; set a ball bearing from a bicycle hub into the bottom point and circle the top's surface with a rainbow of colors; finally, take a piece of bamboo and tie a clothesline around it—this is the whip. The top looked like the spitting image of a traitor being whipped by a vile rogue, the more ruthless the whipping the more it could be tamed into submission; if the whipping halted, it wobbled east and bobbled west in dizzy transport and delight. Or a Beijing boy would yell out: "Hey, ya! You looking for a whipping?" This must have been how the game started.

Hoop rolling. Fasten the hook to the big iron hoop, then balance and guide it while pushing it in any direction. I wrote an early poem called "Blue Hoop" that clearly came directly out of my childhood experiences. The hoop must have been the first circular form to emerge from humanity's dreams: add another circle to make a bicycle; add two more circles to make a tricycle; add three more circles to make a car; add several more circles to make a train.

The diabolo. This toy looks simple but is actually quite pro-found; like the game of Go, its skill levels can be divided into *dan* ranks, so upon reaching the ninth *dan* one must surely be an acrobat. Two sticks one rope between; loop three coils around the diabolo's neck, then lightly pull one side up, loosening the yo-yo as it begins to spin; as it slightly trembles, gently yank up again with more strength and soon *weng weng weng* the yo-yo hums, like a gale passing through a bamboo forest. But the real climax comes when, with arms spread, the yo-yo's flung high up into the open air. Eventually, we weren't satisfied with just the diabolo and moved on to spinning pot covers, teapot lids....

Violent tendencies and a spirit of risk are the unwritten rules of boys' games. In the mid-1960s, the film *The Knife Thrower* became the flavor of the moment, the flying knife hijacking our imagination. We started by sharpening a few pencils while the parents were out and pockmarking the door into a honeycomb; then switched to a fruit knife, using a chopping board as a target. But these, naturally, weren't true knife-thrower's flying knives. For a long spell, Yifan and I went crazy searching for those knives, from the realm of heavenly jade to the Yellow Springs, until at last, in a scrap pile of an iron factory, we "swiped" some heavily rusted knives. First, we furiously honed the knives on the cement sidewalk outside our gate, frightening passersby to respect the ghosts and gods from a distance and detour around us. Then, with increasing savageness, we propped up the wooden lid of the garbage can in the courtyard, and from a distance of roughly twenty meters, let the knives flash and flicker by, dazzling the eyes and cheering the heart. Later, we were told that we had caused a disturbance and both our school and the neighborhood committee joined forces to investigate—which is how our flying knives got confiscated.

What the populace looks forward to most each year is Spring Festival, the New Year—for boys, being allowed to play with firecrackers is the main allure. No matter a family's circumstances, each child is always given a little "money to ward off evil spirits," and most boys use it to buy firecrackers. Firecrackers come in all shapes and sizes, each akin to its military counterpart according to firepower: Little Whip, a bullet; Big Whip, a hand grenade; Fire the Lantern, a flare; Double-Kick Cracker, a mortar; Soaring Rocket, a ground-to-air missile; and as for the Numbing Thunder, its closest equivalent would be a TNW, a small-scale tactical nuclear weapon.

At age seven, for the first time in my life, I could go outside and light a firecracker by myself, electrifying my soul beyond anything. Before setting out on my mission, I first made some important preparations. I broke off one firecracker from a bundle and stuffed it into my pocket, then took a small wad of toilet paper and rolled it into a thin joss stick. Such a toilet-paper stick, or wick, when soaked with saltpeter, released a stream of pungent smoke once ignited, giving off a lovely odor, though you needed to blow on the wick evenly to keep it from dying out. As I stepped out into a snowy and icy land, fireworks exploded above me, blooming into twinkling stars that illuminated the dark night. I lit my first rocket; at the end point of a parabolic arc it burst crisp and clear, a lonely echo, like the first gunshot fired in a military attack.

Courage grows with age, for instance, pinching a Double-Kick Cracker between two fingers while lighting the wick, then dropping it to the ground with a loud pop before it comes to life again, flies into the air, and explodes. Then there's the Yellow Smoke Cracker, a special kind of weapon analogous to a smoke bomb, or poison gas bomb, and actually released enough yellow smoke to obscure the sun and sky coupled with an intense sulfuric smell that made you cough and wheeze. Yifan and I took a Yellow Cracker and snuck over to apartment 211, the Ma family's residence, lit the weapon, slipped it under the crack of their door, and scrambled away. Their New Year's dinner turned to mayhem, and eventually one of the Mas arrived at our door threatening to file a lawsuit. Father and Mother pulled me by the collar back to their place so I could offer a formal apology. Fortunately, in those days, this type of lawsuit didn't exist in our judicial system. Otherwise, I imagine that would've been the downfall of our family—to be sued into ruin by another family.

One Spring Festival afternoon in 1959 remains a vivid memory in my mind to this day. The boys of our building complex had split into two warring factions—one group defended the courtyard gate, the other took advantage of the rock garden's "mountainous" topography to launch an assault. Double-Kick Crackers and an array of firecrackers big and small catapulted and slingshotted across the battlefield, shuttling back and forth in a riotous weave, creating an earsplitting havoc, deafening bliss. Our defenses consisted of dustpans for shields. Soon a thick cloud of niter smoke filled the air, as if we were in an ancient city under siege, until the day darkened ... until the voices of our parents beckoned us in....

After that we practiced our maneuvers annually, as if we were preparing for a war with real guns and live combat. The day the Great Proletarian Cultural Revolution broke out I remembered the pungent smell of toilet-paper smoke the night I set off my first firecracker. The revolution unleashed a tremendous amount of energy (converted into violence that reeked with blood); countless boys and girls served as the source of that energy. They seemed to have grown up overnight, disguises shed, games and toys tossed far, far aside.

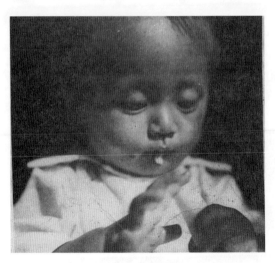

Eating something

With my little brother

With my little brother and sister, 1956

Siblings portrait, 1959

*With my sister at Three Never
Old Hutong No. 1, 1958*

Rowing in Beihai Park

Rowing with my little brother

Furniture

1

IN MAY 1948, my parents married in Shanghai and moved to Beijing, first to Dongdan Duofu Alley, and then to Dong Jiao Min Alley, the former foreign legations quarter. Father worked at Central Trust of China while Mother stayed home for a period of time. Daily life passed prosperously, as evident from the furniture we gradually purchased: Simmons spring mattress, dressing table, large armoire, hardwood dining table with chairs, and so on, all evoking entrenched petit bourgeois tastes.

A rocking cradle was my first abode, the furniture surrounding me as lofty and grand. I rocked and rocked my way out of the cradle, then wove between the legs of tables and chairs, until one day I stood tiptoe peering over the tabletop to glimpse, at last, the horizon.

From Dongdan Duofu Alley we moved to Fuqian Street, then to Fuwai Avenue, until finally settling at Sanbulao Hutong No. 1. During our migrations, pieces of communal furniture burst into our lives like strangers. They included two writing desks—one dark brown with three drawers across, the other a pale yellow "heavy-at-one-end" desk with a large drawer that could hold files and which belonged to my father, who used it to lock up all of our family's secret documents—in addition to a bookshelf, two chairs, and two beds. Communal property assumed the unmistakable appearance of military communism, penetrating the interiors of each and every household; its unit market price followed that of sheet iron. Rental fees for this property were automatically deducted each month from my father's paycheck.

The establishment of communal furniture led the way for privatized furniture, both undergoing a very long transition period during our growing years. I never could have imagined that this wholly unattractive communal furniture would be so sturdy and durable, demonstrating its indomitable spirit while at the same time opening the door to the privatized furniture of bourgeois tastes, and then suddenly disappear from our lives in the blink of an eye.

The first sign of revolt involved the Simmons springs, each coil struggling free of the mattress, breaking out east, popping out west. Not to mention sleeping with the springs pressed painfully against one's legs and back, along with the creaking *zhiga zhiga* all night, as if the tireless twangs of a broken *qin* zither. But how to find someone to fix it, overwhelmed by the difficult times, when even food and drink weren't a given.

After asking around, it was said that a small factory purchased old mattress springs, five kuai for one. Father became ecstatic after hearing the unexpected news and spent one weekend taking out the springs and changing the planks on the bed.

Altogether there were twenty-eight springs; on the black market, a single spring could be exchanged for a head of white cabbage. Borrowing a flatbed pedicab from his workplace, he left in high spirits and returned in low spirits—apparently the information was wrong: five kuai not for one spring but for all of them. He piled the springs onto the balcony; wind blew rain poured rust bloomed, until finally they were sold to the scrap yard nearby for some fruit candies, which we three children shared.

Next in line to revolt were the springs of the four dining chairs, echoing the others from a great distance; perhaps they were manufactured in the same factory as the Simmons mattress, their allotted time now up at once. Father took five pieces of plywood, sawed and nailed, and suppressed a rebellion. Although the five boards couldn't be said to please the eye, one could perch firmly on the seat. Then the Cultural Revolution subsumed everything and there was no chance to lacquer them; the chairs remained bare, though through the years a butt-shaped stain darkened the wood.

2

As the eldest son, I learned how to do the household chores early on, helping Qian Ayi to prepare the vegetables, wash the dishes, light the fire, sweep the kitchen. What always bewildered me were the glass doors of the old hutch cabinet—no matter how or how much you washed them, nothing worked; wipe the glass to a shine with a wet cloth and once the water streaks dried the glass would darken again. I longed to see my parents come home after work and stand before the cabinet with delightful astonishment, so much so that I even used soapy water and scouring powder to scrub and scrub, but my efforts ended in failure. This seriously affected my mood. Only later did I learn it was actually called "crow-black glass," and made that way to deliberately hide things from view. For many years my mood stayed like this darkened glass—no matter what scrubbed it made no difference.

When I started middle school, I finally got a drawer with a lock, causing a most wonderful feeling inside me—I had my own secrets to keep now. Early on I wrote poems like this: "Use a drawer to lock up your secrets, / Leave commentary in your favorite books." Writing felt like pure ecstasy. In my locked drawer I kept my allowance, notebook, report card, New Year's cards, and my first short-story attempts, plus a photograph of my secret love, Cousin Mei, though really it was only a group photo of my extended family standing in front of the Nine Dragon Wall in Beihai Park.

Furniture cycles from birth to old age, sickness unto death, just like a human being. By my second year of middle school, they suddenly turned old—the rails of the five-level dresser broke, open drawers impossible to close; bookshelves wobbled, sagging under the unrelenting weight of the classics; chairs creaked *zhiga zhiga*, grumbling about their own fate as well as humanity's; the thick glass covering the dining table cracked and looked like a Balkanized state. My father used adhesive plaster to patch it up, but the plaster quickly lost its effectiveness and it began to give off a rancid odor.

The appearance of plastic overlay had a revolutionary significance, my father among the earliest ones to comprehend this little fact—the interior-decoration movement that would eventually spread across the nation still far beyond the horizon. One day, Father returned from the hardware store with some scraps of plastic overlay, their yellowed condition reminiscent of excrement, which was probably why he could buy them at such a steep discount. He used some latex glue to join four of the scraps together, took some editions of the classics along with various household items to press it flat, and a few hours later the experiment proved a success. Plastic overlay seemed much more durable and longer lasting than glass. My father felt utterly pleased with himself, and with emboldened unrestraint purchased more and more scraps until he had covered nearly all the dressers, kitchen cabinets, nightstands, and tabletops in plastic.

For twenty-five kuai, my father recruited a leather sofa chair from our neighbor Uncle Zheng; enormous and unwieldy, its proportions beyond any standard furniture made for public or private use, it was like stuffing a cushion for a giant to curl up on between my parents' wardrobe and bed. It also proved to be a dubious business deal: soon a spring stretched outward from the middle of the leather cushion, looking like a lead-the-cow morning glory in full bloom; unable to hide in the open, each spring one after another popped up, *rising here once buried there*. The leather also started to flake off, peeling away like an gigantic orange.

The dressing table was my family's only other extravagant piece of furniture, no doubt born sometime before me. On either side of the large mirror sat two small cabinets, between which a connecting glass passageway looked like a rectangular fish tank; the glass top had long since shattered, the vanity stool had also *flown away without wings*. The large mirror had turned hazy with the passing years, as if it suffered from amnesia, only reflecting the springtime of my mother's youth. With its back turned to the age, its presence troubled me, especially during the Cultural Revolution when it essentially existed as proof of guilt.

My parents were sent off to a cadre school. One day off from my forced manual labors, I borrowed a tricycle cart, hauled the dressing table to the Dongdan Antique Market, and sold it for thirty kuai, a heavy burden lifting from me. I used the money to treat my brothers to a meal at the Old Moscow; we commemorated our fleeting youth that had passed by in a blink.

3

When my parents returned from the cadre school, our home resumed its usual *Lebensordnung*. The furniture resembled a bunch of drunkards, leaning to the left, tilting to the right, and my father continued his repairs, spreading his plastic overlay patches all over the place.

We also purchased our building's first nine-inch black-and-white television set (outside of the CAPD secretary-general's family), causing an ever-so-quiet entertainment revolution. The television found its place against the north wall in the outer room, centered on top of the plastic overlay of the five-lever dresser and replacing the plaster bust of Chairman Mao. Whenever a movie started, the neighbors would swarm inside, carrying a wooden stool or folding chair. Those were happy times of communal bonding. As each family, one after the next, acquired their own television set, a calmness cooled through our house.

Television began to alter our lifestyle—first, the viewing position made our waist ache, back sore, and forced us to move to a bed, where we became wholly dependent on cotton padding. Then just as our necks turned rigid and our vertebrae warped, Little Qu appeared. He lived in Building Six, worked as a public servant for the municipality, his wife a ticket seller on the trolleybus. His ordinary Mongolian face always displayed a smile as he let out a soft *heh heh,* eyes asquint, as if spying an oasis through a sandstorm. Little Qu told us that the times had changed, television must be watched from a sofa, and he proposed to help us acquire a pair. He proceeded to show us a simple sofa he had made himself, as cozy as it was economical. This happened during the nationwide subtract-communality-from-the-people era, and to have it instantly flip into addition made my father and me a little giddy.

I went with Little Qu to the hardware store in the Xinjiekou district and bought shoulder poles, springs, hemp rope, canvas, and other sundry items of various shapes and sizes. Every evening after work Little Qu would come over. This was grueling coolie labor that demanded a quick mind and skillful hands, and I could only play the role of the helper. With his singular eye precise as a plumb line, he sawed the shoulder poles in half, used a carpenter plane to sand them evenly, and coated each with three layers of colorless lacquer; after waiting for the lacquer to dry and turn as diaphanous as a cicada's wing, he used long screws and latex glue to fasten the poles together in a crisscross pattern, then tied layer upon layer of springs tightly onto the frame with the hemp rope, draped the structure in canvas, and covered it with colorful bath towels. He even cleverly built two tea tables to insert between the sofa pair.

Sitting on the makeshift sofa, I'm not sure why but a sudden *cling-to-life-fear-of-death* feeling came over me, as if sitting on the Sovereign King's dragon throne. Of course it brought many benefits—receiving guests no longer resembled a business meeting, sitting face-to-face a dignified distance apart. The crux of the issue was that, because of the sofa, our relationship with television changed, that at the center of modern life a correspondence formed between the television set and the sofa, the two not only becoming desirable but a bare necessity. In due course, those neighbors with a television set came in thronging succession to seek enlightenment, busying Little Qu relentlessly as he worked away, always happy, never tiring. And so this new wave set free by the makeshift sofas' link to the television set transformed the life ways of the whole apartment complex.

4

Since the day I met Lin Dazhong, my feelings of inferiority have only deepened; this despite the fact that he was primarily a peddler of nineteenth-century art and literary theory. Lin's eloquent words flowed out of his mouth like a torrential stream, sentences trailing clouds of smoke, lilting in the thick fog. When poor he smoked Cannons, when rich he smoked cigars. For a brief burst, the Xidan Department Store sold *Romeo y Julieta* Cuban cigars, that metal cylinder of the highest-grade brand-name tobacco cost a mere one yuan. It must have been part of Cuba's strategy to export revolution. With a Cuban cigar in his mouth, Lin Dazhong spewed out even more mountainous fogs of discourse.

One night at my home, assuming the mask of the intellectual Vissarion Bellinsky while puffing on his Romeo y Julieta,

Lin Dazhong declared that no matter in the name of aesthetics or freedom, all of our family's shabby, ragged furniture should've been thrown out a long time ago. With a graceful gesture he calmed my rage, saying, furthermore, that it was imperative to think about reversing the family's steady decline, which presented, really, only one solution: build a bookcase. As I motioned toward my teetering, ramshackle shelves, he checked me with another firm gesture. "I'm talking about a respectable bookcase, one with glass doors to pull open and a modern-style feel that would then, and only then," he said, "properly symbolize the sanctity of knowledge."

Fully convinced of his argument, I proceeded to persuade my parents. There was a pile of hefty lumber heaped in a hallway of our house, ready for use. Li Dazhong started to draft some blueprints, measure the wood, but first he appointed himself head architect and asserted his need to hire a few unskilled laborers. In those days there were plenty of idling brothers who'd fight over fixing a house or making some furniture, and once called on, always on call. I found Sun Junshi and Li Sanyuan. Sun was of medium height and stocky; Li was tall, over one meter ninety-three, and strong as a horse—they both frequented the same literary arts salon. Lin Dazhong handed over his blueprints, lit up a Cannon, turned, and disappeared.

Each morning around ten thirty the two arrived at my house for work. First they brewed some tea for themselves and sat down for a chat; at the moment, they were in the middle of reading *Animal Farm*. Sometime after eleven they'd rise and get to it. The first step involved cutting the lumber into eight-centimeter thick planks. I helped move the lumber to the courtyard, tied a piece to a tree; the two bros retrieved a huge whipsaw and began to saw and chat—"All animals are comrades" was discussed—and in a wink, noontime arrived. I hurried inside to cook up some noodles along with a few dishes, and poured us cups of sorghum liquor. Both bros had unusually large appetites, especially Li Sanyuan who could eat for three. Once Sun started on the liquor, his white face turned into a red face. By the time the conversation reached "All animals are born equal, but there are some animals even more equal than other animals," it was past three in the afternoon and we were ready to get back to work. Before daylight erased into blackness, we drank two more rounds of tea. Naturally, some more dishes to go with more liquor had to be whipped up for dinner, and by the time our talk turned to "Four legs are good, two legs are bad," Sun's red face had deepened to purple.

Lin Dazhong as foreman would show his face every once in a while, sometimes puffing on a cigar, sometimes a Cannon. After pontificating about the Cold War ideology that served as backdrop to *Animal Farm*, he vanished again.

We sawed the wood planks for more than two weeks while witnessing my family's rapid conversion to ruin—our rations of nonstaple foods emptied, our jug of cooking oil bottomed out, and yet the engineering project still seemed far from completion. Mother grew more and more worried; Lin Dazhong tried to console her, saying that the manufacturing process was entering the final phase.

One day, Lin Dazhong brought over a roll of dark-brown wood-grain paper; he rolled up his sleeves, brushed sheet after sheet with glue, positioned each sheet carefully on the pieces of wood, then finished it off with a layer of colorless lacquer. On the second day, after he conducted a detailed inspection, the bookcase was finally assembled and moved into place. Once the glass doors were mounted, the bookcase stood before us with an imposing grace. We dried our cups with a toast to the sanctity of knowledge.

Who knew that this modern bookcase would deteriorate so fast? The wood-grain paper bubbled up, the planks warped from the dampness, the glass doors jammed—its appearance grew distorted and its functionally changed accordingly, books replaced with hats and shoes and junk, until at last it was moved into the kitchen and stuffed with pots and pans. Nevertheless, this bookcase bobbed about in the drifting tides and persevered through each ordeal, enduring a decade of multiplying changes that involved our whole nation.

Vinyl Records

AROUND THE BEGINNING of the 1960s, our father spent 400 RMB to buy a Peony radio–record player. The record player, in particular, was quite high-tech back then: four-speed selection with automatic stopping coupled with a speed-detection regulation system. I imagined the flood of music that would flow out of the tiny red-and-green power light, turning our lives totally transparent, as if we lived inside a glass house.

Father, however, didn't particularly understand music, his purchase, while linked with an infatuation with modern technology, was more a reflection of his romantic temperament, a sharp contrast to the ominous age taking shape around us. An age when people endured constant hunger and busied themselves just trying to scrape by, living hand to mouth—idle ears seemed superfluous. Father also bought a few vinyl records, including *The Blue Danube* by Johann Strauss. I remember after the Peony was first set up, Father leaping about, dancing along to the waltz, almost making me choke with shock.

On the 33⅓-rpm album cover, Russian text printed across an image of the Danube seemed to indicate a performance by the USSR State Symphony Orchestra. My illuminating initiation into Western classical music made me feel like a child tasting his first piece of candy. Many years later when I visited Vienna, Strauss's waltz mingled with an Austrian pastry, causing my stomach to perform a somersault.

The Cultural Revolution arrived. I'm not sure why but that hurricane now reminds me of those black vinyl records. The epoch had shifted—it was the mouth's turn to be idle while the ears cocked at attention. I positioned a loudspeaker outside a closed window, lowered the volume, and played my favorite record.

Sometime in early 1969, my friend Da Li, who had been a year ahead of me in high school, borrowed *The Blue Danube* and took it with him on his move to Hetao Prefecture in Inner Mongolia, where the Great Bend of the Yellow River flows at the foot of Daqing Mountain. In autumn of the same year, I went to visit my little brother at the Construction Corps site on the Mongolian border and, on my return to the capital, I hopped on a train at Tuzuo Banner to pay a visit to Da Li and other former classmates, staying in their village for two days. They materialized as a group at sunset, each carrying a hoe over their shoulders, waists tied with grass rope, a raucous pack of happy chatter and laughter. Upon returning to the Educated Youth commune, Da Li put on *The Blue Danube*. The graceful melodies of the Austrio-Hungarian nobility melded with the choking clouds of cigarette smoke, rising up to the roof beams of a farmhouse on the northern borders of China. Years later,

Da Li returned to Beijing but that record album disappeared without a trace.

The second record I remember listening to was Tchaikovsky's *Capriccio Italien*, a Columbia 78 rpm Bakelite recording. At the start of 1970, Yifan, Kang Cheng, and other comrades, gathered at my family's apartment, as if huddling around a bonfire with our backs turned against the cold wind. In that salon raised to books and music, there was a taste of the forbidden fruit of happiness, there were girls who brought their romantic affections. That was when we started to write, each of us an author doubling as a reader-critic. The melodies of the *Capriccio Italien* must have infused these early writings, as we listened to it more than a thousand times.

It quickly became a kind of ceremonial ritual: hang up some heavy curtains, fill up the wine cups, light up the smokes, let the music carry us along as it broke through the night's tight besiegement and advanced into the faraway distance. We listened to the record so much that the needle soon needed to pass through the noisy static zone of the dust-filled world before it could enter the splendor of the theme. Then a brief pause. Kang Cheng's hand gestures established his tone as he began to expound on the second movement: "As dawn breaks into brilliance, a small band of travelers walk through the ruins of ancient Rome...." Deep in the night, the song ended but no one dispersed, each toppling over here and there to sleep, the needle lingering on the music's coda *zhi la zhi la zhi la* spinning on and on.

Yifan developed his own photographs at home. One time the red safelight of his darkroom was reported to be a military spy signal; the police went to investigate and, sadly, they confiscated his vinyl records, including the *Capriccio Italien*. That small band of travelers had crossed into the archive of the dark night to never emerge again.

Album number three: Paganini's *Violin Concerto No. 4*, a 33⅓-rpm Deutsche Gramophon recording, given to me by my uncle Gufu, the husband of my father's sister, upon his return from performing abroad. He played the flute in the Central Philharmonic Orchestra, and only retired a few years ago.

Talking about his musical tour through Europe, Gufu couldn't help but joyfully clap and kick up his heels. While in Vienna, he witnessed a Manchurian manifesting cloak performance that took the city by storm. From within the long cloak and robes the magician wore under a *magua* horse-riding jacket, he conjured up fire pans, doves, flowers, colorful streamers on the open stage; and for his final inspired act, somersaulted to the side and manifested a giant Beijing opera drum. After a hushed moment of silence, the audience broke out in thunderous applause. This amusing little anecdote, due to its countless retellings and a displaced cognitive association, caused me to conflate Paganini's record with a Manchurian manifesting cloak, as if it too was part of the magic act.

During the Cultural Revolution, Gufu was sent to a May Seventh Cadre School; I often worried about those wonderful records of his, especially the Paganini, its cover wondrously labeled with "Stereophonic Sound," filling us with awe—no household could own any stereo equipment at the time. The acoustics of monophonic sound, no doubt, shaped our monophonic ears, and monophonic ears constituted our unique way of listening attentively to the world. Whenever I borrowed an album, Gufu would eye me with suspicion and warn me again: *For the ten millionth time, don't lend it to anyone.*

Recalling our initial listening experience of Paganini, it caused a bit of a feverish obsession in everyone. Kang Cheng taught himself German and word for word, sentence by sentence, translated the liner notes on the LP cover for us. When that rousing *Sturm und Drang* theme resounded bold and unrestrained, he waved his arms as if conducting the strings with the rest of the orchestra. "Just like a bird in the wind, rushing into the open sky, rising to new heights, then falling, and yet unyielding, unwavering, it rises higher, and rises still higher."

In our cultural salon, material possessions belonged to everyone, the question of borrowing or not borrowing simply didn't exist. It stands to reason then that Kang Cheng packed the Paganini album into his book bag and pedaled back home with it. One early morning, I arrived at the Ministry of Railways residential apartments on North Altar of the Moon Street. I looked up at the second-floor window where Kang Cheng and his brother lived and observed the figure of a policeman moving back and forth. Trouble electrified the air—my forehead beaded with sweat, chills ran down my back. I immediately sped off to inform Yifan and the rest of our friends, and we converged en masse to plan our counterattack. We first wrote out every possibility of what could have gone wrong, detailing a variety of conjectures plus countermeasures for the right response to any given scenario. The summer of 1970 had just begun and that day felt like it would never end.

Then, as night fell, Kang Cheng mysteriously appeared at my home wearing a dust mask.

It turned out that Paganini had caused all the trouble. So-and-so, a girl at the secondary school affiliated with the Normal University, and so-and-so, her boyfriend, the son of a cadre officer, had brought the exact same record to their own literary salon and it had disappeared. They heard from so-and-so that he had seen it at Kang Cheng's place and assumed Kang Cheng must have stolen it. One morning before dawn, the strangers appeared at his door wielding some crude weapons. As Kang Cheng's paternal grandmother opened the door, they pushed her aside and rushed inside, the two brothers still fast asleep in their room. A dousing of soy sauce and vinegar led to a close-quartered fisticuffs. A "little feet investigation squad" instantly reported the incident and the police appeared at the crime scene, ignoring the black-and-white and whatever red-or-green-between in the situation, arresting everyone first to ask questions later. Paganini, though, couldn't be held as the chief counter-revolutionary, and so the intruders spent several days in jail for "disturbing law and order," where they wrote the compulsory self-criticism report, and that was the end of it.

Paganini could never have imagined that his music would circulate in such an extraordinary physical form of preservation and reproduction, circulate, moreover, into such a tangled situation: Almost half a century after his death, halfway across the world, it would be the cause of a bloody brawl between some random Chinese boys. Even more inconceivable is that these two identical vinyl recordings, through whatever unknown channels, found their way into a completely sealed-up China, each mingling, to further the mystery, with the warm blood of youth caught up in two separate underground salons, to eventually meet in a final confluence. Indeed, this all had something to do with magic.

Fishing

I WAS ELEVEN OR twelve when I first went fishing. After school the day before my excursion, I busied myself with preparations. The tools for fishing can be easily assembled: Mama's clothes-drying bamboo stick can serve as a rod, a sewing needle can be bent into a hook, a short piece of pencil lead can make do as a bobber. When Mama wasn't looking, I took a bit of noodle dough for bait, kneading in a few drops of sesame oil. I hardly slept that night, rose before dawn the next morning, and set off with my fishing pole over my shoulder, heading toward the moat by Desheng Gate, the Gate of Virtuous Triumph.

There's an old saying in Beijing: "First there's the Gate of Virtuous Triumph, then Beijing City behind it." During the Yuan dynasty, Dadu, the Grand Capital, was called Khanbaliq, and the Gate of Virtuous Triumph was known as Jiande Gate, or the Gate of Strong Virtue. In 1368, Xu Da led an army of one hundred thousand soldiers to conquer the city and Emperor

Shundi fled, escaping through the Gate of Strong Virtue, which was subsequently renamed the Gate of Triumph. Zhu Di, the Emperor Chengzu of the Ming dynasty, spread virtuous governance under heaven, and its name changed again to the Gate of Virtuous Triumph. By 1420, as a result of Beijing's reconstruction guided by the designs of the chief adviser and astrologer Liu Bowen, the Grand Capital's north wall was moved south a couple of kilometers, the city gate and outer walls fortified, the moat dug out, and nearly six-hundred years of Beijing's former façade swept away. The city's inner walls once possessed many gates, each with its own specific use, the Gate of Virtuous Triumph mainly a passageway for war chariots. In 1644, Li Zicheng's peasant rebellion defeated the Ming army outside Desheng Gate, the rebels stormed through the city walls, and Chongzhen, the last of the Ming emperors, hung himself on Coal Mountain.

From the beginning of the last century, following the demise of the imperial regime and the new needs of modern traffic, Beijing's city gate towers and walls were torn down first here, then there, until hardly a ruin remained. The Gate of Virtuous Triumph was razed piece by piece, growing smaller and smaller, down to a single surviving archery tower. The gate left standing in the early 1960s: crumbling walls, rubble strewn everywhere, weeds and grass soughing *se se se* in the wind. Onward the moat flowed around the archery tower. City walls indicated the boundary between the metropolis and the pastoral, that desolate wasteland one entered upon leaving the Gate of Virtuous Triumph for the northern outskirts. According to legend, the ghosts of lost souls roam the barren fields there.

It was about three kilometers from my home at Three Never Old Hutong, following Deshengmen Inner Street, to the gate; at the average walking pace of a ten-plus-year-old child it took about an hour to get there. The narrow Desheng Inner Street only allowed room for two opposing lanes of traffic. The No. 14 bus took this route and ended at the gate. That old relic of a bus looked a little savage on the narrow street, doors and windows quaking *hua hua,* billows of black smoke *pen pen tu* tu blasting out, any hint of clear blue sky instantly absorbed.

Back then, the most common means of hauling goods around was either by mule cart, horse cart, or tricycle cart. As the day grew lighter, I could hear the crisp, calm sound of horse hooves, from a distance coming nearer, then from nearness fading out into the distance. If anything could be said to embody the rhythm of Beijing in those days, it would be the sound of horse hooves.

And how profoundly this rhythm changed along the graded incline of Deshengmen Inner Street to the Changqiao intersection. Going downhill, a cart driver must hold the reins tightly to keep the horse or mule in a controlled gait as their metal shoes can easily slip on asphalt; going uphill requires a waving of the whip plus hollering encouragement, to the extent of leaping off the cart and cheering alongside. One day, in order to "Learn from Comrade Lei Feng," I helped push an old flatbed-tricycle driver slowly pedaling up a slope, putting my whole strength behind his cart, and then used all my pocket change to buy four pieces of *huoshao* bread for him, my behavior bewildering him with the nameless mystery. Afterward, I wrote an essay about it in the form of a diary, reaping the praise of my teacher.

I'll return to this Lei Feng story later, but right now let's go back to that early morning of fishing. When I arrived at my destination I was already a bit sweaty. The moat was in the throes of its low-water season and no more than a ten-meter-wide band of thick yellow-green soup, as turbid as it was smelly. I sat down below the decaying stone bridge and cast out my fishhook.

Most enthusiasts would describe fishing as a kind of meta-physical sport: physical energy expenditure is basically zero, externally it appears to be an exercise in meditation, its end goal really moral and spiritual self-cultivation. "Grand Duke Jiang fishes, the willing one is hooked" doesn't apply here. His way of angling unusual by any standard: line hanging straight down with a baitless hook hovering three chi above the water. And as Grand Duke Jiang had declared, it wasn't a fish he hooked but a sage-king—his strange technique luring the attention of the benevolent King Wen of Zhou.

When I started, I felt agitated and fidgety on my seat below the bridge, anxious about having too little bait on my hook for too many fish, the competition too fierce. My worry proved unnecessary—not one fish even nibbled. A shoal of them swam with mighty flips and flops not far from my line, undulating along and spitting out strands of bubbly foam. Ripples over-lapped as if tangible echoes colliding with one another. My heart began to ache for our household sesame oil.

A venomous sun shone down from the open sky—in its re-flections the bobber spun round and round, dazzling my eyes shut. The stench from the water drifted up, permeating the air. My whole body felt hot and dry, my throat parched. Then sud-denly a small fish floated toward the shore, coming so close I could nearly pet it. With quick-witted resourcefulness, I conveniently found a stiff piece of cardboard to retrieve it. But the fish sensed danger, its tail swayed back and forth as it swam into the heart of the water's torpid flow. Gone the golden moment fled, my spirits crushed.

But then, miraculously, the fish drifted back over. It *followed the ripple and chased the current*, as if a mysterious force carried it toward the shore. On closer inspection, it must have been sick, or in a dreamless sleep, as it waited for the cardboard to close in before languidly swimming away once more. Dejection turned to rage, followed by a cool serenity. I waited again, making my calculations in advance, selecting the perfect point of attack, and finally, I scooped it out from behind. My heart plummeted *ge-deng*, and I whooped in victory.

The little fish was about three inches long, shiny shiny black and slimy against the cardboard where traces of water bloomed out. It looked like it lay in a bed, its body still, no attempt to flounder, both cheeks working in and out. My triumphant joy abruptly faded, giving way to wonder at the cold detachment I felt toward my prey. The fish seemed to be observing me, too, with a sense of cold detachment as it faced the cold detachment of a fisherman's power over life and death. Time slipped away in our mutual gaze. Then the fish died.

I had forgotten to bring any water or food and my stomach began to rumble, my mouth felt dry, tongue swollen. As shadows lengthened in the light of the western sun, I packed up my fishing gear. Out of curiosity, I flipped over the rock I had been sitting on, and there in the shady depths squirmed a dozen or more brown leeches tangled together, scattering in the sunlight. Terrified, my whole body broke out in a sweat and I scampered off.

On the road home, I put the fish on the hook and carried the pole over my shoulder, head raised, chest out, *strolling through streets and alleys great and small*, thinking the eyes of the whole world watched me. I caught a glimpse of my shadow cast on a wall, the pole twice as tall as me, the small fish swinging at the end of the line. Smoke from stovepipes melding into sunset clouds waved like flags and turned to greet me.

I arrived home and Mama exclaimed, "O, my dear son! You show so much promise catching such a big fish." Those were the famine days. She disappeared into the kitchen to make preparations. Enjoying the laziness of the victor, I slumped onto the edge of the table and fell half asleep. Until Mama brought over a large platter with the small fish placed at its center, the fish roughly the size of a pencil stub and crisped to a golden yellow. I stared at it blankly for a moment, then devoured it in one gulp.

Swimming

1

I LEARNED HOW TO swim when I was eight. Aside from Ping-Pong, swimming was the most popular sport at the time. Once the weather warmed, kids everywhere swarmed to the waterside. Rather than swimming, this would be more fittingly described as "the great benefit of bathing to escape the heat while having fun."

The closest swimming pool to my home was located in the Shichahai district. I'd set off on foot with my pals from next door, walk the half-hour distance with the sun beating down on our heads, withering us into listlessness. But then, from half a mile away—salvos of boisterous clamor followed by a head-on olfactory attack of urine, bleach, and Lysol mixed together made our blood surge and boil. In stark contrast, when we staggered back home, wet swim trunks on our head, our shadows seemed to swim on the ground alongside us. We'd stop at the tomato stand, five fen for half a basket—the red mushy mess covering our faces and bodies rinsed away under a roadside faucet, where we filled ourselves with a bellyful of cool water.

I first imitated the freestyle stroke in the mushroom kiddie pool, two hands alternately paddling the water, and both feet splashing furiously, yet I remained in the same place. From the mushroom pool I surveyed the *deep waters and burning fires* of the grown-up world: dangerous movements and extreme cacophony clashed with frenzied competitive play, as if on a field of battle.

At home I used a washbasin to practice holding my breath. A quick glance at the alarm clock, suck in a deep deep breath, dunk the head into the water, air bubbles emerging *gu gu gu*, until the agonizing last moment of no breath causes the neck to snap violently back. Competing against my buddies I could hold my breath longer and longer, but with a heave a gasp a pant, my face looked ferocious, as purple as an eggplant. Along with breath-holding, I also practiced keeping my eyes open underwater, to the point where it looked like I suffered from pinkeye. To master the skills of a fish, *Homo sapiens* must reverse millions of years of evolutionary progress.

Moving from the washbasin to the swimming pool, the world expanded with the level of difficulty. One slip of a held breath and, *gu-dong*, a mouthful of water went down, leaving behind an acrid taste—piss in the pool. And yet, for those reluctant to swallow the water, how could they ever learn the skills of a fish? The mushroom kiddie pool became my drill pool. Both hands barbed to the gutter grate, I'd take a few breaths, hold it, cat-bend into the water, push off hard from the wall, and bob 'n' flop for seven or eight meters in one breath.

Having drunk large quantities of the undrinkable water,

my technique eventually did improve: Unable to breathe while freestyling, I popped my head above the water surface while frantically working my arms and feet, and managed to swim twenty to thirty meters. The adept are bold, as the saying goes, and so I ventured with my friends to the "swimming wilds" of Houhai. So-called swimming wilds denote the *rivers streams lakes seas vast heaven and earth*, which, for one, are free, and secondly mean no one present appointed to save you and so, if need be, you better save yourself. Houhai was a swimming wilds paradise for poor children, no lifeguard naturally, plus you could fish, catch shrimp, and even clam. And kids there didn't just thrash and splash in the water to keep from drowning; they swam *like a fish to water*, and looked like a little black brood so darkened from the sun that their teeth and eyes gleamed white. Although we couldn't keep up with their ranks, we could drift across the light waves of the lake, to our heart's ease and delight.

The *Beijing Evening News* often ran stories of people drowning, which didn't deter me, a water demon, in the least. Houhai waters weren't deep; even if there was the threat of full submersion, you had nothing to fear if you could tread water. Clamming proved the most difficult skill to learn. I watched others dive into the water, forked feet pedaling twice in the air then vanish, only a thin trail of bubbles floating to the surface showing the diver's whereabouts, and the next instant, the diver rocketing into the air, hand clasped around a big clam. I tried many times, each attempt ending in defeat: one hand pinched my nose, back arched, butt sticking out, legs fanning convulsively with spasmodic kicks, my body like a crossbeam spinning in the same spot. My open eyes were blind, only the bubbles gurgling from my mouth visible—not even close to clamming when I couldn't even reach the sludgy bottom.

2

I marched farther on toward wider watery realms.

Summer break, age ten—my classmates and I visited the Gardens of Nurtured Harmony at the Summer Palace. It was a tranquil day, gentle breeze, calm waters. We rented two boats and chased each other around the lake, our bodies soon drenched with sweat. We docked at the Pavilion of Literary Prosperity, climbed ashore, and headed straight for the waters nearby. The seasonal swimming area had some simple changing rooms and wooden signs that marked the water levels and safety zone.

Wading away from the stone levee, I tested the depths on tiptoe, the lake bottom mucky mud interspersed with sharp stones. Sludge oozed soft between my toes and sucked the soles of my feet; the undercurrent surged, mud loaches threaded in and out right under my crotch. The water rose up to my chest; I began to swim forward, reached the wooden sign that warned of the depths and turned around. Back on shore I caught my breath and rejoined my friends. Hungry, I bought some provisions at a food stall, ate and drank with relish, and returned to the water.

The more I swam the braver I grew and soon I left the safety zone behind. The people on shore looked smaller and smaller, the world silent save for the sound of the wind, the water, my breath. Shimmering sunlight, scrolling clouds. That sudden feeling of loneliness so entrancing as anxiety elevates.

A ferryboat sped by, triggering a series of big waves to roll toward me, *blocking the sky sweeping the earth*; I went under fast, swallowed gulp after gulp of water in quick succession. I got caught in the middle depths—unable to reach the lake bottom in order to push off to the water surface above. Darkening sky, sun a turbid blur at the center of the vortex. Choking, my whole body went limp, my head cleared to lucidity, and in a split second dinner, schoolbag, parents, pet rabbits ... coalesced and scattered, like the brilliance of fireworks bursting, as I bid farewell to everything, each and everyone, before my awareness of death gave me a jolt—in a flash transforming into a powerful will to survive. I flailed with all my might until, at last, I made it to the surface; with my equilibrium totally ruined from choking so much, I bobbed up and down in the water, sinking and rising while swallowing several more mouthfuls of lake.

But once again I floated on the surface, then flung out my arms and floundered toward shore. Reflecting further on my swimming technique, just think of a child's "tortoise-fist style" of fighting. Finally, my toes could reach the lake bottom; I exerted the rest of my strength in finding my footing while hacking out the water that had collected in my lungs. At last, climbing onto shore, my whole body weak and limp, I found a rock to sit on. Surveying the scene, I saw my friends frolicking and chasing each other in the water—not one of them had noticed my plight. Life moves on. The sun dipped in the west and would soon fall behind the hills, this sun, the same sun I had glimpsed underwater.

I didn't tell my friends anything, and of course didn't tell my family. This was my first near-death experience, which I could share with no other.

3

The first time I met my older cousin Kai Fei it must have been a Sunday as that was the only day he could ask for leave. I was about thirteen. We ate lunch at the home of his maternal uncle (who was also my father's elder brother), and afterward went to the swimming pool at Taoranting Park together. The Taoran Pavilion was built in the Qing dynasty and got its name from a couplet by the Tang dynasty poet Bai Juyi about yellowing chrysanthemums and drinking, "happy and carefree." My cousin met me with his head hung down, *as silent as an oyster*. This never changed.

Cousin Kai Fei was a student at a Red Flag School. "Famous schools with reeducation through labor characteristics," is how teachers and parents put it to threaten children. Anyhow, my father encouraged us to get together as, after all, we were cousins. Whatever my cousin had done was guarded by the whole family as a dark secret. Though children may not really grasp the moral universe of adults, whatever is treated as taboo, illegal, heretical only piques their curiosity, to the point of fostering a natural reverence.

From Legation Street we rode the No. 6 streetcar to the Taoran Pavilion Swimming Pool, hardly exchanging a word the whole way. My cousin was three years older than me, short and stocky, dark-skinned, with a laryngeal lump rolling up and down—that mark of adult maturation. I hadn't reached this advanced developmental stage yet and, compared to him, looked like your everyday thin-boned, helpless, firewood chicken.

While inching along the metal railing of the ticket line, we each wished to speak, then stopped, glanced at each other, chuckled, and when it came to be our turn, fumbled in our pockets for change and each paid his own way. At the entrance he bought two popsicles and handed me one, waving me off when I tried to thank him. On the way from the changing rooms to the pool, sunlight blinding, chaotic hubbub of the crowds, the sky swayed for a moment—I slipped on the wet ground and nearly crashed onto my back. But before disaster could strike, my cousin grabbed me with his hands, held me steady, his arms strong and powerful.

After swirling his hips around and stretching his legs, Kai Fei prepared for entry, then dove into the pool. His freestyle stroke was efficient and fluid, flutter kick barely splashed, as if he were a professional swimmer. I was floored—my eyes wide, jaw slack. Entranced, I stared with admiration.

When we climbed out for a break and stretched onto our stomachs on the boiling cement, black droplets fell from his arms, drop after drop soaking into the rough ground, water stains fanning out. I voiced some words of praise, which were drowned out by the ambient noise; I wanted to repeat them but he seemed lost in thought and I quickly clammed up. My cousin lived in his own closed-off world, unwilling to let anyone inside.

The sunlight shifted ever so slightly, waves glistened in the light, dancing papercut-figure shadows. My cousin stood up, headed for the depths of the lap-and-diving pool, guarded by a metal railing around its perimeter, the deep waters a clear cerulean blue, a near emptiness, while high above sat a lifeguard with sunglasses on. My cousin first climbed the three-meter-high diving board, jumped twice on its end and soared up, spreading both arms wide before bringing them together, outstretched above his head, and then plunged straight into the water. Emerging from the blue bubbles, he ascended the poolside ladder and climbed again, up and up to the ten-meter-high diving board. He didn't hurry, but stared out into the distance from his lofty perch.

When he came back over he smiled as before but his mind wandered elsewhere, his gaze like a blind man's. Try as I might, I couldn't make him see me at all, which caused a profound sadness within me. That day we didn't exchange more than ten sentences, and upon parting, didn't even say good-bye. It would be the first and last time we'd ever see each other.

4

I started to take notice of the fairer sex, especially young girls my age, in the thick of puberty. During a time of suppressed desires, the swimming pool became the public space where the human body bared itself the most gratuitously. I would often lay on the cement with my head resting on my folded arms, feigning sleep while peeping at those graceful, mysterious curves. I secretly sighed to myself, *Such beings exist in this world—how could I have looked without seeing before?*

As the pool was small and people numerous, one often bumped into female strangers, accidentally brushing a breast, or thigh, and triggering a sudden surge of electricity. For the most part this moment ended in mutual peace and harmony, but every so often one was confronted with a tricky situation of hurled abuse: "How gross, you disgusting pervert!" During these troubling encounters, there was no recourse but to pretend nothing happened and trade barbs in order to prove one's respectability. Actual indecent behavior, however, did occur at the swimming pool. What would begin as a small disturbance would quickly attract a gathering, watertight layers, a jam-packed crowd with not a few depraved, jeering hecklers, and end with the offender being wrenched away to the local police station—presumably a case of a real pervert being caught red-handed.

In all male sports a libidinal factor plays an inherent role. As I attentively observed my cousin Mei with whom I was secretly in love, along with those dulcet strangers at the pool, my swimming skills soared to bold heights. And yet my ultimate dream was to be like Cousin Kai Fei—sashay and sway over to the deep end, scale up to the heights of the high-dive, and casually stare out into the distance.

The lap-and-diving pool represented the supreme privilege of the whole swimming complex—experience the pure blue cool chill of an Arctic iceberg. At the entrance, a sign noted this pool's water temperature: eleven degrees today, reminding me of that quality product, the Arctic Pop. And yet us commoners waded through murky waters of a hue difficult to describe, its temperature unmentioned. Because so many people populated the shallow pool, and its water was never changed, the temperature always felt warmer than body temperature, making it feel like you were soaking in a public bath.

However, to enjoy the privilege of the pure blue cool chill, one needed to pass a two-hundred-meter swimming test. I increased the intensity and hours of my training, including a night session. The key to breaking through to the two-hundred-meter mark was figuring out how to overcome the "false fatigue state" that hits you within the first fifty meters. The night session proved beneficial; fewer people meant less disrupted swimming which in turn focused physical and mental energy. Each time your head lifted for a breath, you could see a row of lights, hovering like a strand of pearls that belonged to the person you loved, or will soon love.

Blue firmament on high, I finally passed the test and earned my lap-and-diving pool certification, sewing the patch onto the most eye-catching place on my swim trunks.

The very next afternoon, I sashayed and swayed over to the gate of the deep pool. In that moment, I felt the gaze of every girl there as if a spotlight focused on me, its singular intensity. Nonchalantly, I lined up for the ten-meter diving board. Feeling dizzy from the heights, I couldn't look down let alone gaze out into the distance. I stepped onto the diving board, *threads of panic tangling mind and heart*, no open path to beat a hasty retreat; I could only pinch my nose and, straight as a brush, bounce into the empty air. With a great PENG! I felt a violent slap as the perfect storm swallowed me with a fearsome wave. The icy waters felt like needles, my scalp a tingling numbness, my whole body stung. I straggled up the ladder and out of the pool, shivering uncontrollably, half of my body red and swollen like a cooked shrimp curled over. At a loss for words, I couldn't stop shivering. I only prayed that the persistent spotlight pursuing me would immediately switch off.

Raising Rabbits

1

ONE DAY, WHILE exiting our building, a peasant with some baskets balanced on a shoulder pole and a tattered straw hat on his head called out his high-to-low hawking cry, luring many children around him to circle in for a peek. I followed my father over and leaned in to take a look; the baskets at each end consisted of multilayered bamboo trays, each tray crowded with newly hatched chicks, golden yellow down feathers so fluffy and light, tickling our hearts. After my badgering, Father went back upstairs to fetch a cardboard box and bought six or seven chicks. At home, he used a pair of scissors to poke some small holes into the top for air and, *Bian*!, an instant chick nest.

Their faint murmuring cheeps really turned your innards inside out with worry. After school I rushed home and charged straight for the box, first observing and petting, before cupping each one with both of my hands. The baby chicks used their claws to hook my fingers, each one trembling like a silk string and wailing plaintively on and on. I couldn't help but feel a thread of ecstatic delight.

It was the late 1950s and food supplies grew scarcer with each passing day; I could only give my brood minced pieces of white cabbage. Their crops swelled out; soon their feces turned a watery ash-green, attracting countless houseflies. Soon they turned into yesterday's yellow flowers—heads featherless and bald, bodies covered in filth, claws curled sharp. From the beginning, the adults harbored a secret plan for them that they kept from the children: The hens would be used for eggs, the roosters for meat. But that plan was still far from becoming a reality when, one after another, they fell ill and passed away.

By comparison, raising silkworms was much easier—as long as you didn't expect to spin and weave, let alone expect the bugs to spit up a single thread of silk. Start-up costs were low, just spread out ample mulberry-leaf bedding onto the bottom of an empty shoe box. The silkworm larvae looked as small as cadelle beetles. Their so-called nibbling away difficult to perceive with the naked eye—tiny black specks of larvae droppings evidence enough. In fact, their appetite and growth rate turned out to be astonishing in proportion to their tiny size. Mulberry leaves soon became hard to find, almost every mulberry tree around the neighborhood totally bare, save for a few lone leaves at the branch tips. I suffered from vertigo. The Tang poet Li Shangyin famously wrote about "spring silkworms spinning silk unto death," but my silkworms died before the silk-spitting stage—just as well, given my fear of moths; I had nightmares of cocoons breaking open and moths rising out.

Goldfish were the easiest to raise—they're equipped to endure hunger for ten days, half a month, no food no problem. Regular water changes the only inconvenience, though even this could be a fun chore: carry the fishbowl to the sink, use a bamboo strainer to scoop the fish into a dish, watch the fish gasp for breath, the innate wickedness of children manifesting itself so naturally. The life of a goldfish is wholly transparent. It made me wonder: Did the goldfish adorn our lives, or did we adorn theirs?

2

The Great Famine awakened my growing body during a time of daily desperation and fear. Everyone talked about how to get enough to eat, how to survive. Chairman Mao issued his own directives: "Ration according to the people, so when busy eat more, when idle eat less, when busy eat dried foods, when idle eat lean foods, when neither busy nor idle, half dried half lean, mix yams and greens and radishes and cluster beans and taro root and so on." School hours were reduced; physical education class suspended; teachers urged everyone to save their energy, move less, recline more, go straight to sleep after dinner. Visiting friends and relatives brought their own ration coupons, accounts settled after the meal. Inventive means were *born into their fated purpose*: We used various containers to store rice-rinsing water and grow chlorella, each month harvesting two to three catties of precipitate—rather than calling it "rice flour," it'd be more accurate to call it a soybean equipartition system according to their own computations. Little Jing and his older brother divided up fifteen hundred soybeans, which the two brothers gambled away playing marbles. We circled around to watch a match, this fight for survival rattling each and every one of us to our very soul....

An outdoor farmers' market in Guanyuan Park turned into the black market. The prices there truly frightening: one white cabbage for five kuai, one fish for twenty, one chicken for thirty, but our whole family still went every weekend. Father would occasionally buy a pestilent chicken at a discount; back home he'd quickly hone his knife and the chicken would flap madly around the room, trying to flee death's pursuit, covering the floor with feathers. Eventually the chicken would make it into the pot, where it'd braise in soy sauce, its ribs ultimately gnawed with the most exquisite care, as if carving jade.

One winter afternoon, Father brought my brother and I to the Guanyuan Park market. As we strolled up and down the rows of stalls, my eyes caught sight of a fluffy mass of small rabbits, huddling together for warmth, mouths opening and closing, red eyes shining—it was, as the saying goes, *a love once clutched no way to let go*. We both pleaded and begged Father with piteous persuasiveness. He wavered, smoked a cigarette with the rabbit seller who puffed a pipe, casually haggled, the price bouncing back and forth between them, until they finally agreed upon twenty kuai for a male and a female.

At home, the rabbits were released from the satchel: a sniff sniff east and a sniff sniff west. We hopped alongside them, much happier than they seemed to be.

Father found an old wooden trunk and some planks, and with a little sawing and hammering, he renovated the trunk into a modern rabbit hutch: two levels divided by planks and connected by a small ladder with wire mesh covering the passageway, plus a sloping roof and a small door in the right corner secured with a metal hook. The rabbits played, ate, and made waste downstairs; upstairs, they slept peacefully. We kept the hutch on our apartment balcony.

The rabbits ate and ate, as if they could never be satiated, and no matter what went in it always came out as the same, black, bean-size pellets. My brother and I carried bags in our pockets to hunt food for them outdoors, first in the courtyard and then farther away, from Houhai Lake to Purple Bamboo Park. While putting nature into practice in an open field, we discovered among the weeds a bounty of wild herbs perfectly edible for human consumption, some even tasted good. It seemed that humans and rabbits were more or less equals, positioned at the starting line of subsistence.

One afternoon, me and Pang Bangdian, a boy one or two years younger than me who lived downstairs, decided to focus our attentions into changing the living situation of our family's rabbits and his family's hens. We used some iron wire to make a hook 'n' hoe and set to work on building No. 1's dumpster, continuing our search all the way to building No. 8's dumpster. The sun trailed our bottoms, crossed over our heads, then plummeted behind the buildings. We collected 146 white-cabbage "heads" from the eight dumpsters—a brilliant victory on the battlefield. The first thing Beijing locals do with this vegetable is chop off the "head," or root section, of the cabbage; we planned to feed these discards to our respective pets.

Under the dim lights at the gate of building No. 8, we divided up the white-cabbage heads, each bundle of seventy-three filling up two empty cement bags—we were thrilled beyond belief; our faces as red as a hen's, our steps as nimble as a rabbit.

I returned home around nine and went straight into the kitchen to soak the cabbage heads in the sink, scrubbing each of them while recounting everything to my parents. With a strange look, they both stared at me. They told me that on this planet called Earth, there exists a hierarchy in the food chain. Without further explanation, they proceeded to take over my labors, wash the roots clean, pile them into a pot with water, boil them to softness, cut each in half, dip one in soy sauce, chew its tender heart, *zaba zaba* sucking and lip-smacking and praising its savory tastiness. I had been famished for a while, and so I, too, joined the white-cabbage head feast. The rabbit hutch on the balcony *dongdong dongdong* thumped and thumped.

3

Hunger gradually devoured our lives. Dropsy became commonplace. Everyone's usual greeting to each other changed from "Have you eaten yet" to "Have you gotten dropsy yet," then the pant legs were pulled up and each used their fingers to test the other's degree of illness. One could press a coin into Mother's calf and it wouldn't fall out; this was considered stage three dropsy, a very serious diagnosis. People clicked their tongues in amazement, as if it were a great honor.

The female rabbit got pregnant. The reproduction process still remained a riddle for me. She grew clumsier as the days passed; besides meals, she mostly reclined upstairs, pulling off tufts of her own fur to make a nest.

One evening, I noticed some strange happenings in the rabbit hutch; wielding a flashlight, I discovered five baby rabbits burrowing around their mother. Eyes tightly shut, bodies hairless, they looked like tiny, tailless mice. With my little brother and sister, I opened the cage door and gently picked up the kits; we cradled them in the palm of our hand and softly petted them. Who knew this would lead to catastrophe? After putting the kits back into the hutch, the mother rabbit began to push them away with aggressive nips. We soon realized that the mother rabbit recognized her offspring through her sense of smell, and once their scent changed, they changed into five strange kits she didn't know.

Emergency measures were quickly adopted: We transferred the baby rabbits to a shoe box lined with cotton batting and fed them through a straw. Besides rice water, we also found a bit of powdered milk, a scarce item as precious as gold. The kits greedily sucked down the rice water and milk, a heavy weight lifting from us.

Then one night I slept in fits and starts; the next morning, I opened the lid of the shoe box to find all five baby rabbits dead, their bodies rigid, four limbs curled. We wept, blaming ourselves. The mother rabbit acted as if nothing had happened, eating and drinking as usual. Who can comprehend the emotions of a rabbit?

The appetites of the parents continued to grow and grow while the grassy spaces around us shrank and shrank. My little brother and I trekked farther and farther out, exiting the city gate, heading deep into the wild fields where we were often chased away by village children. In the name of the rabbits, we exhausted our already quite limited energy reserves given our rationed existence. At the same starting line of subsistence, it wasn't who ran fastest, the rabbits or us, but who ran farthest.

And then came the critical juncture: My older cousin visited our family. She was a second-year physics student at Beijing Normal University; her family lived in Guangzhou and so she stayed in the dorms. After hearing my parents' complaints, she suggested that she take care of the rabbits—in front of her residence, a wide expanse of grass opened out, *take what you want, eat what you can*; plus, a stairwell on the ground floor usually saw little foot traffic and the rabbits could graze there during her breaks between classes.

The rabbits had found their celestial paradise.

That was around the time my little brother and I were learning how to swim. We'd blindly flop around the Beijing Normal University pool then pay a call to the rabbits, our trunks half wet atop our head. The rabbits hopped with vigor and gamboled with joy; they nipped our sandals with affection. Tending rabbits seemed akin to the ideals of tending sheep, the orderly cycle of the natural world freeing our hearts and easing our spirits. Sometimes they'd move as stealthily as the wind and sneak into the depths of the tall grass; other times they'd stand at alert, forelegs tucked in, taking in the sights and sounds around them.

But a good thing never lasts; someone complained and the school authorities stepped in, declaring the raising of rabbits in the dorms a disturbance of public space. After freely enjoying a bounty of food and warmth for three or four months, the rabbits moved back into the hutch at home.

Rumors together with famine spread *neither here nor there but everywhere.* Students circled around the classroom stove to roast corn-cone buns and talked feverishly about the international situation. One popular theory making the rounds was that our Big Brother, the Soviet Union, demanded the repayment of a debt, a debt owed from the Korean War when they had sold China weapons on loan, so that everything from chicken and duck, to fish and pork, to fruit and grains secretly made its way across the border, including each and every apple, one by one. I worried about our rabbits—a film I had seen showed Russians wearing rabbit-fur hats. I imagined a somber, stirring scene of a cargo train full of rabbits crossing the Siberian desert.

The mother rabbit's stomach swelled once again. We spread dried grass and old cotton batting onto the second floor of the hutch, then waited patiently for the moment of truth. At long last the birth took place, six babies total; this time, of course, we were sure not to touch them, focusing our efforts on finding food for the mother. Spring had just begun; the grass and wild plants had barely broken through the ground. While my parents weren't looking, I tore off the wilting leaves from the last of our stored winter-white cabbage and minced them up, adding a little lotus root powder, which we usually mixed into water to make a nutritious drink.

The hutch was too small for a family of eight. My brother and I found some bricks to line the bottom of the balcony railing, forming an enclosed pen that gave the animals a much larger space to roam. The kits curled around their mother, sucking her milk, while the father rabbit patrolled the area—eagles, fortunately, an uncommon sight in Beijing.

The following morning our faces turned white with fright: Three of the kits had disappeared! To our horror we discovered a gap in our "brick wall." The babies had plummeted off the balcony, their corpses we recovered in the Gongs' small vegetable garden. With heavy hearts we reinforced our "brick wall." But on the morning of the second day, another one was missing; it had dropped into the flower pot on the Gongs' windowsill. We became crazed: Their blindly suicidal behavior totally unfathomable; their eyes hadn't even opened yet to see the wide world. We had no choice but to shut the survivors in the hutch again.

As spring passed into autumn and the babies grew up, it became increasingly difficult to provide for this family of four. Our legs turned to noodles looking for grass to feed them—my little brother and I walked the whole "four-nine city": Beijing's walls in the four directions and its nine city gates, then walked the wild fields outside the city, a whole summer vacation spent serving the rabbits' struggle for survival. This, though, would be the final struggle. With winter around the corner, what could be done? Even if every white cabbage in our stores could be fed to them, it wouldn't be enough. And then there were those Russians seeking a settling of debts, waiting for their rabbit-fur hats.

My father, our family's commander in chief, issued forth a decision: Kill the rabbits and eat our fill, solving all our problems with one stroke. I imagined he had plotted this end from the moment of purchase—from wild rabbit to house rabbit, truly this pattern of excess has passed down to us from our hunter ancestors.

My brother and I put up a fierce fight, wailed and wailed *kuhu! kuhu!*, and even declared a hunger strike. But the words of the lowly carry little weight—the dictatorial decree of the food-chain hierarchy could not be overturned.

It happened on a Sunday. My brother and I set out early in the morning, one fleeing east, the other west, unable to step onto the balcony to bid the rabbits one final farewell. I found myself along the shore of Houhai Lake, crossed the Silver Ingot Bridge, passed Slanted Tobacco Pipe Street and the Bell and Drum Tower, lost myself in the crisscrossing alleys of the hutong weave. The posture of a rabbit standing on its hind legs, surveying the scene, is, in fact, nearly equivalent to a person's posture. I fell into a trance, the streets seemed to be packed with standing rabbits.

The day darkened; my brother and I arrived back home around the same time. Everything was very quiet and still; it felt like the massacre had ended a long, long time ago. The commander in chief lay in bed, reading a book. Mother spoke to us softly, mentioning there was some food left in the pot. She didn't say anything about the rabbits; we understood without a word. Our empty stomachs rumbled with hunger, but we firmly refused to enter the kitchen.

I climbed into bed, covered my head with my comforter, and cried.

Three Never Old Hutong Alley No. 1

1

ONE WINTER MORNING in 1957, my mother guided me along the hutong alleys, thick with mud after a snowmelt, to a newly built red-brick building. The muddy lane was about one *zhang* (3.3 meters) wide, full of potholes; a small hut stood in the middle of the lane, thick smoke pouring out of it, the charred scent of roasting yams wafting in the air. While we walked, my mother the doctor kept reminding me: "It's dirty—walk on this side."

As if I were a hound, that charred scent of roasting yams was forever ingrained in my brain with the memory of our new home: Three Never Old Hutong Alley No. 1. Setting out from here, I've walked for many years....

That winter morning, I raised my head to look up, followed the drainpipe, windows, balcony, all the way up until I reached the Beijing sky behind the eaves. The famous explorer Zheng He had once lived here—where were the carved balustrades and jade steps of yesteryear? Only a rock garden remained, as if today's blind witness.

Zheng He's family name was Ma ("horse"), his nickname San Bao ("triratna" or "three jewels"); the third emperor of the Ming dynasty, Zhu Di, later bestowed on him the name Zheng; this is how San Bao Lao Die ("Triratna's Old Man") Hutong got its name, until the late Qing when the Beijing dialect must have swallowed a jujube red date whole while the choking northwest winds further garbled the homophones to form San Bu Lao ("Three Never Old") Hutong Alley—a most auspicious name. As for Zheng He's travels around the globe, the riddle remains—if he was neither flaunting military strength nor involved in commercial trade, what drove him exactly?

Before transferring to the People's Progress of Min Jin, my father worked for the People's Insurance Company of China, and we lived in the company's Fuwai apartment complex, which stood in what is now the city's second ring road, the area still mostly wild fields. At Fuwai Elementary School, I recited the Winter Solstice "Nine Nines Song," counting down the nine nine-day weeks until spring: "First nine second nine keep your hands inside / Third nine fourth nine walk the ice outside . . ."; after we moved, I transferred to Hong Shan Si ("Temple of Great Benevolence") Elementary School, and continued to recite in perfect sync with the times: "Fifth nine sixth nine see willows riverside / Seventh nine river runs, eighth nine swallows come . . ."; then settling into our new home, spring arrived: "Ninth nine add a nine, oxen roaming far and wide."

To an eight-year-old, the excitement of moving surpasses any feelings of nostalgia. We had been living in the same unit of the insurance company housing as Uncle Yu Biaowen's family, sharing a common kitchen and bathroom; but our new place was a fourth-floor walk-up, single-family apartment. Faint whiffs of fresh paint, natural light reflecting off glass, a view of the rock garden from the balcony, and farther out, as if waves rolling away, layer upon layer of tiered clay-gray roof tiles of the *siheyuan* four-walled courtyards, pushing forth northward to the capital's low skyline, as flocks of pigeons flicker by, whistles echoing against the lonely sky, jujube trees withstand the wind from eight sides, green drupes deepen to red, enticing children who pass by to reach up on tiptoe, unable to resist a try.

I met Cao Yifan—his family lived on the third floor right below us. Yifan was only a month older than me, yet precocious far beyond our years: While I lingered among children's books, that prodigy hid under the bedsheets with a flashlight to read *Dream of the Red Chamber*. His physical development also shot off the charts—by junior high he was already half a head taller than me, and by high school he could pretend to be another student's uncle. We attended different elementary schools, then merged into the same secondary school, different classes, until finally we both tested into Beijing Middle No. 4 and placed in the same homeroom. If not for the Cultural Revolution engulfing everything, Yifan certainly would've been my sponsor to join the Communist Youth League.

2

The insurance company didn't insure anything at all. Uncle Yu Biaowen leaped from the company's residential building and killed himself. When I heard about it later the same morning, bewilderment flooded over me—it surpassed my capacity for comprehension. He made a widow of his wife and left behind two boys—the eldest, Yu Meisun, three or four years my junior, trailed after me all day, and the youngest still a baby. The inconsolable widow spent half the night sobbing alone next door, her weeping swallowed by the abyss of history. Besides myself listening through the wall we shared, who else could have heard her lamentations?

Moving to Three Never Old Hutong No. 1 actually made me feel light and carefree. To me, a change of address meant a change to a new life.

Of all the children at Three Never Old, Zhenkai (a "rousing spirit" indeed) is making his name as the most mischievous. The elderly grandmother in the courtyard often raps on our door, producing the child with red iodine spread over all his wounds for me to see, reproaching me with questions of why I haven't bothered to teach my own son better. I know automatically that Zhenkai has been the cause of trouble again, and like always I can only apologize and apologize once more. Kicking a ball, or throwing a brick, through someone's window, glass smashed to bits—more of the same, ordinary occurrences. (*From my father's notebook*)

In 1958, the large courtyard of our building bustled with excitement, an unceasing stream of novel tasks unfolded before us, each day like the celebration of a festival. First, the residents set up a canteen in the courtyard; Qian Ayi went to work there and me and my brother and sister joined to help. A small blast furnace was built in the vacant area in front of building

No. 8—Father, along with several uncles, worked busily from morning to night, surrounded by smoke and flames, until at last the smelting produced a heap of slag mixed with lumps of iron, whereupon drums and gongs resounded, filling us with envy and admiration; compared to us, the grown-ups really knew how to have fun.

Playing sparrows (mahjong) had reached a peak that year, the whole city caught up in the madness: Boisterous fanfare and cries shook the skies, raucous cacophony went on for three days and three nights straight. I stood on the balcony and drummed an empty cracker container with all my might, arms aching, voice hoarse; I hardly slept—even if I wanted to sleep I couldn't fall asleep it was so noisy. According to the statistics, in the Beijing area alone more than forty thousand sparrow tiles were eventually confiscated and destroyed.

What broke our communal heart was the razing of the rock garden. One piece of Taihu stone after another hoisted up onto a truck and, with a puff of smoke, the garden disappeared. Our favorite place to play hide-and-seek vanished with it. I later heard those chunks of Taihu stone were relocated to the Military Museum, one of the Ten Great Buildings constructed in Beijing in 1959 to commemorate the tenth anniversary of the People's Republic. A bulldozer busied itself for several days in the former rock garden, leveling the ground, then row upon row of Lombardy "leap-into-the-sky" poplars were planted, the trees growing at a rapid rate, leaping up three to four stories high in just a few years.

Yifan and I would often set out on long hikes, using our own two feet to measure Beijing, not a single coin in our pockets but filled with boundless imagination. He spoke highly of *Around the World in Eighty Days*, and we were convinced that we'd circle the globe together one day. And sure, we'd need to bring a few assistants, preferably female, from our building, too, to help us wash clothes and cook meals.

We walked out the Gate of Virtuous Triumph onto Qijiahuozi Road, spied around to make sure the coast was clear, and dove headlong into the vegetable fields. Just as we picked a few green chili peppers, some village kids discovered us; rocks and clods of dirt rained down in torrents; we shielded our heads, scurrying away like rats.

3

The turning point came when the white yams on the balcony started to rot. The smell of rotting yams transformed into one word: dropsy.

> I remember a three-year period of hardship, when there wasn't much food to eat; the children cried out from hunger and I told them not to run around outside and play but to lie down in bed and rest more. My second child, Zhenkai, looked at me and said, "Mama, eating just two meals a day, we're still hungry when we lie down to rest...." I thought to myself that Ji Nian and the children shouldn't go without proper nourishment, so I bought two chickens with the hopes of raising them for the whole family to eventually feast on. I asked Zhenkai to go downstairs to let the chickens out for a bit, never expecting that someone would

steal them. Ji Nian got so angry, and even beat his own son. Once, I felt so hungry my hands trembled and my body broke out in a cold sweat; it was truly agonizing, and so I stopped by a Sichuan restaurant on my way home and ordered a bowl of soup. Back at the apartment, I saw how the rest of my family was starving, too—my heart sank with anguish; Ji Nian tried to console me, saying I shouldn't be too hard on myself. He said that even in our suffering we should try to enjoy ourselves. And so the following Sunday we went to Purple Bamboo Park together for an outing. I remember Ji Nian and I seeing the malnourished condition of our children that day; we gritted our teeth, and at a fresh-fish house in Purple Bamboo Park, spent twenty-six kuai on a meal of fish.... (*From my mother's interview*)

The fresh-fish house stood just inside the east gate of Purple Bamboo Park, an aquarium in front of it where they kept their catch, ready to net ready to cook. So-called *hongshao yu*, or red-braised fish, is really just fish simmered in soy sauce, plus a dab of oil that blooms onto the surface. Compared to the wages at the time, the cost of the one dish was shockingly expensive. Finally, only bones remained on the plate, the three of us siblings still licking our lips, eyes widening, blinking, staring at one another in blank silence.

Chao bing, doughy noodle strips fried with cabbage and garlic, proved to be a much better deal than red-braised fish. Every Sunday our family frequented a small restaurant on Xi'anmen Street to eat *chao bing*. This establishment used more generous amounts of oil than other places.

From 1960 to 1961 I worked at the Socialist institute.... Those were really difficult times, the three siblings coming to the institute to eat the better meals there. We looked at our children and felt wretched; sometimes we'd buy them some fancy candy, which they devoured with glee, comforting us a little. (*From my father's notebook*)

As the eldest son, I felt obligated to help my parents maintain the ecological balance of our family, looking after my little sister and brother, making sure they received at least the minimum intake of calories. My brother and I ate lunch in one of the communal canteens that had been popping up everywhere, our stomachs still constantly rumbling with hunger; our little sister went to the July First Kindergarten, where the food wasn't so bad and on occasion she could even bring home half a steamed bun. The tricky meal was dinner, which demanded meticulous planning and calculation, each person allocated no more than two taels (less than half a cup) of rice. Though Qian Ayi possessed divine skills, she couldn't conjure up any miracles either. She went through a spell of making vegetable steamed buns day after day, outer bun a thin skin with lots of filling within. I tried to set an example, facing my little siblings and preaching the benefits of eating one less steamed bun, but I couldn't fool them.

My uncle Da Gufu got his doctorate in Germany; after liberation in 1949 he became one of the esteemed "first-class" engineers in the country and enjoyed special perks from the state. It was during this time of the Great Famine that he regifted his Chunghwa and Peony cigarettes to my father. My pangs of hunger intertwined with the clouds of smoke pouring out from my father's mouth, as if a fantastic hallucination swirled around me.

It was also a time when people rarely invited guests over; during New Year's or other festivals, if a relative happened to drop by, the grown-ups would inevitably circle around the table after the meal and wave their fingers, arguing over each ration coupon they fished out of their pockets. On the good-natured faces of Chinese citizens, this was clearly an extremely awkward situation.

Toward the end of the month one evening, my father gave me a one mao coin plus a couple of almost-expired ration coupons to treat myself to a bowl of wonton soup. There was an outdoor wonton shop on Dingzi Street in the Xinjiekou district. As I waited to be seated, it already neared eleven o'clock, leaving only an hour before the coupons turned into worthless scraps. I handed over the coin plus the crumpled pieces of paper to the shop assistant who verified the coupons, then smoothly pinched some tiny dried shrimp, scattered them into a bowl, rinsed five or six wontons in a bamboo strainer, and ladled out the pork-bone broth from a huge pot, the generous steam rushing past my face. My stomach rumbled with hunger, and yet I didn't immediately pick up my chopsticks; this being my first time dining out alone, I wanted to prolong the pleasure for as long as possible. The cauldron boiled as the shop assistant drummed its rim with a iron ladle; the suspended lightbulb glowed a faint yellow as a few moths fluttered to and fro.

4

Like the faithful attending church, our family frequented the Huguo Temple Theater every Sunday to watch a movie, in this way passing our days of hardship and want, as if it could compensate for our hunger.

Leaving Three Never Old Hutong Alley No. 1, turn left onto Mianhua ("Cotton") Hutong Alley, then head west on Huguo Temple Lane East, the trip roughly fifteen minutes by foot. The theater's façade looked inconspicuous. Air-regulator vents popped out from the roof, making the building look at first glance like an old factory fallen into disrepair over the years, flaking paint exposing the mortar in the brick walls. Only the glass doors, the movie posters, and the little ticket window disclosed its true identity.

My parents subscribed to the *Beijing Evening News*, a four-page newspaper with the movie listings printed in a column between pages two and three. Father, a movie addict, also subscribed to a few cinephile magazines; he usually chose the films we watched, his favorite ones being foreign films, which I often found totally baffling, and yet I, too, quickly caught the exoticism bug. All the early films from the Soviet Republic were dubbed by the Changchun Film Studio into thick Manchurian accents, which I initially mistook for Russian.

I silently reveled in the momentary darkness before a movie began, expectations and mental associations rising from within; the gap when a reel cut off while still running I appreciated even more, the screen a blank space, circles and scratches at the head and tail of the reel scrolling by, the sudden quiet, when one could hear the spinning machinery rewinding, mingling on occasion with crickets chirping *qu qu qu*.

After the movie ended, as I followed the audience members slowly out of the theater, a feeling of despair always washed over me—unable to charge on with the hero, unable to walk beyond the horizon, no choice but to return to the boredom of reality. Mother's head swirled with heavy fogs; while walking home, Father would clarify the story's principle threads, as well as the connections between characters.

Movie ratings didn't exist in those days. Once, while watching a film from Argentina with my whole family, a scene unfolded that I will never forget for the rest of my life. In a bar, an evil tyrant strips off the clothes, piece by piece, of a gorgeous female dancer—her blouse, ample skirt, bra, garters, underwear, all thrown into the air to her utter humiliation. My heart skipped and my flesh tingled; I was filled with both longing and terror to see her naked body. Then, at the climactic moment, the hero steps bravely forward and fights the evil tyrant, while also managing to throw the skirt back to the dancer so she can cover herself. The camera exposed nothing, I couldn't catch a glimpse of anything, and yet, for many nights afterward, I slept in fits and starts.

I started to go to the movies alone, especially on the first day of exams as it was the best way for me to relax. I'd usually watch a double feature, immerse myself completely in another world, forgetting everything about any exam. Strangely, I'd still do well; watching movies before battle turned out to be more effective than polishing a gun.

One day when there was no school, Father took my little brother to the Huguo Temple Theater. As the audience dispersed after the film, crowds thronging along the aisles, Father's glasses dropped to the ground and the lenses shattered. He was extremely nearsighted and couldn't walk a step farther, so my brother had to run home to retrieve another pair of glasses. This incident amused me immensely (though I stifled my laughter);

I could see my almighty father so clearly before me, standing outside the theater entrance, alone in the cold wind, looking blankly about with a helpless expression in his eyes.

5

Three Never Old Hutong No. 1 consisted of two multibuilding complexes; a gate between them served as the main entrance where a reception hut blocked the way, evoking an atmosphere of fleeting indolence. Arrogant Idler Wu guarded the main gate and also controlled the telephone, notifying residents of any calls. When the telephone rang, he'd put his rice bowl down, step into the middle of the street, and yell into his megaphone: "443, phone call—!"

No. 443 was our apartment, in building four right next to the main gate, four units on each of its four floors; most of the residents of the building worked for the CAPD. I'll start with the neighbors to the left and right of us.

In 441, Uncle Zheng Fanglong, a bachelor, roomed with the widow Aunt Tian. After being labeled a "rightist," Uncle Zheng married and moved to building seven. Aunt Tian, always cheerless and blue, had a son in college who loved to sing; we secretly called him Skylark—that "hundred spirits" bird of folk mythology that exists as the soul of one returned from the dead. Every day he went up and down the building's corridors trilling his songs to the skies, the stairwell's acoustics perfect for the timbre of his soprano voice.

In 442, the Wu family. Uncle Wu Chan, my father's elder brother, was from Haifeng County in Guangdong Province; he had lived for a while in Japan, then emigrated to Malaysia, later returning to the Mainland whereupon he joined the China Zhigongdang Party (CZGD) and was soon promoted to vice chairman. The CZGD, the youngest brother of the eight democratic parties, mostly consisted of residents who had returned home after living overseas. To me, Wu Chan personified that political party completely—smiling silently while sharing the motherland's secrets of wealth and power. He had three taciturn daughters. Strangely enough, I never heard any loud voices on the other side of our shared wall. Only when I went to retrieve the utilities bill could I could spy into one corner of their lives, though upon looking and looking, discovered nothing.

In 444, the Zhang family. Grandmother Zhang, kind and affable, always called me "young master" in Shanghainese. I'd tiptoe up the stairs to try to evade her address, but inevitably she'd softly turn the corner in the corridor and deeply bow with a "Young master has returned." The Zhangs were as ordinary as their family name—Mrs. Zhang worked at the childcare center at a foreign consulate and had two children herself. I attended the same elementary school as her youngest daughter, who was a grade below me. In fourth grade, I developed a crush on her. One day, on the way to school, she turned around and waved at me. Happiness, like an electric current, surged out of the top of my head; I bravely forged my way to her only to realize that she was greeting a girl behind me. They were a well-off, harmonious family using courtesies to maintain their distance from strangers, and silence to resist the violent windstorm.

In 431, the Chen family, a CZGD "alien household." The brother and sister seemed the deepest of the bunch; the younger of the two, Chen Chunlei ("spring thunder"), attended Beijing

Middle No. 13, performed exceptionally well, and ended up staying on to teach physics; he also played the mandolin. The older sister, Chen Chunlü ("spring green"), taught fandango and other Spanish steps at a dance school. She dressed fashionably in a chiffon blouse and a long pleated skirt, like a Gypsy woman. She eventually moved from Beijing to Guangdong, and reportedly was sent to a reeducation through labor camp for having intimate relations with a certain man.

In 443, the Cao family. Yifan's father, Cao Baozhang, had thick facial hair from ears to nose to brow. In the 1940s he served as a county magistrate and National Assembly delegate in Sichuan Province; naturally, after liberation, he didn't smoke with the leaders anymore. Not only were Yifan and I the same age, my little sister Shan Shan and his, Yiping, were too. We children came and went between both families, opening front doors without a knock and moseying inside. Yifan had three older half sisters with the same mother but different father; one married a doctor who worked at Jishuitan Hospital before moving to Hong Kong in the early 1970s.

In 434, the Pang family. Pang Anmin, a former director at the Wuhan Bank of Communications, possessed the cool poise of one who has handled a lot of money. His wife worked as an accountant at the Yili Food Factory, tantamount to holding the keys to the Heavenly Halls (particularly during those hard times). Pang Bangben, the eldest brother, was a painter; his wife Sun Yufan lay sick in bed year round (more on her situation in the next section). The little sister of the family, Pang Bangxuan, high-minded and proud, was a star student at the Girls' High School at Beijing Normal University. Pang Bangdian, the little brother, a mad genius, wrote novels before becoming a mathematician.

In 421, the Ma family. Ma Decheng was the son of Ma Xiang, President Sun Yat-sen's bodyguard. When the military governor Chen Jiongming revolted in 1922, attacking the presidential palace in Guangzhou, Ma Xiang risked his own life to carry Madame Sun to safety; she had a miscarriage and couldn't bear children after that. It is said that at the end of his days, Sun Yat-sen implored Madame Sun: "Ma Xiang followed me for a lifetime, take care of his living expenses and make sure his children are properly raised and educated." Ma Xiang visited the capital each year during those fateful days, going out for walks with a soldier's spirit, looking healthy and spry, back upright. His two grandsons, First Fatty and Second Fatty, eventually chose their own paths, one becoming a professor and the other a famous doctor, neither discrediting the hopes of the Father of the Republic.

In 423, the Liu family. Liu E-Ye was a simple and honest man who tried bitterly to avoid any sort of exercise; he balded early. Liu's wife was a schoolteacher; they had two daughters. The close friendship between our families was bound by an unusual act of fate: For the birth of her second daughter, Mrs. Liu had to undergo an emergency delivery in her own home that my mother performed.

In 424, the Ge family. As the secretary-general of the CAPD, Ge Zhicheng was the building's chief magistrate; each day, a swanky car picked him up and dropped him off. When he had worked in Shanghai as an elementary-school teacher, he had been active in the underground movement, then after liberation moved to Beijing to become an official in the Ministry of Education. Outside of his commuting routine, he lived a secluded life, rarely showing his face as if he were still in the underground. His wife, Hua Jin, worked as the party branch secretary for Beijing Middle No. 8. After meeting their adopted child, Ge Jiaduo, for a while he never said a word to any of us despite our promptings, and so we called him Ge Bushuo ("Ge Doesn't Speak"). They owned the only private telephone in the whole building.

In 422, the Mu family. Mu Shaoliang used to be the senior editor at Commercial Press; he had a weak constitution and suffered from an assortment of illnesses; during the Cultural Revolution he was violently beaten, and passed away in 1969. There were two dragons and two phoenixes in the family—the phoenixes had long flown far away, marrying early. The young widow, Fang Jianmin, gentle and reserved, raised her two sons alone. Mu Dingyi, the older brother, was my age and later tested into Beijing Middle No. 8. The younger brother, and youngest in the whole family, Mu Dingsheng (or, Little Jing), was skillful with the brush and eventually won the country's highest prize for calligraphy, his talents whisking him away from a factory to the National Museum of Modern Chinese Literature. For a time, we were as close as comrades-in-arms; and later, he helped cut the mimeograph stencils of our underground literary magazine, *Today*.

6

A boy entering the springtime of adolescence often needs someone to go to for advice, someone akin to a spiritual guide or psychotherapist, the best person to fill this role being an experienced woman.

We called Pang Bangben, of apartment 434, Big Bro. He

joined the army in 1951, continuing to paint while he served, then went on to university, eventually becoming an art teacher at a secondary school. After being violently beaten as a "right-ist" in 1957, he worked for the Beijing Public Security Bureau as a "rightist" painter, setting up a studio that made traffic signs. During the Cultural Revolution he was banished to the Auto Repair and Assembly Plant at Xingtai, Hebei Province; his design for a big-rig truck looked more or less like the standard space-alien combat vehicle you see in sci-fi films today.

Big Bro's wife, Sun Yufan (Big Sis), was a Japanese "war orphan"—born in the north, in Dalian, she was abandoned by her parents in 1945 when they evacuated the country, so she was adopted by another Chinese family. She had just turned thirty then, her skin dark, her eyes large and prominent compared to her small nose and mouth. Big Bro's photography skills were first-rate and his portrait of Big Sis made her look like a movie star: with a red-checkered scarf wrapped around her head, she leaned airily against a white poplar, the whole image affecting an intensely Russian mood.

Apartment 434 was the building's largest residence with two bedrooms plus a sitting room; Big Sis, always sick in bed, took over the small sitting room; a thick curtain kept out the clamor of the outside world. An exceptionally good listener, she could point to and elucidate the crucial points of a problem with a turn of three words and two phrases, making one feel wholly assured and wholly submissive to her will.

One clear and crisp winter afternoon at the start of 1970, my siblings and I helped Big Sis take the children in our building on an outing. From Three Never Old Hutong No. 1 we all embarked, chatting and laughing, piling onto the No. 14 bus.

We arrived at Zhongshan (Sun Yat-Sen) Park, found a spot on the dried, yellow grass to form a circle, and swatted a volleyball around. Big Sis wore a black turtleneck sweater, and like a coach shouted out tips and instructions. The day grew dark; we strolled to the Hotel Novotel to eat dinner at the Western-style restaurant there. That would be the only clear impression she'd leave me with of herself outdoors.

Kang Cheng, Yifan, and I were as inseparable as a figure and its shadow; Big Sis called us the Three Musketeers. Trying to visit her wasn't easy—one first had to wait for Uncle Pang to return from the cadre school and face him; one also had to endure the nosy nattering of Qian Ayi, who eventually returned to her hometown in Yangzhou; Big Bro, ordinarily at the auto plant in Xingtai, came home during leave once or twice a month.

Pang Bangxuan, Big Bro's little sister, returned to Beijing from the Inner Mongolia rural production team during winter fallow. She had been in her second year at Beijing Normal University, a year above us, and hung out with one beautiful and smart friend after another. One of them, Sister Song, a professional soprano singer knocked the Three Musketeers over, our adoration drawing us into an emotional crisis. As the dust settled, wounds slow to heal, we lined up to visit Big Sis for a private talk; she guided each lost lamb through the maze of his feelings.

Wind-borne rumors from the neighborhood committee spread that Big Sis was "luring in and corrupting the youth"; we had no choice but to lie low and take shelter from the headwinds. Big Sis was like a commissar, educating via positive reinforcement, always encouraging me to be proactive and optimistic, and make a contribution to society; she thought my poems too pessimistic, too gloomy, that they should extol the homeland, extol the proletariat—the workers, peasants, soldiers. Somehow coming from her mouth these words didn't sound annoying. Her voice was a little husky, almost a whisper, and possessed a kind of hypnotic power.

After I got married I saw less of Big Sis; from time to time, when visiting my parents, we'd sit and chat at her place. Fine wrinkles appeared around her delicate little mouth—the etchings of time.

In the summer of 1997, while living in Davis, California, I received a letter from my brother saying that Big Sis, suffering from a heart disease, had passed away, and that during the last few months of her illness she had only read one book: a poetry book of mine that she kept by her pillow.

7

In order to situate Three Never Old Hutong No. 1's position in Beijing's social landscape of the time, one needs to consider the "grand courtyard" and the "hutong alley." The cultural politics of these two spaces differed sharply. In general, the "grand courtyard" existed as an exclusive outdoor area for those in high office to receive strangers, while the "hutong alley" existed as an all-inclusive space for local residents *from rivers to lakes far and wide*; the "grand courtyard" symbolized power, the "hutong alley" zigzagged through the whole of history.

Of course, it wasn't as simple as this; high officials, in fact, preferred a life of seclusion in the hutong. So, for instance, the tenants around our grand courtyard were mostly lower-level cadres, and yet the big shots of the democratic parties imitated the ruling party by stealthily wandering the hutongs, *sharing water through parched times*, so that even if one were a sacked official, one could eat and drink as well as before, just like a so-called last aristocrat.

The grand courtyard was often classified according to a three, six, nine, and so on hierarchy that had something to do with being a spare part of the state machinery. Although the status of the democratic parties rose in specific historical periods, they were basically seen as defective goods, thus Three Never Old Hutong No. 1's awareness of its own shortcomings. This embodiment of class consciousness was passed on vocally, particularly during the Cultural Revolution, as people would introduce themselves with so much hot air: "Of Party Central!" "Of the Planning Commission!" "Of the Navy Yard!" When it fell to our turn, as if sucking a jujube, a garbled sound would emerge: "Of Sanbulao—"

In those days, multiple-story housing was still uncommon in the city and Sanbulao Hutong No. 1 instantly became a landmark building for the neighborhood; one could see it many kilometers away from any circumferential point. At Hong Shan Temple Elementary School, most of the students came from the lowest strata of society. Going to a classmate's house to play, parents would ask me where I lived and my friend would rush to reply: "That big building, Three Never Old!" Usually the parents would roll their eyes and size me up—in the presence of the state machinery's spare parts and surplus defective goods, there could be no distinction between civilians.

The maze carved out of hutong lanes, puddles of water after an early-summer rain, the fragrance of pagoda tree flowers and the crepuscular streetlamps, for a boy growing up in Sanbulao, these things filled me with longing. Compared to the rigid structure of the multistory complex, out there the wild freedom of the masses lived on. Summertime by the public taps, half-naked men and women joked with animated gestures, as if on an impromptu opera stage, while children chased each other with glee. Follow a wall around a corner then turn into a little courtyard with a crooked house, piles of broken roof tiles strewn about. That was another kind of life: From grandparents to grandchildren, three generations crowded together in one place, talk interspersed with swears and curses, yet beneath the coarse surface ran deep attachments and an unwillingness to part, plus the sincere concern of neighbors left and right.... From the abyss of the hutong alleys looking back toward our big building, I actually felt a vague hostility. This must have been related to a rebellious phase of adolescence: the multistory complex stood for the authority and order of my father.

Children of the grand courtyard who ventured into the depths of the hutong were *braving the winds of the narrow passes*—one false move and you could be confronted with taunts, jeers, and even a beating, unless you had a few true hutong friends.

Guan Tielin attended the same elementary school as me, and for a while we were quite close. His family lived nearby in a dead-end little courtyard alley, most of the natural light blocked by our huge building. Tielin's mother died young from an illness; his father, a fireman, worked three shifts and wasn't home much. Their old copper washbasin, dented and scarred, made the deepest impression on me—it looked like a family heirloom. After school, Tielin would light the stove, boil some water, pour the boiling water into the copper basin, test the temperature with his fingers, then slowly submerge both of his hands into the scalding water while closing his eyes with contentment.

Once I boasted to him about my father's wondrous skill with a brush. Tielin stared at me incredulously. How did this relate to his father? He sunk into a deep silence. Fighting fires and writing words are fundamentally nonequivalent—in a raging fire, to climb higher means risking your own life. He couldn't bear the thought of losing his father.

I've forgotten the name of my other hutong friend. He was in the same class as me in elementary school; he lived on the Houhai riverbank. His father, a street peddler, set up a stall that sold candy, as well as needle and thread, while running a small-scale gambling business on the side. A series of wooden boxes were arranged into a grid, pasted with window paper, and after handing over two fen, you stabbed a box with your finger, the probability of winning or losing about fifty-fifty, the prize a piece of candy or marble or some other little bauble. I always played with a winner's mind-set, which was actually quite easy: the peddler's son leaked the game's secrets to me in advance.

8

I was seventeen the year the Cultural Revolution erupted. At Beijing High No. 4, I felt like I was in the heart of a storm—in the throes of a math-physics-chemistry crisis, final exams around the corner. Then the school suddenly announced that all classes were dismissed, the term over; I cheered with relief, flitted about like a joyful sparrow, for the failure of the bourgeoisie educational system as well as for my own victory leaping over the math-physics-chemistry barrier. For me, the start of the Great Proletarian Cultural Revolution seemed like a carnival. Waking up each day I felt unsteady, worried that Chairman Mao might alter his plan and wait until one day, only as an eminent old man, he would make his final heartfelt decision to close the school gates forever.

The rebel movement quickly divided: Those students born into families with "good" class backgrounds became the main force of the army; the rest of us were excluded. Loafing around at home, it was hard not to get a bit depressed; I turned to help my little brother and sister write big-character posters, criticizing teachers for leading us down the "white road" of academia, yet it was far from stimulating—in this unprecedented historical hurricane, teachers existed as mere baby shrimp and not much more.

I became king of the children, and analyzing the situation with some of the younger boys of the compound, we found a big fish: Chen Xianchi of building No. 8. We had heard he once worked for the Kuomintang secret service and after liberation spent a few years in prison, his case a typical slice of "counter-revolutionary history." I rounded up five or six boys and we rushed over to his apartment. Rapping open the door, I first read aloud some quotations of Chairman Mao: "Everything is reactionary: If you don't strike, then he won't fall; like sweeping the floor, wherever a broom can't reach, the dust won't flee of its own accord." Without us lifting a finger, Chen Xianchi fell to the floor, his hands cupping his voter's card to show that he, too, was one of the people.

Without any explanation, we pulled and pushed and escorted him to the entrance of building No. 4, where we forced him to sit on a stool. I went home to retrieve some hair clippers, and surrounded by my entourage, pushed his head down. With the first touch of his greasy hair, I actually swooned a little; then after hesitating for a moment, I settled my nerves and buzzed the matted mess from his forehead around and down the back, opening out vertical windrow grooves. The hair clippers didn't work so well; only after several passes did the base of a groove expose blue-green scalp. This popular "yin-yang head" hairstyle was very fashionable back then. In fact, I discovered that the hair clippers were functioning fine, the real problem had to do with my right hand—it couldn't stop shaking. I had no choice but to put the clippers down, use my left hand to grip my right hand, and pretend nothing was wrong, while continuing to shout out orders.

Droopy-headed Chen Xianchi straightened his faded Sun Yat-Sen suit and brushed off the loose hair. He calmly looked around after his initial panic, his eyes narrowing in the realization that this whole performance was merely some mischief carried out by a gang of Mao's little children. His contempt infuriated us; right away, we convened a mini struggle session with only a few passersby and kids to witness the lively scene. Chen Xianchi didn't assume the infamous "vapor-trailing airplane position"—head bowed, waist bent, arms straight out to the back, three "I don't know"s for every question. We shouted slogans at him: "Down with Chen Xianchi!" "If the enemy doesn't surrender, demand his annihilation!"

We first locked him in the boiler room, but fearing he might do some damage there moved him to the basement of building No. 8. We took turns guarding him, organizing a three-shift system, delivering meals and accompanying him to the bathroom, all the while afraid that he would escape, or even worse, that he'd commit suicide. Two days passed; we were exhausted, *troops crushed horses downed*, yawns reaching to the skies; it seemed we had no choice but to release him.

We brought him out of the basement; it looked like he had been imprisoned for a long time, skin wan, eyes squinting as he raised his head to look at the sun. I first read aloud some quotations of Chairman Mao: "Policy and tactics are the lifeblood of the party; all leaders and comrades must adequately take note, and truly, truly never act with an impulsive heart or careless thought." And then some stern warnings for him not to be defiant in word or deed, and that he must check in with us regularly.

After that, bumping into him on the street was like meeting a ghost; I tried to give him as wide a berth as possible.

Many years later I happened to read Golding's *Lord of the Flies*: His bold vision, alas, had been a ruthless reality for us.

9

The carnival soon turned into a bloody tragedy: Hua Jin, the wife of our building's chief magistrate, Ge Zhicheng, was thrown into the makeshift prison inside Beijing Middle No. 8, where she had been working as the party branch secretary; after enduring endless beatings and insults, she hung herself in the early morning of August 22nd that summer. Soon after that, Beihang University Red Guards raided Yifan's house, forcing his father to return to his ancestral home in Sichuan Province.

Three Never Old Hutong No. 1 became the primary target for searching and confiscating homes for virtually the whole of

Beijing. Consider building No. 3's Zhao Junmai—this fellow had been imprisoned by the Kuomintang mayor of Changchun city during the Liaoshen Campaign in the 1948 civil war; each day he performed his sword dance in the courtyard, floating on air, as if practicing his ascension to heaven. The day the Red Guards raided his house he tried to resist and was nearly beaten to death on the spot. It seemed as if he had completed his preparations for his ascension.

An announcement posted at the entryway to each building declared that every resident was a counterrevolutionary, that on such and such a day each home would be searched, no one exempted … and before this takes place, immediately hand over any of the "four olds" (old ideas, old culture, old customs, old habits) … anyone who resists will be killed under lawful authority. Thereupon, we first voluntarily raided our own home, delivered any books and objects suspected of being among the "four olds" to the neighborhood committee, including an ivory mahjong set, which many years later my father would still mention with a pain in his heart. Doomsday arrived—the threaten-to-search-and-confiscate Red Guards vanished—neither a shadow nor a trace, just our empty fears remained.

One summer evening, it was our family's turn for night duty at Sanbulao's reception hut. Old Wu, who used to watch the front gate, had been swept away—as a fugitive "rich peasant," he had been sent back to his hometown. Tall and lanky, bald and slightly hunchbacked, Old Wu wore a coarse-woven work shirt draped over black Burma-crotch pants, his body like a bow stored in a cloth sack. A strong Hebei accent streamed out of his mouth, making his voice exceptionally loud; those who watched the gate after him couldn't match his roar, even with a megaphone.

Very late that night during our watch, a girl who lived in building No. 2 came toward me weeping. In the morning, she and the rest of her family would be escorted onto a train, forever forbidden to return to Beijing. Under the authority of the Red Guards, more than one hundred thousand Beijing residents were forcibly relocated back to their rural ancestral homes. Beneath the dim lamplight, the girl sobbed and sobbed, crystallized tears tumbled down her cheeks, flowing on and on, glinting in the night.

A summer of bloody rains and foul winds finally ended.

The Cultural Revolution gave the democratic parties an opportunity to put the practice of democracy into action. The CAPD central committee joined up with a group of twenty high officials and party workers, then separated into two factions according to the democratic rules of the game. Father busied himself writing big-character posters, wielding his brush as a weapon, *always happy never tiring*. While on a ladder, brushing a slogan, he fell and landed on his left hand; when he tried to check in at Jishuitan Hospital, the doctors and nurses were also busy with factional fighting; his wrist bone, fortunately, was still in one piece though it looked dislocated.

On the theme of "carry the revolution to the very end," ordinary people's daily lives provided the variations: souvenir-badge collecting, regular chicken-blood injections, arm-swinging therapy, raising tropical fish.... A Mao souvenir-badge market appeared at the Ping'anli T intersection where one could barter and trade. I carried several Mao badges in my chest pocket, and wanted to trade for one as big as the mouth of a bowl, but no one gave me the time of day. Father bravely retreated from the torrent of factional battles and started collecting transistor radios.

In those days, the main source of fuel was the honeycomb-coal briquette. Coal-shop workers originally used to sell them door to door via tricycle cart; then to keep pace with the Cultural Revolution, the workers revolted and no longer served the bourgeoisie capitalists, basket upon basket of honeycomb briquettes would simply be unloaded at the entrance to every building, each family needing to figure out their own method of transport. A basket of honeycomb coal weighed around sixty to seventy catties (more than ninety pounds), blindsiding families short on physical strength who then eagerly sought to take in a son-in-law, first making sure he could pass the trial of the honeycomb-coal basket.

Exploiting the chaos of the Cultural Revolution, an assortment of junk sadly invaded the basketball court on the eastern side of the courtyard, turning the area into a recycling station, though this later proved to be quite visionary: at the end of the 1960s, the great migrations across the country produced unlimited business opportunities. Yifan and I visited the recycling station to intercept clients and sift for old books that were being sold as wastepaper; we even used certain letters of introduction to worm our way in, diving straightaway into the wastepaper heaps to retrieve the treasures.

While the great migrations crisscrossed the country, the citizens of Beijing began to dig out air-raid shelters. Once again, a large-scale construction project took over the courtyard. The first to suffer disaster were those leap-into-the-sky poplars. They were all chopped down and carried away, only a barren landscape remained.

10

The residents of Three Never Old Hutong No. 1 disappeared one by one, buildings emptied—*you could net sparrows at the gate*. The recycling-station business turned bleak. What was once a deluge of overflowing junk shrank, as if a conjuring trick, into a few wicker baskets.

In the spring of 1969, I was assigned to the Beijing No. 6. Construction Company and sent to Yu County in Hebei Province to blast through a mountain. More than a year later the construction site moved to the East Is Red Oil Refinery in Fangshan, in the southwest reaches of Beijing; once every two weeks I could take a day of rest at home.

This was when our apartment became a central gathering place. Closing the thick, coarse curtains, our small group of friends would read, write, drink, listen to music, and, naturally, pursue romance. Our activities were long being monitored by the compound's neighborhood committee. And so the night Yi-fan developing photographs at his place, the red darkroom light glowing, the enlarger lamp flashing on and off, the "little feet investigation squad" quickly informing the West City District Public Security Bureau about the suspicious secret signals, the policemen breaking down his door and storming in, all for a pile of classical Bakelite records.

We invited the tenor Kang Jian to my home. His head as big as the Dipper, face ruddy; like a night sun, he lit up the little room packed full with guests sitting on the floor. His laughter thundered out and shook the windows. By the time his voice rose to Mily Balakriev's "Song of the Volga Boatmen," the audience turned pale; we heard that booming warning could be heard over two kilometers away: "Stamp open the world's uneven road...."

A few years ago, the boys and girls of this building went to live with a production team, to work for the military corps, join the army, reform themselves through labor; these diverse individuals now, one after another, have returned; Ji Nian and I transferred to the May Seventh Cadre School in Hebei's sand-and-river Shahe town, near Beijing, and so we have also returned home; only Shan Shan hasn't been able to come back.... (*From my mother's interview*)

The salon had no choice but to move its base of operations; we forged some monthly trolleybus tickets and met outside the city in a desolate field.

At the start of the 1970s, rising into his early twenties, he was already starting to write poems and novels. He frequently asked for sick leave and stayed home, turning the kitchen into his study, shutting the door, and immersing himself in his work. Sometimes I'd get up in the middle of the night to go to the bathroom and the dull yellow light in the kitchen would still be burning.... (*From my father's notebook*)

Through my father I was introduced to Uncle Feng Yidai in building No. 1, and through Uncle Feng I was introduced to a bounty of books and interesting individuals. I often dropped by his home for a visit. Uncle Feng, pipe in hand, always smiled brightly. Threads of conversation ascended with the wisps of cigarette smoke as we sat and chatted. Aunt Feng, wearing an apron and sleeve coverings, busied herself between the stove and the dictionary they were working on together. She was almost blind. Answering the door, she would stare at me through her thick lenses in total perplexity; grasping a magnifying glass in her hand, she would help Uncle Feng track down the hidden meanings of words, to finally lock them into place.

One early October evening in 1976, I rushed over to Uncle Feng's with good news: The Gang of Four had fallen. Uncle Feng was standing in the kitchen wiping his back with a towel. Then he turned around to face me, as if hand in hand with history.

Later that year, some friends and I launched the literary magazine *Today*. We bound the issues at my place, piles and piles of mimeographed pages rising from the floor past the bed, emanating the pungent odor of printing ink. Our threshold turned busier than a marketplace; I raced around with flailing hands, feet in a flurry. While greeting guests, I imagined that the neighborhood committee and local police must be working overtime, too.

In the autumn of 1980 I got married and moved out of Three Never Old Hutong No. 1.

11

Toward the end of 2001, Yifan drove me back to Sanbulao. This home that has haunted my dreams for so long was now difficult to recognize: a low building, narrow windows, façade recently whitewashed, yet its appearance of decay couldn't be concealed.

We visited some old neighbors, first stopping by the Pang family in apartment 434. Big Bro Bang Ben opened the door and welcomed us in—his hair white, his stature as tall and stately as before. Bang Xuan currently worked as the managing director of an investment company and dressed like one. Everything pointed in the direction of society's remarkable material progress. Big Bro had wanted to host a party for the guests and invited all the children in the building. Our family's apartment was being rented out, an idea that I had suggested as a way to avoid stirring up the dark recesses of memory.

Dusk fell as we said good-bye to our neighbors. An apartment building now stood on the former air-raid shelter. Reverse thirty years, those poplars await their felled fate; reverse forty years, those Taihu stones await their heaving onto a truck and their destination at the military museum under construction; reverse six hundred years, Zheng He leans on a balustrade, gazes out over the back garden, lights a lamp in the twilight, birds return to their nests, the ten thousand things return to silence.

My parents' wedding portrait, Shanghai, 1948

Father at the Temple of Heaven, 1948

Father as a young man

Family portrait, 1963

Beijing, 1969

With classmates at the Temple of Heaven, 1968

Little sister in Beihai Park, 1969

Little sister on the balcony, 1969

Qian Ayi

ACCORDING TO MY father, sometime in early 1950, a village girl named Wang Yuzhen, embroiled in a domestic dispute, traveled from Baoding, Hebei Province to Beijing in order to file a lawsuit. From the start, the legal battle became as drawn out as the day is long, and for a time we employed her as a *baomu*, a live-in nanny plus housekeeper. We were living at Dong Jiao Min Alley, 1 Ministry of Foreign Affairs Street, not a far walk from the courthouse on Ministry of Justice Street. Wang Yuzhen had a strong, robust constitution, her voice sonorous; besides watching the children, she did the laundry, cleaned the apartment, bought groceries, cooked meals, all with an as-if-it-were-nothing lightheartedness. My father said that each day he came home from work, he would find her sitting by the doorway, holding me in one hand and my little brother in the other, taking turns feeding us. Both of my parents worked, and as no one else watched over us, we must have joined Wang Yuzhen during her judicial arbitration whenever her case came to session. Two years later, her lawsuit was finally resolved and she returned to Baoding. By then, my brother and I were already running around.

1

Toward the end of 1957, a new *baomu* joined our family: Qian Jiazhen, from Yangzhou, Jiangsu Province. Her husband ran a small business, found a new flame; she left for Beijing in a fury, first staying with her stepmother, with whom she eventually had an ugly falling out. Gritting her teeth with determination, and with a single-minded resolve to make it on her own, she found her way to our home through the introduction of one of my parents' colleagues. Qian Ayi and I became mutual witnesses through the passage of time—from age eight to my grown-up days as a construction worker; from Qian Ayi's days as a comely young woman, *as graceful as an echo of wind*, to her wrinkled old age.

Before the reform and opening-up policies, my parents' salaries hardly increased and together totaled around 239 RMB per month (enough for a family of five to live comfortably); after deducting some for pocket money, they gave the rest to Qian Ayi to keep house.

Qian Ayi was illiterate; as I was considered the most educated one in our family apart from our parents, bookkeeping duties eventually fell on my head. Every night after eating dinner and tidying up, I'd sit face-to-face with Qian Ayi at the dining table, her big eyes staring into my small eyes, as we went over the daily household expenditures. We used a ruled notebook, sixteen lines per page, cover stained with grease spots, corners curled, several vertical lines drawn down each page with a ruler, columns labeled with dates, purchased items, quantities, total costs. Qian Ayi broke her fingers calculating each and every expense, fishing out jiao banknotes and coins from her pocket, as well as little pieces of paper with circled sums. All those circled figures, depending on their size and shape, represented different purchased items, their visual notation calling to mind certain ancient, originary glyphs and signs.

In truth, I came to wholly detest the job, which continued on and on, year after year, three hundred and sixty-five days with hardly an interruption, and if there happened to be an interruption for a day or two, even more time and energy had to be expended to make up for it. I just wanted to have fun, let my mind wander without a care, and prepared for the right moment to sneak away. Qian Ayi would first put on a serious face, then she'd slap the table and glare; each day we parted in discord. My parents, in fact, never checked the accounting books, and Qian Ayi knew it, yet this only demonstrated her lifelong reputation as an upright individual with an honest name.

I was responsible for another impossible task: writing her letters. Concerning Qian Ayi's personal history, I really didn't know much. She always prattled on and on about how she was born into a rich and influential family. Essentially, she could be described as a germaphobe, her clothes and bedsheets unsullied by the slightest speck of dirt; when cleaning and chopping vegetables, she tossed out more than she saved. Such faults were caused by her wealthy upbringing.

Qian Ayi had a younger half sister on her father's side; whenever she received a letter from her sister, who lived in Yangzhou, it was a major event. To ensure an unobstructed path of delivery, Qian Ayi even offered her matchmaking services to the mailman, Little Zhao. Little Zhao maintained a squeaky-clean appearance; he was also exceedingly shy. Each prospect he readied himself for either harkened from a rural village or lacked sense and sensibility. On the scene for every introduction, I could only knead my fingers and sweat anxiously for Little Zhao, for how could I interfere with the conversation? Nothing could be done about Qian Ayi's limited social circle; back then, the social hierarchy lurked behind a mask of equality. Little Zhao gradually turned into Old Zhao, staying as single as ever.

Finishing her day's work, Qian Ayi removed her apron and sleeve covers, then pulled out the freshly received letter from beneath her pillow. I carefully unfolded the paper and *keke baba* stammered through, reading aloud, skipping over any unfamiliar words. Qian Ayi listened intently, face full of doubt, then forced me to read it over again. The composing of the reply followed. In second grade I could write about two or three hundred characters at most; if I got stuck in the letter, adopting Qian Ayi's notational method, I just drew a circle around the mysterious word. Fortunately, one could follow a pattern in her replies, the opening always running: "Receiving your letter and knowing that everyone's doing so well eases my heart...."

A long time passed before I finally found out that Qian Ayi's sister also used a "sharpshooter": her own daughter. My counterpart happened to be around my age; later, she joined a production team in Jiangxi. For a while we commiserated with each other by inserting our own commentary in the margins of the letters, confounding Qian Ayi to no end.

2

Though illiterate, Qian Ayi, "feet unbound," didn't want to be left behind and sought to participate in various social campaigns; keeping up with the fickle times, however, wasn't easy to do. In the new society, the *baomu* position had become complicated and uncertain, especially during the Cultural Revolution, to the extent that it carried political risks.

Summer of 1958: Great Leap Forward propaganda posters appeared on the brick wall of the hutong next to us, Aviation Alley, their blazing hues cranking up the summer heat. The changing roles of workers and farmers symbolized the changing times; the wind picked up, the sun blazed down, and bit by bit posters covered the whole wall. To children, those were thrilling, exhilarating days, when almost every day felt special, like a festival.

Autumn arrived and a communal canteen was set up in the neighborhood committee's one-story building across the street. Qian Ayi answered the party's call, abandoned the three of us, threw on a white workers' coat, and twirled into the canteen, puffing out with pride. She metamorphasized into another person, brows raised eyes smiling, riding a spring breeze. There was a time when her thick Yangzhou accent knotted its way through her jumbled Mandarin, creating a feast for the ears. Qian Ayi still lived at our house but ignored us, withholding any sort of affection. Did she have a certain agreement with my parents, or was this a unilateral decision? Her posturing seemed like it could evaporate at any moment. The three of us were totally blindsided; we had no other choice but to join her in the canteen. Almost instantly I could see why Qian Ayi felt so liberated: independence; feelings unfettered and untroubled; the camaraderie in the communal space.

The canteen ran at a heavy loss; no more than a few months passed before it shut down. Qian Ayi took off her white workers' coat, slipped on her blue sleeve covers, and lit the stove back at home. All day long she walked around with a long, inconsolable face, sinking into a deep silence; from time to time she would stand with her back to the window in a daze, chimney smoke from cooking fires drifting up behind her, soaking up Beijing's winter sun and sky.

Seven or eight years later, Old Heavenly Grandfather had another joke to play on her. When the Cultural Revolution broke out in the summer of 1966, Qian Ayi initially *halted the troops and took no action,* watching calmly from the side to see what would happen next. Then one Red August morning she suddenly sprang up, changed into an earth-yellow army uniform (different from the orthodox national-defense green), pinned a Mao badge onto her chest, wrapped a leather belt around her waist, and rushed out like a fire in the wind, *peng peng!* slamming the door behind her. She went on a kind of semi-strike. Actually, a coordinated semi-strike, as she just no longer served regular meals; after we had filled our empty stomachs ourselves, she would conveniently appear and offer us some food. Qian Ayi turned forty-three that year—maybe she was making her final stand before life slipped away from her; maybe she felt it was her last chance to alter her destiny.

In the tumultuous torrent, who could clearly see whom anyway? Everyone was duped by revolutionary passion. From what I gathered, during her army days, Qian Ayi danced the dance of loyalty and participated in the neighborhood committee struggle sessions. She had trouble reciting quotations—not just because of her illiteracy but because of her tongue-twisting Yangzhou dialect. As we stumbled about in a half-crazed state, too, sidewise watching a half-crazed Qian Ayi seemed quite normal to us.

It wasn't long before Qian Ayi's brave surge declined; she dug out her little Ming blue padded *ao* jacket and, like a molting bird replacing its plumage, prepared for the winter. What hidden difficulties could she not share with us? No one knew, and yet one could presume: When a little nobody charges headlong into the immensity of an age, how many harmful ambushes await her on all sides.

Father's work unit pasted up some big-character posters that listed names and claimed that employing a *baomu* perpetuated a bourgeoisie lifestyle. My parents panicked; the same night they had an urgent talk with Qian Ayi, asking if she could please leave, just temporarily, making promises that they would still take care of her in her old age.

Qian Ayi acted as if nothing had happened; the next morning she brushed her hair as usual with her double-edge fine-toothed comb and coiled it into a bun. A few days later, she made us a nice lunch, then, carrying a cloth-wrapped bundle, she left. For a while, she still dropped by regularly to see us, but as more time passed, she slowly faded from our horizon. Then suddenly the news arrived that she had married a pedicab driver; in those times when it seemed impossible to be shocked, she succeeded in shocking me totally.

One Sunday morning I rode my bike south on Xisi Bei ("West Four North") Avenue, trying to track down an address. When I found it, I stood before a very large, multifamily court-yard compound, noisy and crowded. A child showed me the way to a door curtain, and when it lifted open, Qian Ayi's head poked out. She brought me into a small room, barely four or five square meters, the *kang* bed taking up more than half the space, the drop ceiling and window paper newly restored. Qian Ayi insisted that I sit on the lone chair while she perched at the edge of the *kang*. I felt a bit flustered, stumbled over a few words, then asked her about married life.

"The old man's at work," she replied. Her facial expression remained as stiff as wood.

An awkward silence followed. Qian Ayi poured hot water over the tea leaves, then asserted that she would make me some-thing to eat. I pleaded that I had things to do, hurriedly said my good-byes, then turned and disappeared into the streaming crowds. A few days later, news came of her divorce, though noth-ing about any upheaval at home, no swelling wave that finally crashed down upon them. We heard that the reason for her di-vorce was actually very simple: Qian Ayi couldn't stand messy people.

3

Around the beginning of 1969, Qian Ayi moved back in again, mainly to look after the apartment. Everyone had left, the place was empty: Mother had gone to the May Seventh Cadre School in Xinyan prefecture, Henan Province; my little brother had gone to the construction corps on the border of Mongolia; I had gone to a construction site in Yu County, Hebei Province; not long after that my little sister had joined my mother at the Cadre School; and for the finale, Father had gone to the May Seventh Cadre School in Shayang County, Hubei Province.

The day my brother left for the construction corps, Father saw him off at the departure point on Denei Avenue and returned home. At the entrance to our building, he bumped into Qian Ayi, who in a flustered frenzy sputtered, "Suppose Bao Bao" (my brother's childhood nickname) "finds a Mongolian wife before coming back home, that would be a disaster! This matter can't be ignored, did you talk to him about it?" "No, I didn't talk to him about it," my father replied, "and no use chasing after him, he's already far away now." Qian Ayi raised her face with a long sigh: "O my Old Heavenly Grandfather!"

Summer of 1970: Our construction site moved from Yu County to the outskirts of Beijing; every other Saturday, around midday, a transport bus would take us into the city for our weekend off, and early Monday morning bring us back. When I arrived home, Qian Ayi would circle me round and round, asking if I felt hot or cold and if I was taking care of my health; she'd first cook me a big bowl of soup noodles, making the base out of soy sauce, vinegar, and chopped scallions, then added a spoonful of lard and two fried eggs on top. She watched my *ravenous wolf devouring tiger* table manners with a look of ease and contentment.

Then suddenly Qian Ayi got old, wrinkles furrowing across her cheeks and forehead. A photograph of her at the time still exists as proof, a portrait I had taken for her residential registration. Here it should be said that though I considered myself a seasoned photographer, having assiduously plied my trade for several years, most of my subjects until then were pretty girls. First, I'd hang a white bedsheet across an iron wire as a backdrop, then adjust three high-wattage lamps for lighting, mount my Czech "hobbyist" 120 twin-lens reflex camera onto a tripod, and pressing my shutter release cable *kacha kacha kacha*....

I admit my portrait of Qian Ayi failed dreadfully, just as she herself assessed: "Looks like a ghost." As for the reasons: 1) overexposure, 2) out of focus, 3) didn't find the best angle to shoot from. No doubt there were also other processing problems later. Before I returned to my construction duties, I passed the negatives to Yifan downstairs to make the prints; the two of us shared one photo enlarger he kept at his place.

Later, Yifan grumbled to me that it was hopeless, the negatives overexposed, even using grade-four photo paper didn't work, the prints came out too dark with zero contrast. But after my errors, he made a more serious one by casually tossing the dozen or so shoddy photographs into the garbage bin. Who knows the rotten kid who dug them out of the trash and pasted each one up along the corridor windows at the entrance to our building. Qian Ayi looked like a wanted fugitive. She flipped out, embarked on a fanatical investigation, until she determined that the chief culprit was none other than me.

Qian Ayi idled around the house doing nothing, her heart troubled; she spent 120 yuan to buy me a Dong Feng wristwatch. Soon after that I received a letter from my father. Apparently more gossip had spread to the Cadre School—as the presence of a *baomu* was considered clear proof of a capitalist lifestyle, Father was being subjected to the usual array of severe pressures: isolation and interrogation, tight supervision during his manual labors, and so on. Despite my father's tactful wording, Qian Ayi listened to the letter and immediately understood; she left immediately for her hometown.

In the end, we never fulfilled our promises to take care of Qian Ayi in her old age.

4

Spring of 1982—as a journalist for the Esperanto magazine *China Report*, I decided to write a piece about the Grand Canal, to set out from Beijing and trace the canal south, where I'd eventually pass through Yangzhou. I wrote a letter to Qian Ayi's sister before I left, telling her about my trip. The day I arrived in Yangzhou, after gathering some information at the city government offices, I visited her sister's home in the afternoon. Qian Ayi looked restless and tense; upon seeing me, her little eyes blinked and blinked, without tears. From her younger sister's tone of voice, I could sense that Qian Ayi had no status in the family and counted for nothing. I suggested that we go inside her room and sit for a bit.

Along the green dampness of a stone path we walked shoulder to shoulder. Qian Ayi had grown so thin and small, her shadow even smaller, as if she could vanish into the earth at any moment. Her so-called home was merely a small, wooden room; besides the bamboo bed there was hardly anything else in it. I had bought a tin of cookies at a shop nearby, and gave this to her, along with a transistor radio; the gifts seemed totally out of place.

In her clouded eyes I could see a flicker of fear—fear of old age, of hunger, of death. She faltered, mumbled, then halted again, until it was time for me to go, at which point she blurted out: "What I really need is money!" I felt like a fool, stunned by the red-bared truth of her poverty. I told her to please set her mind at ease, and promised to send her some money when I returned home (my mother later sent her seventy yuan). At the main gate, the setting sun behind her plated her in golden light. Her mouth twisted; she wanted to smile but no smile broke out.

Through the wide streets and narrow alleys those Yangzhou-flavored words Qian Ayi spoke float on and on. Here, it turned out, would be her real native home.

Reading Books

1

R EADING BOOKS HAS nothing to do with going to school, the two totally separate activities—reading, as being outside the classroom, and books, as being outside textbooks—so that what happens when reading books arises out of a kind of mysterious life power, which has nothing to do with any profit or gain. The experience of reading is like a well-lit road, illuminating the darkness during our brief existence, and at the end of the darkness burns a candle flame that can be called the zero point of reading.

Open up a map of Beijing from the early 1960s, and at the northwest corner of Mianhua ("Cotton Blossom") Hutong and Huguosi ("Protect the Country Temple") Street you will find a *xiaorenshu* ("little picture books") shop. From the little picture bookshop, head west, past the flower sellers, and arrive at the famous Huguo Temple "Little-Eats" Snack Shop, a variety of mouthwatering dainties: sweet ears, rolling donkeys cakes, *aiwowo* sticky-rice cones, fried sesame balls, *miancha* millet mush, jelly bean-curd brain. The bottom half of the little-eats shop's front window will be frosted, the top half fogged over, a blur of shadowy figures, oil crackling in pans *zi zi zi*, the most exquisite aromas permeating the air. With the meager change in my pocket, I'd often linger back and forth between the little picture bookshop and the little-eats shop: stomach rumbling like a motor, mind as blank as an empty pot. If I could've suffered only one of the two, I naturally would've chosen the latter.

Xiaorenshu bookshops weren't big, their primary customers children, their function somewhat analogous to the Internet cafés of today. Upon entering the shop on Huguosi Street, your eyes brimmed over with the serialized covers hanging from the walls, glittering like jade pendants and carnelian gems, your heart fluttering with ardor. Each one of these "bare books" were wrapped with a second kraft-paper dust jacket that displayed the title and series number written out by hand. The transaction took place over the counter: borrow any title for two fen a day plus a deposit; read it in the shop for one fen, no deposit required.

During those difficult years, elementary schools only ran on a half-day schedule. In the afternoon, after finishing our homework, like lambs set free the gang would scatter east and west and the little picture bookshop would be our primary meeting-place. Three to five pals would always show up, each one borrowing several titles, this natural resource pooled and shared among us. Though the shop supposedly had a clear no-swapping policy, the boss turned a blind eye.

Double-tiered benches of different sizes were haphazardly tossed against the walls, their dark brown paint worn away, wood grain faintly exposed. A cluster of stools cluttered the middle of the shop. *Shua shua* the pages flipped in our hands, punctuated by the occasional gasp of wonder or hushed discussion about what we had just absorbed. An old-fashioned wall clock *di da di da* ticked away, chiming on the hour, calling attention to the passing of time. Day darkened to closing time; urged on by the boss, we made a dash for the ending, failing to grasp the final seed of the plot. Leaving the bookshop, it felt like we had emerged from another world back to the land of the human race, unsure of which world was the real one. Rooting around in my pockets, I still had five fen left! I rushed into the little-eats shop and treated myself to a sweet ear.

I enjoyed the perennially popular *Water Margin, Romance of the Three Kingdoms, Generals of the Yang Family,* and other such graphic-novel versions of the classics, but I was even more wild about underground resistance or counterespionage stories, like *Wildfires and Spring Winds,* or *Fighting in the Heart of the Enemy,* or *Military Depot No. 51,* many of these based on movies. The little picture books compensated for not being able to read the original texts due to dyslexia, besides the fact that they were more entertaining. What entertaining means here is simply satisfying the expectations of readers of below-average intelligence, like our gang of boys. The right and wrong of a black-and-white cause obvious at a glance: the hero dies as a righteous martyr, surrounded by green pines; the villain always in the shadows; the traitor remained flawed from the start and would naturally, in the final moment, come to a bad end.

Reading next door to the little-eats shop undoubtedly demanded a measure of heroism equal to the task of resisting the temptations of the diverse dainties and not becoming a defector.

To move on from little picture books to real books took a huge transformation in one's life, as momentous as evolving from an ape to a human.

My father was a literature enthusiast in his spare time. Such hobbies can become the epitome of miscellany—seize whatever you can buy, no picking and choosing. The russet-colored bookshelf in our home, neither too big nor too small, held around three hundred titles; it stood centered against the north wall in the outer room (where Mao Zedong's portrait hung during the Cultural Revolution, and before that, where we displayed the ancestral tablets for offerings), and still exists to this day; just from looking at this bookshelf one could see the importance of culture in our family life.

We categorized our books according to a strict hierarchy: the works of Marx-Engels-Lenin-Stalin-Mao, along with the collected works of Lu Xun, *dwelled in the heights looking down*, and represented the established canon; the second tier, representing tradition, included classical texts plus modern dictionaries, such as *Three Hundred Tang Poems, Ci Poems of the Song Dynasty, Perfected Admiration of Ancient Prose, Romance of the Three Kingdoms, Water Margin*, and *Dream of the Red Chamber*, as well as the first major dictionary of the twentieth century, *Ciyuan: Source of Words*, and the *Dictionary of Modern Chinese* and the *Great Russian-Chinese Dictionary*; farther down, contemporary revolutionary fiction represented a moral, Confucian orthodoxy, like *Steel Meets Fire, Red Cliff, Builders of a New Life, Wildfires and Spring Winds Raging in the Ancient City, Bitter Cauliflower*, among other titles, as well as collections of essays, such as Wei Wei's encomium to soldiers *Who Are the Most Beloved People?* and Liu Baiyu's *Red Agate*. The latter category served as the prime target of my excerpting prowess—those flowery, rhetorical passages embedded into my error-laden compositions littered with wrongly written characters shined with an excessive glare. The lowest rung belonged to the hodgepodge of magazines that represented current cultural tastes, among them *Harvest, Shanghai Literature, Study Russian*, although the bulk of them focused on the movies, so in addition to *Popular Cinema, Shanghai Film Pictorial*, and other more popular ones, we subscribed to a pile of specialty periodicals, like *Chinese Cinema, Film Literature, Cinematic Arts, Screenplay Magazine*, and so on. I've often wondered if, all along, my father harbored a secret desire to write a screenplay.

My reading interests turned the hierarchy on its head, inverting the bottom and top. I started with film magazines, particularly the ones on screenplays (which included the working scripts directors used), probably because the writing was easy to understand, relying mainly on dialogue, tight plots, strong and vivid images—a transitional stage between the little picture books and real books. Although such readings did come with a load of specialized terminology: stop-motion, flashback, fadeout, long take, voice-over, push pull rotate pan, etcetera; and yet, this issue proved to be no hindrance, like being able to sing without knowing anything about the musical staff. For me, reading a screenplay was more or less equal to watching a movie for free, and in fact, felt even more gripping—words created visual scenes with a much wider space for the imagination to roam. The relevance of this became wholly apparent when I started to write poems. I considered Eisenstein's use of montage and, rather than expounding on it as a theory of film, adopted it as a theory of poetry.

Rising up a level, I gradually became obsessed with revolutionary fiction. What aroused my heart most about these books were the descriptions of sex. And admittedly, Feng Deying became my foremost instructor on sexual enlightenment, his long novels *Bitter Cauliflower* and *Winter Jasmine* among the earliest sexually explicit reading material available; they involved brutal violence as well as perversions of the pornographic incestuous variety. Coming upon these passages, my heart leaped and flesh trembled with fear; I wanted to stop but couldn't bring myself to, and due to my issues with my own class status, intense feelings of guilt followed. I'm convinced that these books had an enormous influence on the sexual awakening of our generation: suppressed sexual violence in the name of revolution lay in the abyss of our consciousness.

Reading books brought much praise from adults. At a tender young age, where could one go to gain such approval? I recall I was in third or fourth grade when my mother brought me to the Library of the People's Bank of China; from a shelf, I chose a thick Soviet novel, more than seven hundred pages long, and sat down in the reading room, pretending to read with great pride. A librarian made a loud fuss over nothing, attracting other patrons who circled around and stared at me, as if I were a space alien. And indeed I felt like a space alien, reading a celestial script, bracing myself in the presence of so many new words, leaping forward and backward, unable to string together any hint of a plot.

I scaled up to the ancient classics, owing in large part to my father's willpower—he forced me to recite classical poems from the Tang and Song, typically over the winter and summer breaks, one poem per day. At an age when children only want to have fun and play, where could one find the carefree, idle mood of the ancients? The curtains swayed as I rocked my head back and forth, chanting a poem: "Moss green on the steps / grass sheen through the screen / Harmonize with the plain-plucked qin / read the golddust sutras / Chats and laughs with goose-winged scholars / who come and go, no empty-headed idiots among them / No din of other winds and strings to irritate the ears / no official records to toil over / Zhuge's hut in South-ern Sun / Ziyun's pavilion in Western Shu / As Kongzi once said: 'How could such a room be humble?'"* Concerning those books on the top shelf, everything from their stately grandeur to their thick spines made people wince; it wasn't until the Cultural Revolution that we consulted them for writing big-character posters. Reading and reading page after page I finally under-stood why Father placed those books at the summit—it's so lonely and cold at the top.

3

Around the age of ten I discovered a momentous secret: large stacks of banned books stashed away in the attic space above the corridor between the front door and the kitchen.

The boy was short, the attic high; this proved to be no ob-stacle as curiosity worked its mischief and, alone at home, I

---

* From Liu Yuxi (772–842), "Inscription for My Humble Room." Lines 3–4 and 5–6 are not in the correct order in the child's recitation and are interchanged in the original poem.—Tr.

positioned a tall stool on top of two chairs, each balanced on the other. This required an extraordinary degree of precision for all the furniture to fit flawlessly together. It was, essentially, an acrobatic performance without, sadly, any audience present; or it could be said that I played the sole audience member, determined to climb up and see what could be found.

I opened the attic hatch; the smell of dust and old papers blasted me in the face. I often browsed used bookshops where the odor of old paper—refined, remote—smelled like incense, summoning souls from faraway places. But here, maybe from being shut in the dark for so long, the odor emanating from the books smelled a hundredfold stronger; I felt like a prisoner, brimming with hostile aggression, the fumes making me dizzy. Regaining my focus, I held my breath, steadily adapted to the pungent onslaught as well as the dim surroundings, and with swift intuition, it dawned on me that I had found a real treasure trove.

To this day I can still remember the condition of a number of those books, the degree of damage to certain bindings, as well as that very unique odor. They had come from a range of different epochs and regions, each following a different route on its journey. Consider the source of the paper pulp for one—cotton and rice straw mashed together, then add in the differences of temperature and humidity in various locales, the absorption of each season's fragrances and nourishing flavors. Each book possessed its own life, possessed its own age, birthplace, and name.

My family's attic library could be divided into four rough categories: first, old editions of *Strange Tales of the Tang and Song*, Feng Menglong's *Stories to Caution the World* (unabridged edition), *Investiture of the Gods*, and other classic fiction titles of this sort; second, novels published before liberation by authors such as Zhang Henshui, Yu Dafu, among others, who with Mao Dun had been *banished to the cold palace*, having fallen out of favor largely for their explicitly erotic descriptions; third, assorted fashionable magazines from the 1930s and 1940s, including *The Young Companion, Women's Pictorial, Movie Art Pictorial*; fourth, specialized textbooks my mother used during her medical studies, like *Physiology and Anatomy* and *Comprehensive Gynecology*.

As is evidently clear, my family lived a cultural double life: The public bookshelf, out in the open for everyone to see, embodied the status quo and mainstream culture; the attic stacks, hidden and sealed off, embodied the illicit and taboo. From that day on, after discovering the secret in the attic, I, too, was thrown into a double life.

Coming home after school, I piled up the chairs and stool, scaled to the heights, popped open the attic hatch, groped my way through the dark, and extracted one title after another, first making a preliminary assessment before transporting them below. After finishing my reading, I'd put everything carefully back before my parents returned home from work.

The attic was deep, my arms short; I wanted to reach into the abyss and so added one more little stool to climb onto. And then with the slightest of slips, *rider thrown horse felled*, I crashed to the ground, bloodying my nose and bruising my face. Of my early reading experiences, besides the relationship between the public and the hidden, aches and pains unfailingly established their contrary significance. I think this must have been the necessary price to pay for reading banned books.

From the strange tales of ancient times to the novels of the modernist era, depictions of sex were much more depraved and

fantastic in those books than in revolutionary fiction, something that actually made sense to me as many sexual taboos
had formed fairly recently. *Physiology and Anatomy* and the
other medical books that described the structure and function of
female anatomy really made my eyes spring out and my mouth
gape open with wonder: The mysteries of birth revealed! And
compared with those brilliant May Fourth *sanwen* ("scattered
writings") prose stylists, a writer like Liu Baiyu simply couldn't
touch them; he was a quack selling fake herbs and nothing more.

The disarray in the attic aroused my father's suspicions; he
installed a lock on the hatch, and yet even this couldn't dampen
the deep resolve inside me. I scoured east and rummaged west,
until at last I found the key.

4

My secret attic-reading started at age ten and continued until
age seventeen, when the Great Proletarian Cultural Revolution
exploded. For a time, I would still steal the attic's forbidden fruit
while actively participating in the rebellion. Then that Sunday in
August arrived when the Red Guards posted the announcement
on our building, saying there'd be door-to-door searches, setting a deadline to hand over any "four olds" possessions to the
neighborhood committee—do not delay or risk being executed
under lawful authority.

We busied ourselves for three days. Father opened up the
hatch, brought down the whole hidden library, and piled it into
one heap. These books, so central to my upbringing, exposed
in the full light of the day, now waited to be delivered to the

flames. I imagined them in the fire, the shapes and sounds as the pages curled. While saddened, I unexpectedly felt a stealthy thread of delight.

Going to Shanghai

1

URING THE SUMMER of 1957, the Anti-Rightist Movement spread like wildfire, like roseleaf bramble. Dumbstruck and ignorant, I felt the grown-up world to be a very dangerous place, as if they were all playing hide-and-seek in broad daylight, to the degree that the game was becoming a life-or-death struggle. My older cousin who worked as a teacher at the Conservatory of Music came to visit, and I blurted out the question, "Are you a rightist?" She laughed and didn't reply; father blew a fuse, saying there was no doubt in his mind that I'd get into serious trouble in the future. A couple of days later, around noon on July 19, 1957, Yu Biaowen, whose family shared the same apartment unit with us, jumped to his death. Although I pondered death quite a bit during my childhood, mulling over its depths, to this day I am still petrified by the explicit implications of the word "*zisha*" ("to kill oneself").

It was around this time that Mama decided to request a leave of absence to take me to visit Waigong, her father, in Shanghai. This would be my first trip far from home—imagine my euphoria as I broke each of my fingers counting down the days. This was just when the weeping of the newly widowed Zheng Ayi had been waking me up during the night; the dark shadow of death slowly suffocated each individual within its grasp, but at long last, I escaped.

Waigong had suffered an unfortunate accident the previous year: Out on the street a soccer ball struck him, a ferocious kick by a mere kid toppled him over, face to the sky, back of the head cracked to the ground, resulting in paralysis on one side of his body and severely diminishing his verbal abilities. He used to be quite robust, loved to exercise, insisted on taking cold showers in the winter. In 1953 Waigong had visited Beijing for a brief stay and *roamed the peaks and gamboled in the waters*, soaking up all the sights, his characteristic bright smile everlasting in old photo albums.

At Qianmen Railway Station, I saw a locomotive up close for the first time. Enormous wheels connected by steel rods, driver's cab perched up so high, polished brass tubes shiny and bright next to the tarnished, gloomy boiler, the whole assembly making me quake and quiver with ecstatic delight. The steam whistle shrieked three times, our car violently lurched and rocked for a moment. Sitting beside my mother on the hard seats, I leaned against the window: trees fields villages blurring by. Crossing iron bridge after bridge of different shapes and sizes, each one emitted its own idiosyncratic rolling rumble. Mama bought some roast chicken on the train platform at Jinan Station. The train attendant poured the tea from an enormous pot. We had brought our enamel mugs with us and placed them on the small table, the lids of the mugs vibrating softly with the body of the train, like miniature cymbals....

2

Waigong's surname was Sun, his given name Haixia ("sea-cloud glow"), courtesy name Shuguang ("dawn light"); he was born in 1880 in Shaoxing, Zhejiang Province. From an early age he received a classical education at a *sishu* traditional private school, and later matriculated at the Shanghai Telecommunications Institute. Upon graduating, he was assigned to the telegraph office in Hankou, where the Han River converges with the Yangtze, handling service with Europe and the United States He eventually met Huang Xing, the revolutionary leader, and became a member of Tongmenghui, the United Allegiance Society founded by Sun Yat-sen, Huang Xing, and others in Tokyo in 1905, an organization that played a major role in overthrowing the Qing dynasty. Before the Wuchang Uprising, Waigong sent Waipo, my grandmother, and their children to stay with some relatives in Yueyang, Hunan Province. During the uprising, he joined a suicide squad, swiftly seized a telegraph station, and transmitted orders from command headquarters to mobilize the revolutionary army without delay. The next day, at a celebratory meeting, my grandfather was honored with a first-class medal for meritorious service and handed one thousand silver yuan coins as a reward. Huang Xing wanted him to work for the revolutionary government as the director of telecommunications, but he graciously declined, leaving instead for Zhongxiang in Hubei where he assumed the directorship of the telecommunications bureau there and used his reward to found the Zhong Qiang Secondary School, working a second job as its principal.

Every morning after the flag-raising ceremony, Waigong personally spoke to the students about current news while promoting democratic and scientific principles. In 1919 during the May Fourth Movement, he organized a public assembly to support the cause and led many protest demonstrations in solidarity with the students in Beijing. In 1927, after the April 12 Incident, local crime bosses, in collusion with the *huidaomen* secret societies and religious sects, destroyed the county's party headquarters, the facilities of the Farmers' Association, along with other institutions, including the telegraph office and Zhong Qiang Secondary School. They also stormed into Waigong's house, tied up my three uncles, and beat them. My grandfather's family disguised themselves in rags and mixed in with the masses, drifting with the chaos and out the city gate. Waigong first hid in the telegraph office, then in a wooded grove; under the cover of night, he climbed over the city walls and walked the rugged road all the way to Wuhan.

The central headquarters of the Ministry of Transport and Communications transferred him to Shanghai to help run a few foreign telegraph businesses. Shanghai fell into enemy hands; the Japanese asked him to take over the puppet regime's central telegraph office. Waigong feigned illness and fled to the Suzhou countryside. The Japanese repeatedly invited him to banquets. Knowing he couldn't hide forever, he crossed the blockade line, then tossed about until finding his way to Chongqing, where the ministry appointed him as the inspector general of the local telecommunications bureau. He was separated from his family for eight years, *removed to a corner of the sky*. After the victorious war of resistance, Waigong joined the telecommunications bureau in Chengdu, having been appointed its director. In 1948, the workers in the bureau launched a strike, and with Waigong's support, sent an open telegram across the nation. He was forced to resign immediately. The Chengdu bureau's eight hundred workers tearfully sent him off. Returning to Shanghai, he served as the director of the city's telecommunications bureau after liberation, remaining there until his retirement.

An episode during Waigong's turbulent career directly concerned me. In early 1946, my mother accompanied Waipo on a flight from Shanghai to Chongqing to visit Waigong. At Chongqing's Coral Dam Airport, they couldn't figure out how to use the public telephone and so Waipo let a young man standing in line behind my mother offer his assistance; the phone call quickly went through. The young man had been transferred from Chongqing to Beijing for work; with plane tickets scarce, he and a coworker took turns waiting in the ticket line at the airport. Waipo thought him to be courteous and good-natured upon their first encounter, plus he had the looks of a dashing young man going places. She persuaded him to call on Xiaoyi, my mother's little sister, in Beijing, with the design of finding a match for her second daughter. That young man, however, would become my father.

When he arrived in Beijing, Father called on Xiaoyi but no one was home; he left a note saying that he'd drop by another time. Then lightning struck—unable to endure a broken heart, Xiaoyi laid down on the railway tracks and killed herself. Out of this tragedy, regular letters passed back and forth between my mother in Shanghai and my father in Beijing. In May 1948, they got married in Shanghai and subsequently moved to Beijing. This is how I came into the world.

How many coincidences lead to the birth of each individual? If there had been no war, Waigong wouldn't have wandered far from his hometown, Mother wouldn't have accompanied Waipo on her journey to Chongqing, Father wouldn't have been transferred for work, there'd be no postwar chaos at the airport, no phone call to make, no Xiaoyi tragedy, no letters passing between Beijing and Shanghai—could I still have been born?

3

Mouth tilted, eyes askew, Waigong would often stare at me blankly, a trickle of saliva dribbling down his chin. Sitting face-to-face, the only way we could communicate involved rubbing the table leg with our slippers, *first you then me*—a softly sawing *zizi gaga* noise exchanged—and instantly his opaque eyes lit up like those of a naughty child.

Waipo gave birth to fourteen children, thirteen survived—I had eight uncles and four aunts on my mother's side. Not long after my birth, Waipo died from lung cancer. Waigong remained a widow for many years before he found another wife—a short lady full of energy and vitality, her glances and expressions strangely changeable. After Post-Waipo appeared, Waigong slowly drifted apart from his children, until his sickness and paralysis, whereupon everyone flocked to his side once again. Staying with my mother at Waigong's house, I could witness in close quarters the perilous condition of living a tranquil life.

Post-Waipo needed an iron will and steady nerves in order to resist the hostility of the clan members; otherwise, she'd have long been swept out the door. The adults never evaded me, even for secret family meetings or private discussions. Shanghainese wasn't unfamiliar to me; as far as I can remember, my parents spoke the dialect with each other as a kind of secret language. Though I understood it, they had little choice but to switch to Mandarin. During our visit, I immersed myself in my own world and paid no attention to family disputes. From a few fragments of conversation here and there, I learned that Post-Waipo's greatest offense came down to her mistreatment of Waigong; that, in fact, they saw her as nothing more than a "Wolf-Waipo." Living with this Wolf-Waipo, I needed to try my best to assume the role of a most innocent boy.

When he retired as director from the telecommunications bureau, Waigong moved into a residential unit allocated by the state. What was once a traditional *shikumen*-style terraced building quite popular throughout Shanghai, marked by high brick walls that enclosed a small courtyard in a very narrow alleyway, had become subjected to unceasing division and restructuring according to the changing times, its topography, in turn, growing increasingly complex. Entering the front gate, past the open-air "sky-well" courtyard, a sitting room occupied the space to the left of the stairs, a small kitchen directly under the stairs, a garret-like room called a *tingzi* halfway up the stairs, and the main bedroom, no more than ten square meters, made up the entire second floor. Waigong and Wolf-Waipo slept in the main bedroom; mother and I squeezed into the *tingzi*.

Each day Mother would leave Waigong's place with the grown-ups. Bored out of my mind, I'd stare out the window, the horizon obstructed by colorful blooms of clothes blossoming on lines strung between bamboo poles. A group of boys would congregate regularly in the sky-well, *ji ji zha zha* chattering non-stop; with no action or excitement to speak of, I began to feel anxious for them. After gnawing an apple down to its core, I handily arced it toward the boys and, bent at the waist, head down, stealthily receded from the window.

Around dusk the next day, I returned with Mother; she went upstairs ahead of me, while the boys slowly surrounded me. They were all of different heights, silent as shadows; a thin, taller one, obviously the leader, demanded to know why I had thrown a fruit pit at them. He tried again, asking me where I was from, but once more I refused to reply. We glared at each other, our faces almost touching; it was as if we were playing the blinking game, *who blinked first, no, you did*. My mother called me from upstairs, the leader slapped me on the shoulder, the little bros stepped aside to make a path. Whenever I came or went, they always stared at me in silence, no hard feelings, the day's chattering resumed, a pattern that would repeat itself till the earth expired and heaven fell.

Seventh and Eight Uncle lived in a two-story *xiaoyanglou*, or European-style building, at 698 Huaihai Middle Road. The families of my two aunts, who were sisters, also lived with them, and so the saying, *doubling relations binds the relatives*. One birth followed another and the children grew and grew, while their house shrank and shrank. A mass of cousins I had never met materialized before me, a screaming swarm, their mouths an onrush of Shanghainese; among them, my loneliness deepened.

Eighth Uncle graduated from St. John's University in Shanghai and taught English in a middle school. Seventh Uncle was a pilot, and a hero in my mind. He participated in the Two Airlines Uprising that took place on November 9, 1949, when two airlines in Hong Kong broke off relations with the Nationalist government and, in solidarity with the Central People's Government, declared a revolt, piloting twelve planes back to the Mainland. During the Cultural Revolution, Seventh Uncle was labeled a "suspected enemy agent" and eventually beaten while serving a prison sentence. Some years after his political rehabilitation, he visited Beijing; upon seeing the misshapen pinkie finger on his right hand that had been crushed, I started trembling down to my bones and, unable to control myself, burst into tears.

4

Of all of her siblings, my mother was closest to Eryi, Second Aunt. She headed the nursing department at the Shanghai Hôpital Sainte-Marie. Before liberation, she became a member of the Communist Party. On the eve of liberation, as the personal nurse to the factory director of the Jiangnan Shipyard, Eryi helped to dissuade the director from carrying out an order to demolish the equipment and facilities, and to hand over the shipyard intact to the new regime. In 1950, she was transferred to Beijing to work as a special-care nurse for high-ranking party officials, including Mao's wife, Jiang Qing—this became the "buried root" that led to her tragic fate.

Eryi suffered from illness her whole life and never married. She lived plainly and simply, wearing her blue double-breasted Lenin suit with white cloth shoes every day. Though her wages were high, she economized on food and spent little, giving much of her earnings to her relatives' children. On New Year's and such occasions she always sent us gifts—clothes, book bags, pencils, among other useful items. During our trip to Shanghai, mother spent the most time with Eryi—the threads of conversation between them spun on without end. While riding a pedicab, I'd sit in the middle, soaking up their quick, thick Shanghainese chitter-chatter.

Winter of 1968, in the middle of the night, we received an urgent telegram from Shanghai: Eryi had killed herself. Mother wept and wept, *until her heart split and lungs collapsed*, her pain so great she said she couldn't bear living another day. According to the rebel activists at Guangci Hospital, Eryi had been under investigation and had killed herself to avoid punishment. Family members weren't allowed to receive her body and she was quickly cremated without any of us seeing her again. Later we learned that the investigation had something to do with Jiang Qing and the fear that Eryi knew too many secrets.

I remember standing in line with Mother in the Xidan commercial district in Beijing, waiting for a pedicab, when I suddenly heard her sob. I held back my tears, and quietly hushed her with a cautious "Shhh," not wanting her to cry for Eryi ever again— Eryi had been deemed a class enemy. I soon grew up and, as the eldest son, became responsible for the safety of my mother and family. For several days winds from the north raged on, fiercely rattling our front gate in the middle of the night. I could hear Mother weeping and weeping, and as if a distant bird, the widow Zheng Ayi's cries echoed in my mind from across the years.

Summer of 1957; riding a pedicab through the big streets and narrow alleys of Shanghai, sitting between Mother and Eryi, peeping out from under their bosoms, backs, elbows to see the world streaming by, enfolded in their maternal wing, that warm sense of safety. Of all my relatives, Eryi was the kindest to me, often treating me to the finest-quality two-flavor ice-cream brick.

5

My impressions of that first journey to Shanghai persisted as a confused jumble in my mind, a tumultuous blur of incessant astonishments, the city seemingly a world apart, totally different from Beijing. And yet, beneath the bustling haze I could sense a deeper significance. I realized that being far away from Beijing caused me to see the city of my birth anew; I could discern the limits of its heaven and earth, the extent of its boundaries as well as its possibilities. Much later, I would be forced to flutter here and there, at the threshold of madness, moving from country to country across the globe, though I could always trace my way back to that first journey away from home. At some point during my restless wanderings, I came across this line by the Russian poet Konstantin Balmont: "I arrived in this world to see the sun, to see the blue, blue horizon." These words instantly pierced me to the core, clarifying the impulse to keep moving, keep on moving, that burned deep in my innermost being since that first journey to Shanghai.

We stayed in Shanghai for only ten days or so; I started to miss Beijing, miss my friends, miss my home, the hutong, and all the special scents and familiar comforts; I even missed my boring school. For the first time in my life I experienced a feeling of homesickness.

August 1, 1957, marked the thirtieth annual Army Day Festival. That night my mother along with other relatives took me to Waitan, the Shanghai Bund at the waterfront. On the Huangpu River, numerous warships decorated with colorful lights lined up in formation; steam whistles cried out concurrently; sailors standing along the railings of the ships greeted us with salutes. Suddenly, fireworks tore open the sky, lighting up the surface of the river. Sitting on Seventh Uncle's shoulders, high above the thronging crowds, I let out a rousing whoop. The next day I turned eight.

Elementary School

1

IN THE WINTER of 1957, when I was in second grade at
Fuwai Elementary School, my family moved from the Fu-
wai Insurance Company Apartments to Three Never Old
Hutong No. 1, whereupon I transferred to Hong Shan Temple
Elementary School.

The day the teacher brought me into my new classroom,
some kids were drumming the desks, others horsing around;
in the poorly lit room, all those eyes and teeth sparkled and
flashed. I wore a cotton-padded ushanka hat, earflaps sticking
out, making me look like a seventh-rank county magistrate. A
child transfers to a new school to confront a strange collective
hostility, and does anyone care if harm comes to him?

The Temple of Great Benevolence, once a Buddhist monas-
tery, dates back nearly five hundred years to the Ming dynasty.
Among the groves of temples in Beijing, it was small and lacked

spirits to protect it, the burning of joss sticks dwindled, and eventually they converted it into an elementary school. When the monks fled, the temple fled too, and by 1965, Hong Shan Temple Hutong's name was shortened to Hong Shan Hutong, and Hong Shan Temple Elementary School's name shortened to Hong Shan Elementary School.

I type Beijing into Google Earth, and like an eagle spiral down, following Tiananmen, the Forbidden City, Shichahai Lakes, Denei Street, until at last arriving at Sanbulao Hutong No. 1, then pan over to Hong Shan Hutong. I click the mouse to zoom in—charging down and ahead, Hong Shan Hutong No. 3 disappears beneath some large trees. An ugly new building stands beside it: the Tian Hong Shan ("Great Benevolence of Heaven") Hotel. I investigate further but cannot find any information about Hong Shan Elementary School.

An entire half-century has already passed. Early spring, 1958—after an abrupt warm spell it turned cold again. The spirit-screen wall that faced the school gate bore the inscription: "Study Hard Day by Day, Soar Higher and Higher." Outside the reception office, the branches of a crookneck willow tree had started to bud. It slanted through the front of the courtyard, toward the classroom at the northeast corner, where the door creaked open *zhi ga zhi ga* and a row of small windows tilted east and leaned west beneath a low ceiling. Continuing on to the rear courtyard, past the former ritual purification halls turned into classrooms, past the concrete Ping-Pong tables, to where the playing field swirled with dust—there, on a brick platform at the foot of the north wall, the principal shouted with forceful enthusiasm, "Raise the flag!" All the uniformed students stood straight at attention and loudly sang in one voice, "We children of the New China / We youthful pioneers / Rise up together, unite / Carry on the work of our forefathers / No fear of difficulties, no fear of any heavy burdens...."

Many obstacles needed to be overcome on the way to school. Leaving the front gate, two tigers immediately impeded the path: one the white-yam roasting shack in the middle of the road, the other the breakfast hut facing it at the entrance to Huazhi ("Flowering Branch") Hutong. The burned odor of roasting yams, the fragrance of the oily smoke wafting from woks, *zhi zi zhi zi* sizzling away—one simply couldn't move another step forward. I broke free and redoubled my siege, and with much difficulty left the hutong and crossed the street, only to run head-on into the little grocer's shop that guarded the entrance to the Temple of Great Benevolence Hutong on the northwest corner. I unconsciously rubbed my pockets, swallowed lots of saliva, and forged on. At last I reached the school gate, but a street hawker welcomed me—he resembled a master magician of yore, changing shape with a slight shake, as he displayed an array of snacks on the spot—dried fruits, rock candy, haw flakes, cinnamon sticks, and on and on—causing one to drift away, *no spirit remaining to defend the dwelling*. Then, at the critical moment, the school bell resounded.

I fear that cast-iron bell was the only surviving temple treasure left in the whole school; *dong dong dong* it chimed through the thick fog of the dynasties—we stood up or sat down, started class or ended class. The sound of the bell that symbolized time, sliced time into pieces, while also encouraging us to ignore time—within the very clanging of the bell we whooshed along, growing into adolescence. *First grade little steamed bean bun, one whacked one leaps up. Second grade little speck, one smacked one wink-winks....* Save for avoiding "hanging back" (that is, repeating a grade), we just needed to rise in the ranks, turn around, and denigrate the incoming students.

2

I was known in school for my comic cross-talking skills. I remember the sketch I performed, "Confusing Descriptions," I had first heard on the radio. Later, I found the original script in the magazine *Folk Arts* and, with a dictionary, phonetically annotated each unfamiliar character, one by one, until finally committing it to memory *as ripe as a melon that rolls from the vine*. Those were days of confusing descriptives, and copying this and copying that in our class compositions, more than anything else we'd copy an assortment of vacuous, ostentatious adjectives.

Ascending the platform on the playing field, my scalp felt numb, legs and stomach cramped; the crackling feedback of the microphone gave me a moment to breathe and think silently in my heart: "Being onstage, just think of the area before you as a watermelon patch." Indeed, it worked like a charm—my mouth released a torrential stream, once unleashed no restraining it, the whole audience rolled with laughter. For a week I was the school celebrity, countless gazes acknowledged and cast away. Frankly, being a celebrity is nothing special—it just unsettles the heart and mind. Another week passed and not another glance fell in my direction: I felt a sense of loss, as well as a feeling of lightness, as if a heavy weight had lifted from me.

I switched my trade to recitation, memorized Gao Shiqi's poem "Song of the Times," which I had cut out from the newspaper. Gao Shiqi, a *broken-in-body-but-not-will* popular science writer, wrote poems with scientific overtones that foamed to a froth. Standing on the platform, I first silently contemplated the *Watermelon Patch Sutra* in my heart, then lifted my voice: "O, the times ..."

In fourth-grade Chinese, I wrote my first poem, bricolaged together from a number of poems published in the official newspaper of the CPC, the *People's Daily*, using an assortment of weighty-sounding phrases, such as "the wheel of history rolls forth," "imperialist lapdogs," "mantis arms blocking the cars," "communist tomorrow".... Alarmingly, this was due to the influence of Gao Shiqi "observing the times."

The cost of advancing with the times initially involved hunger. During the three-year period of hardship, people would often gather in groups to relax, a respite that served as "collective food for the spirit." This was when the rumor spread that everything good to eat our Soviet Big Brother had hauled away by train. Everyone burned with indignation, *slapping their fists and rubbing their palms*—and slowly, expending basic physical energy made us even hungrier.

To improve school meals, the cafeteria decided to raise two pigs out on the playing field. When the final bell chimed, nearly every boy in the school made it the object of his pursuit, the two animals chased all over the place, leaping railings and walls, both thin as a bag of bones, eyes a menacing glint—they seemed more like dogs than pigs. In the eyes of the pigs, mankind had gone totally insane: Once the bell clanged, humans stormed out the doors and windows, hurtled and pounced over one another, each one with a savage look in his eyes, emitting the flashing green *pingpingpingping* signal of a carnivore.

3

On the surface, it seemed that the principal and teachers were in charge of the school, but prowling beneath appearances a different system of power thrived, feeding on force and violence.

One day, in the classroom by the playing field, a fellow student Lei and I copied out the "blackboard news" onto the chalkboard. The afternoon sunlight felt pleasantly warm; the fragrance of pagoda-tree blossoms drifted through the air. Most of the students had already gone home, the campus grounds very peaceful and quiet. At first we worked together quite cheerfully, talking and laughing; then a dispute arose over the spacing of the layout, a few sparring exchanges tossed back and forth, and without warning, out of the blue, Lei charged at me, fists raining down upon my head and face. Golden petals flitted before my eyes; from within a haze of pain I could vaguely make out the twisted, malevolent smile on his face. The injustice I felt knew no bounds; my eyes brimmed with tears, but I held them back, refusing to let one drop tumble out.

This was the gist of the fist-clenched truth. Instinctually, I learned the law of the jungle, the crucial point being to seek a protector. A student in our grade, Li Xiyu, played on the school soccer team as a striker. Squat with short limbs, his looks weren't worth talking about, face a pugnacious hunk of meat, squinty eyes made it seem like he was always asleep; one moment he'd be calm like a napping lion, the next he'd strike with ferocity—local hooligans feared him to roughly the third degree.

I don't know how it happened, but after hanging out once or twice, Li Xiyu became my protector. A kind of natural power dynamic develops between individuals, its causes very tricky to discern. In this case, it possibly had something to do with the fact that most of the students were from the poorest strata of society, whereas Li Xiyu's father was a high-level engineer and so we shared a similar family background. He lived in a single-family home not far from school, with a private gate, private courtyard, and a huge jujube tree that was the envy of the neighborhood. He even had his own bedroom, an unimaginable luxury in those days. At his home he seemed very ordinary, very easygoing, like a well-nurtured, well-educated, well-behaved child.

Then one winter morning I entered the classroom as usual about fifteen minutes before the first bell. Students chatted and laughed around the stove, warming themselves. Li Xiyu came over to greet me, passing me a baked bun he said he had buttered for me on top. His excessive eagerness and strange grin put me on the alert; I declined. He angrily replied, "Not good enough for you? You're really no brother to me." It later came out that the baked bun was actually buttered with snot. This incident hurt me deeply, making me realize that, while alive on this planet, one's dignity was of the utmost importance. From then on I avoided Li Xiyu as much as possible, while at the same time steeling myself for a sudden bloody reprisal. I maneuvered along the half-comatose, squinty-eyed perimeter of his sight; he seemed to be weighing things carefully, he seemed to be wavering....

A boy joined our class who had just returned from Japan. Lai Desheng also had an older brother, Lai Wenlong, one grade above us. Tall and athletic, the two brothers first swept the school away with their Ping-Pong paddles, then proceeded to smash each record in every competitive sport. As they had grown up in faraway Japan, they weren't guarded in the least and knew nothing about the subterranean system of power, though no one dared to pick on them. Unintentionally, by imperceptible degrees, they expanded the power vacuum, granting me a cushion of safety. As I lived near them we gradually became buddies.

The Lai brothers brought back the most advanced technology from Japan. One item, an elaborately designed transistor radio with the finest sound, filled me with awe, its buttons and knobs giving it the appearance of a bona fide detonation device. The other, glossy magazines filled with photographs of beautiful women, sent my imagination into flights of reverie: Who knew this other world existed beyond our daily lives?

4

My first head instructor was Teacher Li. Every morning, on schedule, he'd pass by our building downstairs, the soft *tuo tuo* steps of his leather shoes rising above the mishmash of other footsteps like rice tassels popping out of a husk; in haste, I'd leap out of bed. Teacher Li was taller and thinner than most, with dark skin and a grave face; whenever he spoke his Adam's apple would roll up and down. He wore a blue uniform, faded from frequent washing, collar always buttoned up tight, black leather shoes polished to a shine. Teacher Li suffered from recurring colds; at every turn he'd fish out the large handkerchief from his pocket and *chi chi* clear his nose, or spit a mucous gob out any which way (though never in the classroom). His spitting technique was matchless—posture graceful without the slightest stoop, delicate turn of the head, mouth angled down, eyes forward: *Ptooey!*

Between the dull, dry-as-dust lessons from books, Teacher Li would often intersperse some cautionary tales. Once there was a wastrel who every day loved to eat mincemeat buns, but the last corner pleat of each bun he'd bite off and throw into the trash. The old man next door secretly picked up each of these bits and stored them away. Then the sky fell, fortunes reversed, and overnight the wastrel became a beggar. One day, he went scrounging around his former neighbor's gate, and the old man brought out a big, bulging sack for him. Opening the sack, the beggar discovered it was full of bun pleats, and while stuffing his face, he sighed, "O, that such a tasty delicacy exists under heaven!" The old man replied, "These are all the bits you had thrown out yourself so long ago....!" Here, Teacher Li would raise his intonation with profound implications of meaning and sweep his gaze across the whole class. Too bad none of us had a fortune to lose back then.

Because of his persistent cold, Teacher Li used the classroom to pitch his remedy of choice, Yingqiao Jiedu Wan, or Honeysuckle-Forsythia Detox Pills: "You know what the nectar cure is, right? It's made out of honey, yes, and you're all, in fact, being reared in a cozy honey pot. What is a wax pill? It's just a pill coated with wax, to seal it and keep it from going bad. Only two mao a pill, not so bad, right, and moreover the flavor's especially...." The way he talked about it, it could have been immortal cinnabar, and of all the students, only I believed him. Two months later, I walked into an herbal medicine shop as tenebrous as a dark grove. I placed the change I had scraped together onto the high counter and received one pill of "immortal cinnabar." I turned down a narrow alley, found a spot with no one around, peeled off the wax shell and popped the pill into my mouth, the pungent, bitter taste instantly making me wretch....

In fifth grade, the ore-cast bell switched to an electric bell and our head instructor switched to Teacher Dong Jingbo. Bobbed hair, glasses, double-breasted button Lenin women's wear—Teacher Dong was as clean and neat as she was refined. Always sunny and smiling, at least to me, she often praised my compositions in class as examples of model writing; apparently, I was her prize pupil. I fell in love with Chinese class; writing filled me with a heartwarming confidence that I didn't get out of math. I worked hard on my calligraphy and the words flowed from my fountain pen with a Yan-style intensity, which received Teacher Dong's profuse praise, along with the admiration of my classmates. My sky opened out, clearing to a bright radiance. A lifetime later, I'd write in the preface of my collection of *sanwen* essays, *Book of Failure*: "In elementary school, my compositions often received favorable critiques from Teacher Dong, who'd read them aloud to the class. I remember how wildly my heart thumped and fluttered as she read. Indeed, it was analogous to being published at an early age, Teacher Dong my first editor and publisher...."

During class I'd often daydream, somnambulate between imaginary worlds. Teacher Dong would wake me in a gentle way, for instance, by prodding me with an obvious question and ushering me back to reality. "Absolutely correct, Zhao Zhenkai," she'd say, brandishing her pointing stick. "Would every student please focus and pay attention."

Drifting with the waves during my wandering days overseas, I finally tracked down Teacher Dong through my mother and initiated a correspondence. In the winter of 2001, upon returning to Beijing after my long separation, I made a special trip to call on Teacher Dong. Her hair had fully grayed, her legs crippled—all day she could only lie in bed, unable to get up on her own. She showed me our old class picture, though couldn't find me in it, my former appearance too difficult to match with my present one. She spoke with a heavy Hebei accent, and grew visibly emotional talking about our memories of those times. At last, she muttered: "Hai … move along now. Don't waste so much effort on me." Though I could sense that it was time itself she reproached.

Toward the end of last year, I was eating lunch with my mother in a Shanghainese restaurant in Hong Kong's Kowloon Tong, when my mother casually mentioned that Teacher Dong had passed away. I froze, powerless to hold back the tears streaming down my face.

The year I took the citywide placement exam to transition from elementary school (fifth grade) to junior high, Teacher Dong served as the supervising proctor. A dreadful calm permeated the testing room; other than the hushed sound of pens scribbling away, sparrows chattered noisily on the rooftop. I let out a breath of relief, inwardly pleased about the easy essay topic. Then in the "correct the wrong words" section I came upon the two characters *ji ji* (極積), my gaze pausing for a moment, then continuing on. At that moment, Teacher Dong strolled up beside me; I could feel the pressure of her gaze. She rapped my desk with a finger, turned around to face the others and said, "Students, don't be careless. Before turning in your exam, check it over very thoroughly one more time." It was clear that Teacher Dong's words were meant for me. I earnestly checked over my exam again, found no errors, and convinced of a perfect score, turned it in well ahead of the allotted time.

But because I had inverted the word *ji ji* (積極, "active"), two points were deducted from my score and I didn't test into my top choice, Beijing Middle No. 4.

Beijing Middle No. 13

1

I N T H E S U M M E R of 1962, I tested into Beijing Middle No. 13. It was twice as far from my home as my elementary school, and my own world seemed to grow twice as big.

The school had been the residence of the Kangxi emperor's fifteenth son, Commandery Prince Yu of the Second Rank. More than a century and half later, in 1902, Commandery Prince Zhong of the Second Rank adopted Zaitao, the seventh son of State Prince Chunxian of the First Rank, who inherited the title of *beile*, Noble Lord, and moved into the official mansion, which then became known as Tao Beile ("Billowing Noble Lord") Mansion. During the reign of Xuantong, the last emperor of China, Zaitao, as the little brother of the Regent, was given the appointment of Minister for Training the Imperial Guard. When General Zhang Xun regained power during the brief Manchu Restoration, Zaitao assumed the position of Commanding Officer of the Imperial Guard. A few decades later, the founding of the People's Republic of China in 1949 changed everything in one swoop, and Zaitao became a member of the National People's Congress and the Chinese People's Political Consultative Conference, a political advisory front composed of delegates from various parties and organizations. Back in 1925, Zaitao had leased Tao Beile Mansion to the Catholic Church to establish a university, which eventually became known as Fu Ren Catholic University. In 1929, Fu Ren opened an affiliated all-boys secondary school, and in 1952 its name changed to Beijing Middle No. 13.

The school's campus lay on a north-south axis; the main gate opened east. The path that ran through the center of the grounds and the one that bordered the eastern edge each passed through four courtyards. The western path led to an amphitheater-stage platform, continued along a long covered walkway, and on to a pavilion and a rock garden. Through the years, the howling hordes of boys flanked the three paths, nimble little legs churning their feet *dongdong dongdong, rising from the halls into the chambers*, until at last they disappeared into the dust of the playing fields at the western border. Our classroom happened to be situated right next to the entrance of the playing field, the sound of those thronging footsteps so familiar to me, the movement and direction of those years.

The first day of class, clutching my schoolbag tightly as I walked through the gate, I came to a halt, stupefied: Staring at the backs of the high-school students *blotting out the sky, blocking the sun*, I caught a glimpse of my future—grade after grade leading to the single-plank bridge of the college entrance exam (below it, the abyss), and from there into university and on to the dreaded world of adulthood.

Middle No. 13 used to be an all-boys school, no girls to form a buffer zone, which at first I thought would translate into an even more savage law of the jungle. But it didn't turn out this way. I discovered that at a certain age, man becomes more cunning and begins to use his intelligence more adeptly which, coupled with his will in place of his fists, forms the fountainhead of power and authority for grown-up society.

I was thirteen when I started my new school that year, and with respect to both my physical and mental development, a late bloomer. I still have a photograph to prove it—me and my peer Yifan standing with others in front of a building: Yifan is tall and brawny, his gaze behind thick-rimmed glasses emanates self-confidence, his Adam's apple prominent, his upper lip bears a slight trace of stubble; I'm shorter than him by half a head, shorts exposing thin hemp-stalk legs, a childish grin across my face, confused look in my eyes. It was a transitional year for us—we had tested into Middle No. 13 from different elementary schools, Yifan into Class 4 and I into Class 2, separated like opponents in a sporting competition before we'd meet again in the final round.

A student in my class called Big Neck had to "hang back" two grades due to learning problems, and it'd come as no shock if he'd have to hang back even further. We met by some chance permutation and combination of our rising and falling grade levels. He possessed the limbs of a tiger and the trunk of a bear, his arms thicker than my thighs. The fat collar he wore around his neck earned him the nickname Big Neck. He claimed that he had slipped while practicing on the parallel bars, wrenching his neck between them, and long-term traction was necessary in order to recover. To this day I still remember his contrite smile, as if he were offering his sincere apologies for accidentally intruding upon the world.

At the time, we still lived in the shadow of the Difficult Three-Year Period of the Great Famine. There were no chairs in the cafeteria, so everyone stood around the tables to eat, each meal ending with Big Neck singing. He used to work as a manual laborer at a construction site and still ate as if he spent the hours hammering away, his appetite astounding. As it was hard for him to live off the food rations, he sang for food, each tune varying in price, from half a steamed bun to a corn-cone bun.

Big Neck didn't have a great voice, but he sang with an earnest intensity and never goofed around; when he reached for the upper register, a segment of pale neck would stretch out from beneath the fat collar. When the singing stopped, he'd scarf down his bartered buns in two or three bites, and then, like a dog, look around to beg for more. The songs he sang lacked subtlety and mostly concerned the riffraff of life. In fact, most could be classified as explicit "yellow ditties" that doubled as our earliest enlightenment about sexual issues.

Our class moved on to the second year of junior high, except for Big Neck, who once again hung back, though this time he exceeded the grade's age-limit policy and so subsequently was expelled. He would return to the bitter ranks, *our paths diverging, reins raised*. At our final farewell lunch, almost everyone gave him a steamed bun. He sang many songs, this time not for bartering but for friendship and for his own unpredictable fate. His singing reached a passionate pitch—his huge mouth pinched into a tiny circle rooted to his neck—and then ended with a screech.

2

In the fall of 1962, an unexpected guest arrived at our house—my uncle Biao Jiu's comrade-in-arms up in the Great Northern Wilderness, Lu Shushu ("Uncle" Lu).

Yong Yao Biao Jiu used to be a young officer in the Air Force Logistics Department in Beijing; not particularly tall of stature but handsome and rugged, and to my inner childhood eye as mentioned before, my hero. For New Year's and other festivals he'd wear a dark green military uniform, along with collar insignia, epaulets, leather arms belt-and-strap, and topped his lofty airs with a peaked cap. When we chatted outside by the gate of our building, my little comrades would look on in wonder, massaging my vanity with their admiring stares. After Uncle Biao Jiu left, I would boast till the cows came home, saying that he had shot down who knows how many American fighter planes. Our shirts, our family's window curtains, all could be traced, light as air, to the parachute fabric Biao Jiu had given us, as if visible proof to the world that he had hopped out of an aircraft and dropped from the sky.

In the early spring of 1958, Biao Jiu was transferred to the Great Northern Wilderness, far in the northeast bordering the Soviet Union. The last time he came to our house to say good-bye, Mother had been demoted to a cadre and was also preparing to leave, her destination the Shandong countryside. He took off his military uniform, and in an instant the spell had been broken, his splendor gone, filling me with sadness. I silently withdrew from the grown-ups' field of vision and slipped out the door. "I'll come to see you," my uncle said to me on parting, then turned and disappeared from the horizon of my childhood.

Lu Shushu's appearance made me secretly happy: Biao Jiu had indeed sent us someone from far beyond the horizon. Lu Shushu operated and maintained a tractor; while using a hammer to bang away at some machinery, a sliver of metal flew into his right eye. He couldn't get proper treatment at the local clinic near the farm and so was transferred to Beijing Tongren Hospital. Through Biao Jiu's introduction, he stayed at our place.

"The doctor wants to fix me up with a dog's eye," he said to me. This made my heart palpitate uneasily—what would it be like, exactly, observing the world through the eye of a dog? But of course he was only joking; the doctor fitted him with an artificial eyeball, which looked pretty much the same as one of the glass marbles I flicked around. He'd often sneak into the bathroom to pop it out and put it in a little glass to wash.

Biao Jiu regularly appeared in my dreams. He wandered through a land of ice and snow, directing an army procession of ten thousand horses and men. I tried to pester Lu Shushu for details of the Great Northern Wilderness, but he evaded my every question and wouldn't reply, presumably because it involved secret military affairs.

One night, Lu Shushu finally told me a story. Between the luster of his two discrepant eyes under the electric lights, the glass one looked excessively limpid and bright. "In the middle of the night, a black bear broke into the storehouse on the farm, flipping over boxes and baskets, searching for food. A sentry discovered the disturbance and we surrounded it, first firing some warning shots, but then it bounded toward us. Unfortunately, no one aimed for the critical spot, that white patch of fur on the front of its chest, and instead fired away haphazardly with their submachine guns. It toppled over, a total of thirty-nine bullet wounds later found in its body...." This story made me quite despondent, but in the edited version I told to my classmates, Uncle Biao Jiu became the commander of the military campaign against the enemy black bear.

That year Beijing remained unlit and pitch-black, while the stomachs of its citizens emptied, forcing people to go home early just to rest. Lu Shushu, though, discovered Beijing's "high life": the dramatic arts. He was a stranger in a strange land with no friends and so he always took me with him. Together, we saw the plays *In the Name of the Revolution, The Man with the Gun,* and *Aesop,* among others, though the last made the deepest impression on me.

A late-autumn evening after a rain, the scent of moldering leaves. The Capital Theater was located on Wangfujing Street. Its windows were as majestic and clear as the cloudless twilight sky; the spectators moving up the staircase seemed to be leaving for another planet, among them a thin, small boy (me) and his uncle with a glass eye. The enormous chandelier glittered softly, making me a little dizzy. After the bell rang out low and deep, the lights dimmed, the red curtain slowly pulled open *xu xu xu,* and, lo and behold, the columns and steps of ancient Rome emerged....

I didn't sleep at all that night. Bewitched, I had memorized passages of the play's dialogue and proceeded to recite them, emulating the actors' exaggerated onstage delivery. At school, half crazed under Aesop's spell, I declared to the other students my concept of freedom—that it would be better to die than to be a slave to examinations. In class, the teacher asked for the molecular composition of water, and *as if putting a donkey's lips onto a horse's mouth,* I replied in Aesop's intonation: "If you can divide the river from the sea, I will drink the sea dry, my master...." The teacher assumed I had experienced a psychotic break.

Those were the famine days of dinner guests needing to bring their own ration coupons. Because Lu Shushu didn't bring enough coupons to the table, some friction arose between him and my parents. I remained furtively on his side, for the simple reason that he took me out of the darkened hutong alleyways into a brilliant, illusory world, a world wholly unrelated to the reality I longed for.

3

The endlessness of middle-school year three, exams like doors after doors obstructing any chance of reaching eternal life. How I loathed exams—to me they were one of the most sinister plots of mankind to make children prematurely experience the bitterness of life.

In elementary school I lacked arithmetic chops; rising into middle-school mathematics, I found a boundless sea of suffering: besides chopping up integers, reversing positive and negative, and then squaring and square-rooting to dismember the universe, there was no other choice but to go mad. I lost my way completely. If the final exam for this subject was the last judgment, quizzes were like being served in the Hall of Great Torture. Nevertheless, each individual has his own way to survive and endure. The day before the final exam, I watched two movies, forgetting everything in the darkness. Due to this mental-emotional relaxation, I could muddle my way through the test with a passable result, *as if mistaking a tiger for a horse.*

Next to mathematics in affliction came Russian. China and the Soviet Union had flip-flopped and become enemies, but the majority of middle school students still learned Russian as before. Retroflex sibilants proved to be a primary impediment; fortunately, these sounds were also present in the hawking cries of northern cart drivers, and so it would seem better to first learn how to drive a cart, then learn Russian. I wrote words and phrases on little slips of paper, Russian on one side, Chinese on the other; from early dawn till reaching Houhai, I'd rote memorize each syllable to death, some by way of Chinese homophones that I'll remember forever: "Saturday" (суббота)—*shu bao da* ("book bag's big"); "Sunday" (воскресенье)—*wazi ge zai xie limian* ("sock placed inside a shoe"); "home" (домой)—*da maoyi* ("hit the sweater"). When the Cultural Revolution blew up, the trend shifted to English. There were no classes at the time, though using the homophonic method I can still recall one sentence: "Love live Chairman Mao!"—*Lang laile qianmian pao!* ("The wolf has come, run on ahead!")

Chinese class, too, was losing more and more of its appeal, as politics started to make inroads into our writing assignments. In order to answer the call to "Learn from Comrade Lei Feng," one not only had to practice good deeds but also had to learn from Uncle Lei Feng in keeping a daily diary of them.

It was around then when I waited in ambush that afternoon at the Changqiao intersection—Deshengmen Inner Street running north up a steep incline for three or four hundred meters. A flatbed tricycle piled high with goods slowly headed up the slope, the bare-backed boss struggling with all his might to pedal; I dashed over, assumed the bow stance behind him and pushed, pace for pace following his pedaling, the old boss glancing back every so often, nodding his head at me. I pushed him all the way to the top of the slope. Then noticing we had just passed a little eatery, I asked the old boss to wait a moment, rushed inside, paid two mao for four pieces of *huoshao* flatbread, and stuffed them into his hands as he stared at me wide-eyed and tongue-tied.

Back home I wrote about the incident in my daily diary, then copied it out in my composition book, handing it in to the teacher the very next day. During our Chinese lesson, the teacher asked me to stand up in front of the whole class and read it aloud. As I began, I still felt puffed with pride. Reading on, this feeling turned to shame, until in the end, I couldn't find a hole to crawl into to hide my face, the wretchedness I felt worse than committing a bad deed and being caught on the spot. From that day on, I never wrote another diary entry.

4

The second year of Middle No. 13 wound down, final exams imminent. The teachers' cafeteria simmered with a variety of small dishes, while the students' cafeteria boiled large cauldrons of grub; fortunately, though, the grub rotated three times a week, keeping faint glimmers of hope alive. One Wednesday lunch hour, the student cafeteria served vegetable steamed buns plus egg drop soup—everyone lined up as one beaming ocean of happiness.

I returned to the classroom with my veggie bun and egg drop soup, half eating half chatting. Suddenly, I bit into some alien matter in my bun. I spit it out and before my eyes lay a dead cockroach. I slapped the table and leaped up; surrounded by a swarm of students, I charged into the cafeteria. The head boss was ladling out the soup, nearing the end of his shift. He replied evasively, saying that the cafeteria manager should deal with this matter. Like Danko in Gorky's tale, lifting up his flaming heart, I raised my vegetable steamed bun and led the masses to the cafeteria office.

Old Li Baixi the manager—pointy mouth, monkey cheeks, triangular eyes—supervised the cafeteria and purchased the food; all day long he leisurely cycled through the campus with basketfuls of chicken, duck, fish, meat, none of it going to the student cafeteria. After listening to my vehement speech, he said, "I know what can be done, just ask the head boss to exchange your veggie bun."

"What?!" I was livid, and raised my voice. "Just exchange a bun and everything's fine?"

"Then you tell me what should be done?" he asked serenely.

For a moment I was at a loss for words, gazing at him blankly, then with bold conviction and righteous indignation, I asserted, "From now on there must be a regular health inspection and the quality of the meals must be improved, and furthermore a public apology must be made to the entire student body."

"But how you can you even prove it was really a cockroach and not a dried shrimp?" Old Li countered.

I turned around to mobilize the masses: "Everyone, speak out now! Has our cafeteria ever put dried shrimp into the veggie steamed buns?"

"No way!" A rush toward Old Li with a great yelp and a

roar, "I protest the cafeteria!" "Protest! Protest!" The incitement spread, everyone shouting the slogan over and over, and for a moment it got a little out of control.

"You dare to rebel?!" Old Li howled, his face a ghastly white. "Zhao Zhenkai, you're always up to no good, stirring up trouble. Let me tell you, if you cause any more needless problems, first your mess hall privileges will be revoked, then I'll take you to the headmaster's office and you'll be punished with demerits until you get expelled! Any other students who want to follow his example, the same ending awaits you!"

His threats were quite effective. Most dispersed, only myself and two or three classmates remained. I thought about being expelled, my parents' reaction, and also started to waver. Then those two or three others vanished and only the lone stalemate between me and Old Li remained, mutual rage focused in our gaze. The class bell rang; I furiously chucked the veggie bun onto the floor and stomped away in a cloud of wrath and resentment.

That was my first time leading a rebellion, and it ended in failure. I realized there was no arguing with authoritarian power—a cockroach is but a dried shrimp. I also realized that to truly rebel, your heart must be strong enough to bear any consequences whatsoever.

5

Middle-school students in Beijing used to parrot this adage: "Middle 8's assemblies, Middle 3's fees, Middle 4's poor eyes, Middle 13's marching band." The marching band, indeed, was the pride of our school. A number of brass instruments had been inherited from Fu Ren's affiliated secondary school, pockmarked and scarred, the French horns in particular covered with patch-ups. Nevertheless, at Beijing secondary school sports competitions and large-scale rallies and assemblies of every kind, Middle 13's band proved to be the most impressive.

During summer break in 1963, Yifan and I both went to the Little Eighth Route Army Camp, open to any junior-high student in the city. Yifan, a squad leader, marched at the front of squad two's line formation; I was but an empty-headed idiot, a commoner, and also short, and so drifted toward the back of squad four's formation. Setting off from the school's playing field, the marching band led the way, the rays of the sun glinting crow-bright off the brass instruments. Suddenly, the drums let out a rolling salvo, shaking the earth. As the line formations shifted, Yifan and I crisscrossed and passed each other, exchanging a triumphant glance.

Beijing Middle No. 4

1

IN THE SUMMER of 1965, I received a notice that I had tested into Beijing Middle No. 4.

Middle No. 4 was considered the best secondary school not only in Beijing but in the whole country—its existence had been as remote to me as the Heavenly Halls. After elementary school, I had originally aspired to test into first, Middle No. 4; second, Middle No. 13; third, Middle No. 14—this basically the same ideal for all of us comrades with above-average grades. Because I didn't see through the *ji ji* (極積) deception in the language section of the exam, I was ensnared by a word-reversal trap and, midway on my journey to the Heavenly Halls, I took a turn into Middle No. 13.

That scene played over and over in my mind—Teacher Dong on proctor duty, halting beside my desk, sighing deeply, reminding the whole room to carefully check things over again before turning the test in. How I skimmed it one more time, saw nothing amiss, confident of a 100 percent mark, handed it in early. But then, as the old saying goes, *my name fell behind Sun Shan's* (Sun Shan of the Song dynasty, whose name appeared last on a list to pass the imperial exam), and my father chewed me out, and that summer vacation passed in a gloom-glum, my face felt filthy, my head hung low, impossible to lift.

In my third year of secondary school, the swaying of the grand pagoda tree outside the classroom quietly died away. By the middle of the first term, Father pressured me to rise early, study late, and *step by step from the shallows to the depths* "actively" *ji ji* (積極) hasten on my journey.

The comprehensive exam loomed; I became more and more superstitious, particularly toward the numeral 4. One day walking home from school along Da Xiang Feng ("Big Soaring Phoenix") Hutong Alley, I closed my eyes for four steps then opened them, closed my eyes for four steps then opened them. Walking and walking like this I soon reached Liulin ("Willow Shade") Street and, flipping my eyes open, stood before an old lady with a look of awe on her face. She giggled and giggled with glee: "I said to myself, why does this pathetic little blind boy have no stick to guide him?"

You can even ask Heaven how I, a little blind boy, finally groped his way to the Gates of the Heavenly Halls.

In the summer of that year, my social status clearly improved: Father saw me through new eyes and treated me with deference, relatives and neighbors offered effusive compliments, saying there was no higher school badge to bear—it seemed I had become the darling of humanity. What made me even happier was that Yifan downstairs had also been accepted to Middle No. 4, and moreover, the two of us had placed into the same class.

Beijing Middle No. 4 was established in 1907 and originally called Following the Mandate of Heaven Secondary School Halls; its name changed to Public Secondary School of the Capital No. 4 in 1912, and to Beijing Middle No. 4 in 1949. It was about the same distance from our apartment as Middle No. 13, taking about twenty minutes to walk there.

The day school started on September 1, I got up early, restless, mind wandering, dillydallied and puttered around, opened my book bag and closed it, then set off for school with Yifan. The school's gated entrance, built in an arch out of gray brick and stone, reflected the style of the late Qing and early Republic era; the poet Guo Moruo had carved the red-painted inscription 北京四中 (*Beijing Sizhong*, "Beijing Middle No. 4") onto the stone lintel of the gate. The gray walls combined with the wrought-iron gate evoked something sinister, and even appeared once in a feature film as the headquarters for the Japanese military.

The first day of school mostly consisted of meeting the teachers and students. I belonged to Upper 1, Class 5, and save for Yifan, all the faces were new to me. I felt slightly uneasy, the uneasiness of being out in public with your clothes buttoned up wrong, knowing it's too late to fix and there's no hiding it.

The school day had barely begun when, lightly flicking the beads of an abacus, I suddenly realized the seriousness of my problem: The dominance of the language arts was over, its halcyon days past; mathematics, physics, chemistry held the keys; the nightmare smothered me until I couldn't breathe, especially thinking about math, one glance at an integer and a thick fog swallowed me, east confused with west, north with south. All my peers were in you-leap-and-I'll-leap-farther math-mode, some already using the Junior 3 calculus textbook. I moaned bitterly to myself, regretting that I had ever wormed my way into this Heavenly Hall of Numbers.

Truthfully, the mood of the whole school felt oppressive, though the reasons why were very difficult to discern, *like trying to trace dragon veins in a mountain*—something always seemed off. The clothes students wore, for instance, looked plain and simple to the point of suspiciousness: sweat-stained tank tops, perfectly new pants with patches on them, military sneakers with holes that exposed bare toes. As everyone knew, Middle No. 4 possessed the highest concentration of children of high-ranking officials of any secondary school. Obviously, anything could be covered up, like an infectious disease in an incubation period, ready to break out at the critical moment.

Our head teacher Tian Yong, eight or nine years our senior, doubled as the math teacher. White-rimmed glasses, face ruddy, energy boundless—every day he'd join us for a jog, or play basketball with us, dribbling and jumping as if he were the King of the Children. A recent graduate of Beijing Normal University, salary fifty-six yuan a month, not married, and able to stay in Beijing while teaching at a prestigious school—he exemplified fate's good faith.

Tian Yong accompanied us on our toils in the fields; besides leading the class into the countryside, he looked after our labor force's daily cares and meals. With a rope belt tied around his waist, he personally tended the cooking fires and handled the wok, while another student and I acted as his assistants. Pour out the pork fat, dice up the white yams, sizzle the pieces in oil and add a plash of soy sauce, the mouthwatering fragrance wafting into the air. When it was time to eat, Tian Yong, ladle to ladle, served each of us.

Those were the days of the Four Cleanups Movement, the reinnervation of class struggle. Mother was transferred to Guiyang for a year, to participate in the Four Cleanups of the local banking system there. In the countryside, the first problem hit us immediately: When greeting the peasants, what should we say if we happened to run into a well-off, landowning farmer? Discussing it among ourselves, we agreed they must be loitering in the shadows like ghosts. We asked the village cadre official only to discover the doubtful status of this social stratum—better not to greet anyone.

One day while on break from our labors, K., a fellow classmate, wrapped his arm around my body and put a knife up to the small of my back, first as a joke, then in earnest: I refused to beg for mercy; he furtively increased the knife's pressure ever so slowly, the point piercing deeper. Our faces nearly touched, stares deadlocked for at least a few minutes. All at once, unable to endure the pain any longer, I pushed him away. He laughed, saying that he was only putting my revolutionary willpower to the test. From then on, I kept my distance from K. Combative aggression had been awakened along with class consciousness.

In the spring of 1966, a violent thunderstorm threatened to make landfall, signs of it could be seen everywhere, putting all of us on alert like small animals. Between lessons, students chatted about revolutionary ideals and life-or-death situations; everyone seemed to be facing the last judgment. I secretly thought up a slogan to shout before the sacrificial act, rehearsing it over and over to myself, imagining myself encircled by pine trees. I put my fingers in the crack of a door, slowly closing it, tighter and tighter, until the pain caused me to drip with sweat. I relented, as if punishment had been served—the possibility of me turning traitor to the cause seemed almost assured.

I didn't belong to the Communist Youth League, and worried about being excluded, though I had no idea how to infiltrate the organization. Yifan acted as my sponsor, which is to say he represented the league. This gave me hope—we were brothers after all. I prodded and probed him; he kept his mouth corked like a bottle.

3

The Cultural Revolution launched with a bang. June 1, 1966, the *People's Daily* published an editorial with the headline "Sweep Away All Ox Ghosts and Snake Demons," and Middle No. 4 officially terminated classes. Hearing the news in the classroom, I whooped jubilantly along with the rest of the students, knowing my motives weren't pure: The announcement coincided precisely with my mathematics state of emergency, the final exam around the corner. Old Man Heaven took note, whisking me into the Heavenly Halls that year, once more saving me from the watery abyss and scorching flames. Waking up each morning, I felt unsteady, anxious that Chairman Mao would change his mind again and alter his plan. Finally, the grand statesman decided to close the school gates forever.

A couple of weeks earlier, in mid-May, my comrades and I had set out early each day and returned late. We went to the western outskirts, and in front of the immense red gate of the

Beijing Food Industry School, tried to fan sparks into fire, inciting the students to strike and carry out revolution. We spread the slogan "Don't bake cakes for the bourgeoisie!" though the instant "cakes" issued forth from my mouth, having gone through the famine years, I couldn't help salivating, starry bits of spit spraying out as I gave my speeches. Most of the students at the Food Industry School were from the poorest classes of society, and however persuasive the arguments, they didn't understand the need to strike, what good would it do, and why to not bake cakes. In the middle of a heated debate, a female student asked me, "Okay, then, you explain it: What does cake have to do with the bourgeoisie?" Their animosity couldn't be tempered, their hostility was resilient, invincible; we eventually had no choice but to retreat.

When Middle No. 4's party committee suffered a paralysis of action, each Youth League branch for Upper 3 joined forces and assumed control. I transcribed big-character posters at school—I didn't sleep for three days and two nights. On the third night, my comrades and I went to Qinghua University's affiliated secondary school to show our solidarity with the downtrodden Red Guards there. In a trance, half delirious, footsteps feeble like walking on cotton padding, stage lights dazzling our eyes, raucous clamor near and far. The carnival of the revolution caused the blood to surge and boil with righteous anger.

Entering the classroom one day, I received a huge shock upon seeing the students' attire. Overnight they had all morphed as one, each dressed in a brand-new green army outfit that moonlighted as a school uniform—waists bound with a broad leather strap, Red Guard armbands proudly displayed, feet pedaling in big leather boots as they rode the most coveted bicycles, whizzing around in clusters. I remembered when I had first walked through the school gates, their ineffable oppressiveness, which, in fact, turned out to be a superiority complex; now, having passed through the incubation period, the infectious disease had broken out.

"If the father's a hero, the son's a worthy man / If the father's a reactionary, the son's a bad egg in a pan"—this slogan was born out of the moment, bundling everyone into its folds. It was quickly adapted into the "Battle Song of the Red Guard," our class leader, Liu Huixuan, composing the tune—it brought him fame in one stroke. The last section of the song went: "If the father's a hero, the son's a worthy man / If the father's a reactionary, the son's a bad egg in a pan / If you make revolution, come take a stand / If you don't make revolution, go flip your mama's egg!" And always, "go flip your mama's egg" would repeat endlessly in unison, like an echo in an empty valley.

In the debating sessions of those days, the opposing side's first question would inevitably be: "What is your family background?" If your family background wasn't acceptable, you were ushered onstage for a tongue-lashing or a harsh beating. I was born into a family of functionaries, but in the old, pre-liberation society, my father had worked in a bank, and so I was included on the list of the suspicious. Once again, I was excluded from the campaign and pushed out to the periphery.

At the edge of the playing field, while leaning against the school wall by a thicket of trees, I discovered an unlocked bicycle—its brakes worn, rust spots dotted the frame, wheel-spokes sparse, bell tied with a thin piece of rope, when pulled, *ding-a-ling!* After keeping watch for a few days, no one claimed it, and so I nonchalantly seized the treasure, just planning to borrow it for a while.

There's an advantage to riding a ramshackle bike—wherever you park, there's no need to lock it. Although it can't exist in the same breath as a high-cadre official son's Yongjiu Forever Model 13 Manganese Steel Bicycle, it suited me fine, the old bike being the first means of transportation that belonged to me. The thrill that arises from speed is something a biped cannot know from the daily experience of walking. I rode in and out of the revolutionary current, no longer relegating myself to the periphery, a self-deceiving illusion expanding in my mind that I was actually part of the front lines, the central core, the eye of the hurricane of the revolution. Much later in life I experienced a real epiphany reading *Don Quixote*, realizing that the Ingenious Gentleman of La Mancha had, in fact, gone mad not from books but from mounting his steed.

One day riding along Denei Street on my way to school, as I approached the Changqiao intersection ahead and coasted down the steep incline, the bicycle suddenly jolted up, sending me flying over the handlebars and tumbling headfirst toward a police sentry booth. A crowd instantly gathered around the rollicking scene of a man down. My whole body felt like an injury, though the worst thing was the utter public humiliation. It seemed like a serious warning to me, so I bravely retreated from the rushing torrent, and oh so quietly put the bicycle back in its original spot. Not half a day passed before it mysteriously disappeared.

4

On June 4, the Beijing municipality appointed a work team to be stationed in our school; on June 5, the whole school convened for the struggle session of Principal Yang Bin.

Later the same month, the second-year student Liu Yuan placed a letter on his father's desk—which also happened to be the desk of the nation's president. The letter was part of a behind-the-scenes scheme planned by a group of Upper 3 and Upper 5 students, the sons of high-cadre officials, who upon hearing through inner channels that the central government was considering the possibility of abolishing the college entrance exam, decided to seize the historic occasion and take action. On June 18, the *People's Daily* printed separate articles about the written proposals of Beijing Middle No. 4 and Beijing Girls' Middle No. 1 to abolish the antiquated college entrance exam system.

On August 4, a "reactionary student" disguised as a Red Guard was unmasked in the Wangfujing area, dragged back to the school, and beaten half dead on the playing field. Meanwhile, more than twenty school leaders and teachers were struggled against and paraded through the streets, then punched and kicked by several students; on August 25, some sons of high-cadre officials in Middle No. 4 organized the Capital City's Red Guard Western District Policing Squad, or Xi Jiu ("western policing"), and then issued ten general orders in quick succession....

Middle No. 4 became one of the central hubs of cultural revolutionary activity. Apart from big-character posters that *made the land quake and skies shake*, all kinds of secret activities were plotted there, leading the way to the emergence of many different factional organizations. Because of the family background issue, relations between students slowly disintegrated. This is how an "aristocratic" school unexpectedly shed its guise of elegant simplicity, exposing its sinister face.

What shocked me most at the time concerned C., a timid student in our class. He wrote a "thought report" for the Youth

League about his intimate sexual fantasies, which included explicit descriptions of breasts and female genitalia. Who would've thought that the details of his confession would be publicized on a big-character poster and become the object of everyone's gossip and laughter? And that C. would then be labeled a reactionary student and vanish from everyone's life? And who publicized his confession in the first place?

August 18, I joined the crowds at Tiananmen Square to see Chairman Mao give an audience to the Red Guards for the first time. We lined up early at Liu Bu Kou, the crossroads of the Six Ministries, and while waiting, the streaming hordes swallowed us, pushing us forward in an enormous wave toward the square. We hopped like sparrows and whooped with delight; turning our gaze to the Tiananmen Rostrum, we couldn't see anything, only numerous green specks, among which, I figured, mingled Chairman Mao. In the depths of that feverish memory, all those green specks remain strangely hypervivid in my mind.

The violence intensified with the summer heat—everywhere there were struggle sessions, public paradings, household ransackings, beatings. The stench of blood spread across Beijing City as the infamous Red August pressed on, making people shiver in the swelter.

August 2, 1966, marked my seventeenth birthday. Daylight, no one home. I opened the curtains, lay on my bed, stared at the ceiling, my mood hitting bottom. At this pivotal point in my life, I tried to reassess the past and peer into the future, but everything seemed fuzzy, indiscernible, my heart empty, vacuous.

Thirty-five years passed, and I returned to Beijing to see my ailing father. I rode in a taxi with my brother past Ping'an Avenue on the way to our parents' home. My brother pointed to a white, modern-looking building behind a wrought-iron fence, asking offhandedly, "You recognize that place?" I cast about for clues in my mind, but nothing clicked; I blankly shook my head. "That's Middle No. 4."

5

Back then, in the whole of Beijing there were only four designated "exceptionally distinguished" secondary-school teachers: Two of them belonged to Middle No. 4, the chemistry teacher Liu Jingkun and the physics teacher Zhang Zi'e, both of them officially recognized as "national treasures." One year, Teacher Zhang also taught Upper 3 physics, and reportedly wrote four of the six physics questions for the college entrance exam that year. Handing in their tests well before the allotted time, the students loudly shouted, "Long live Teacher Zhang!"

The trigonometry teacher Li Yutian had triangular eyes and a chin shaved to an ashen hue. He always arrived to class a few minutes early to draw the day's problem on the blackboard, his scrawl indecipherable to me, like a ghost-repelling charm. While my vision haloed out, the rest of the class *could already see the bamboo in their mind before painting it*, mentally preparing their answers and readying a hand to raise before anyone else. Teacher Li didn't fret, didn't hurry, as he scanned the room in an arc with his triangular eyes, habitually rubbing his ashen chin, slowly, leisurely, his voice calling out a name in a thick Li County, Hebei accent, "Zhao—Zhen—Kai," lengthening the "kai" as a falling-rising third tone, rather than first, hooking the heart and soul even further. For every question posed I gave three I-don't-knows. As a matter of fact, this became the source of a long-lasting anxiety for me: Many years later when helping my daughter with her homework, she mentioned the word "trigonometry" and I instantly felt dizzy and nauseous.

Study magazine stopped publication in 1958, its editor switching jobs to become a teacher, and, as chance would have it, Huang Qingfa came to be our Chinese instructor. A little over forty and balding, his wry smiled made him look as if he were apologizing for his own existence. Teacher Huang taught classical prose with remarkable proficiency, while even letting us write our own annotations. Reading aloud Liu Zongyuan's "Account of Little Stone Pond," he'd rock back and forth, head nodding and rolling: "Walking west one hundred paces from the little knoll, to a bamboo grove, distant trickle of a running stream, like the clinking of jade belt rings, heart's music—" Breaking off here, he'd quote his annotation for "heart's music": "That is, 'to be happy," then continued to read the passage aloud. I never expected that I, with my uninspired imitations, *painting a tiger from the image of a cat*, would receive recognition for my annotative marginalia. And so, strolling up to the front of the class, *as if the young urchin could expound*, I delivered my rendition. Pleased as pleased could be, I embarked on the "Little Stone Pond," rocking back and forth, head nodding and rolling, pleasure elevating, and coming upon "heart's music," I also broke off and proceeded to read my own marginalia—"rather not bad" (*powei bucuo*), though mispronouncing '*po*' as a '*pi*' sound, thus noting it as "farting's not bad"—the whole class doubled over with laughter.

Our Russian teacher Ling Shijun had a plump head and big ears; he wasn't particularly conceited, and yet a certain amount of arrogance did seep through his bones. Every class he'd carry a tiny card with notes on it pinched between his fingers, though somehow he'd prattle on and on without end, *dulu dulu dulu*, as if some kind of linguistic magic trick. He had published a monograph on Russian grammar, and was also fluent in Japanese—rumor had it that he had taught himself Russian from a Japanese textbook. Teacher Ling had another brilliant feat up his sleeve—he could recline on the surface of the school's swimming pool while reading the newspaper at the same time, hands and feet motionless. I didn't study Russian very attentively, but studied this brilliant feat on the sly, one unmindful slip and two mouthfuls of water poured in.

Whenever our English teacher Xiang Lixie strolled around campus, he always attracted attention. In order to teach English, he had learned how to behave like an English gentleman: In the summer he wore a white suit; in the winter he wore shorts with suspenders, long, white gartered socks, and polished leather shoes. He brought a whole set of cutlery to class, displayed on a napkin, to demonstrate the customs Western-style food involved. We heard that he had tested at the top of his class at a missionary school, where the foreign teacher there once invited him to her home for tea, and while serving him a piece of pound cake, he said something incorrectly in English, whereupon as punishment she took the cake away....

The two physical education teachers, Han Maofu and Wu Jimin, both refereed in the national basketball league. Han Maofu was smart, competent, and of average height. Wu Jimin was tall, strong as a horse, and asked everyone to call him Big Wu. As the story goes, the Soviet women's national basketball team came to the capital to compete against China's national team. Han Maofu wore the whistle on the floor; Big Wu commanded the referee's table. In the grueling game's final minutes—the teams neck and neck, neither able to pull away—the two secretly conspired to stop the clock and add more time. The Soviet team discovered the ruse and raised a protest, which resulted in Big Wu being demoted to a lower-level referee. •

Principal Yang Bin emerged out of the Yan'an Shanbei Public School, and after the revolution, contributed to important eyewitness accounts regarding the activities of Ye Qun, savvy political leader and the wife of military commander and vice premier, Lin Biao. During the post-liberation years, she served as headmistress of Girls' Middle No. 1 before moving on to Middle No. 4 in 1965. It was said that between being the director of the Beijing Municipal Education Bureau and the principal of Middle No. 4, she chose the latter.

Vice Principal Liu Tieling puffed and puffed with smug self-satisfaction. The Red Guards brought his diary to light, which exposed details of his personal ambitions: age twenty become school party committee member; age thirty become district party committee member; age forty become municipal party committee member; age fifty become central committee member. Everything progressed according to his plan—at the start of the Cultural Revolution, he was just over forty and already a municipal party committee member.

Who could have foreseen that these teachers and principals would become a disgrace overnight, all their culture and learning swept away with a wave of the hand? The eruption darkened the sky and rushed across the land in the form of big-character posters and endless struggle sessions. High tide arrived on August 4, 1966, a Sunday. More than twenty teachers and school leaders were paraded around with tall paper hats atop their heads and wooden signboards around their necks, until at last they were led to the playing field, where they staggered through the throngs of screaming students, who shamed them with epithets while punching and kicking them. Then they were forced to sing the "Battle Song of the Sorrowful Ghost" in unison: "I am an ox-ghost snake-demon / I am guilty before the people / I am guilty / I am damned / The people's iron hammer / Has smashed me and mashed me up...." Among the numerous voices, Vice Principal Liu Tieling's projected out with the most resonance.

During one struggle session organized by the People Liberation Army's Propaganda Team, Big Wu leaped up and pointed his finger at Principal Yang Bin, saying, "Yang Bin, you dare to oppose the PLA!" followed by an arm-flapping shout, "Down with the PLA!" Bewildered, startled awake, he slowly realized his huge mistake as his face turned pale with fear, and Big Wu stammered out, "I am guilty ... I confess my guilt to Chairman Mao and ask to be punished." Then, as if in the presence of the chairman himself, he stooped forward, butt sticking out, large bean-size beads of sweat *pipa pipa* tumbling down.

The suicide of the Chinese teacher Liu Chengxiu filled me with terror. During the Clean Up the Class Ranks Campaign, she was put under investigation, which led to her son's discharge from the army. Around five in the morning that day, behind the cafeteria in a narrow street, she cut open her throat with a pair of scissors, *a sight too horrifying to bear*, people said. That an accomplished, healthy middle-aged woman could go as far as this, to such an extreme and end her life. As news of the tragedy reached the little courtyard of the dorms, I had been lighting a fire in Study Six, the smoke so chokingly thick I couldn't open my eyes.

6

I moved onto campus at the start of August 1966. The student dorms were on the southeast corner by the Teaching and Research Courtyard, an isolated area with two rows of single-story buildings facing each other. Each room, furnished with bunk beds, varied in size and were arranged sequentially with the label "study" followed by a number. I first moved into Study Thirteen, then to Study Six, my life in the dorm totaling more than two years. The dorms originally housed only those students who lived far from the school, but due to the chaos of the Cultural Revolution, no one cared and everyone moved in, one after another.

News and rumors spread quickly under one shared, rundown roof, along little byways and walls with ears. Whenever the furnace spit out its thick billows of smoke, neighbors would start to cough at the same time. Before the revolution, it had been lights-out at ten p.m., the warning bell ringing ten minutes before ten. One needed to cross the dorm courtyard a ways to reach the bathroom, and as it was just us boys at the school with few scruples, residents would rush out in a constant stream to piss into the pond or under a tree. The foul, pungent smell of urine wafted out from the courtyard incessantly. Ten minutes to ten every night, the student counselor Yu Qizhong would frequent the area for an inspection; mission accomplished, his actions turned into the tale, spread far and wide, of "Yu the Great taming the urinary waters."

One of my roommates, Z., the son of a high-ranking cadre, loved to boast and speak in jokes—as well as lust after girls—a very fun comrade to have around. One night at the end of August, he came to tell me that he had caught some local felons, locked them in the dorm basement, and asked if I wanted to take a peek. Out of curiosity I followed him, and crouching outside the basement window, I peered inside.

That night, with Z. as the head interrogator, two "veteran soldiers" dressed in army fatigues played the role of thugs. Those "felons," naked from the waist up, knelt on the floor. Z. proceeded to ask them something in a sharp voice, his words vague and ambiguous; one thug swung his crude iron shackle up and brought it—*huala huala!*—crashing down onto Z.'s shoulder, a bloodstain immediately soaking through his clothes. The shackle whirled up again and Z. quickly restrained it.... Unable to watch anymore, I returned to the dorm room and lay down on my bed. Z. didn't come back until around midnight. With a bit of pride mixed with exhilaration, he asked me what I thought; I changed the subject. I couldn't remove him from that cruel scene in my mind, so we gradually drifted apart. Not long after that I moved to Study Six.

The fluid living situation in the dorms continued through the revolution. In the spring of 1967, a new boarder, Liu Yuan, moved into Study Six; his father had been the nation's former president. Liu Yuan slept in an upper bunk and, downcast and sullen, usually went straight to sleep whenever he returned to the dorm. During our almost nightly ritual of sharing ghost stories, however, he'd tilt his ears to listen, too—the lights switched off, the spooky vocalizations, the washbasin and bed rail ready to be tossed to the ground at the key moment. Then, more than a month later, he mysteriously disappeared.

The school meals were dreadful, and so, under the cover of night, we'd sneak into the cafeteria to pilfer some white cabbage and coal, and cook for ourselves. And because stoves remained unlit in the classrooms that winter, students came to Study Six to warm up. To gain admittance, though, each visitor needed to hand over sufficient coinage before the door could be opened. Many stamped their feet and cursed, and yet, in a world of ice and snow, with nowhere else to go, better to pay the bandits at the pass. We also collected unwanted papers, books, and newspapers, to sell to the salvage station. Empty bottles quickly filled up with change and, rubbing our palms with delight, we'd first agree on the menu, head out to procure provisions, and then heartily gorge ourselves until we couldn't stand up.

7

Beijing Middle No. 4 functioned as both an "aristocratic" school and a school for the general public. This dual identity manifested itself as a kind of inner schism, a schism that wasn't so obvious at first, possibly even deliberately concealed as suggested before, but the Cultural Revolution pushed it to the fore, transforming it into a vast chasm.

The classroom building consisted of one two-story structure; conditions were frugal, with no central heating during the winter, and once it got cold, charcoal stoves had to be brought in. Most of the children of impoverished families brought their own lunches, which they fixed in an aluminum container carried in a mesh bag, and during the break between classes, dropped the containers off at the cafeteria's big steamer to heat up. Some simplified the process and just put their lunch on top of the coal stove, causing wonderful smells to drift through the classroom air.

To eat in the cafeteria cost three mao three fen for a regular lunch, and one mao six fen for just the staple foods, like rice or noodles. Several hundred people could fit in its enormous space, and ten people could sit around a table, but given the absence of chairs, it was standing room only, dine where you pleased. The staff bosses used wooden poles to carry in the huge casks, triggering a stir of activity in the stomachs of the youth. Each table sent a representative with two washbasins to stand in line—one for a staple food and the other for a vegetable dish. Principal Yang Bin realized the school lunches weren't meeting the proper nutritional requirements and proposed raising the cost for students to four mao per meal in order to add a quality meat dish every other day; more than half of the students, however, didn't respond to her proposal, which showed how poor the average family really was in those days. When the Cultural Revolution intensified, this initiative would be brought up as one of the many criminal charges against Yang Bin, for her revisionism and for inciting division between the students.

As we grappled with puberty, the sour taste of hunger followed us everywhere. Students pasted up a big-character poster: "Praise a meal of two corn-cone buns / The food line stretches clear to the sky / Boss Feng's fat face laughs in the window / Students wait at the gate weak and cold-to-the-bone."

After the Cultural Revolution broke out, the suspension of classes led to bedlam in the cafeteria. The school stipulated that it could only refund staple-food meal tickets at one mao six fen per diem. Yifan told me that he had gone to the cafeteria window to return his meal tickets, and Liu Yuan, ahead of him in line, began to argue with the cafeteria manager, Liu Qingfeng. They exchanged some heated words, and then Liu Yuan got slapped with a complete snub: "Not good enough—bring written proof of receipt and come back." Liu Yuan's face and ears turned red with anger as he stormed away in a fury. Not long after this, Liu Qingfeng was swept away by the Clean Up the Class Ranks Campaign, and eventually drowned himself in a river.

This mulberry-field world, where the immortal Magu watched the sea turn into a mulberry field, and a mulberry field turn into the sea, where a noble son meets with misfortune according to the changing of the tides—this is an old tale for all ages. Much later I heard Liu Yuan made his mark high up in the world of government politics; I only hope he never forgot those down-and-out days, the atmosphere of utter abjection, and that they enable him to act with more empathy toward common citizens.

8

Toward the beginning of September 1966, I built a small case of wood and painted these words on it in red: "Engrave Chairman Mao's words in your brain, let them melt into your bloodstream and translate into real action." Soon after putting four volumes of Mao's writings into the small case, I rushed to Jishuitan Hospital to visit my father. He had fallen off a ladder while brushing a slogan, breaking his left wrist. I didn't bring any fruit or other nourishment, just a little bust of Mao that I placed on the stand beside his bed.

Through a letter of recommendation, six of us, all classmates from common family backgrounds, signed up for the nation's Great Linkup, where students traveled from village to village as a way to build revolutionary ties. After spending two days with my father in the hospital, I strapped the small wood case with Mao's books onto my back and hit the road.

Returning to Beijing in early November, the situation had changed dramatically due to the criticisms emerging from the "bloodline debate," which thoroughly destabilized the central position of the old Red Guards. Children of the masses relied on all sorts of rebel factions to rise to the occasion, including the one our class organized called the Red Summit Battle Patrol.

At the start of spring 1967, the rebel factions on campus combined to establish the New Middle No. 4 Commune. Secondary schools throughout Beijing were divided into the April Third Faction and the April Fourth Faction—the New Middle No. 4 Commune belonged to the former. The *April Third Battle Bulletin* issued the following declarations in "Considering the New Zeitgeist: The April Third Faction Manifesto": "to carry out the redistribution of property and power," "to dismantle the privileged class." Beneath the turmoil of factional infighting, such political and societal appeals seemed quite reasonable. I later became close friends with the philosopher Zhang Xianglong, whose older brother, Zhang Xiangping, worked as one of the chief writers for the commune.

Two years ago marked Beijing Middle No. 4's hundredth anniversary, which I heard was commemorated with much pomp and circumstance. What, I wondered, should my alma mater celebrate? The former principal Liu Tieling gave a speech at the ceremony, his voice presumably as clear and resonant as ever. But I can't forget that summer day in 1966, the sight of him with the other teachers being struggled against, all of them singing the "Battle Song of the Sorrowful Ghost" together in one voice.

9

"Let me tell you: If any of you in Study 6 lose something, it will involve me, Zhang Yuhai!" I looked out through the dirty glass on the small window and saw his tall, slim frame, his hands on his hips, wearing a worn backpack, and his pimples bulging out of his face as he shouted. I told him Yifan wasn't in, and he left, cursing under his breath. Ever since Zhang Yuhai grew tight with Yifan, Study 6 knew no peace; everyone grew weary of his spleen, and urged Yifan to spend less time with him.

Zhang Yuhai belonged to Upper 2 Class 2, which had no dealings with our Upper 1 Class 5. Apart from all of us belonging to the New Middle No. 4 Commune, we spent time together in Study Six, drawn together by the same stink—an antiestablishment ideology. Even though we were pulled into the tidal wave of the Cultural Revolution, we still preserved our playful spirit of mischief. As Zhang Yuhai put it, "Politics overflowed with theater, and theater overflowed with politics."

It must be said, though, that he was an exceptional student. The school offered an advanced placement system for certain classes, where students could study the subject on their own and test out of the class. In the advanced placement test for math, Zhang Yuhai only used up half the time before turning in his exam, and received a perfect score. Apart from math, he also tested out of English. During the revolution, he presided over a discussion forum on mathematics reform, the distinguished teacher Zhang Zi'e also participating. He *turned from a host to a guest and back again*, weaving linkages seamlessly onto the blackboard, eyebrows dancing, face beaming. If it weren't for society's current upheavals, he already had the makings of a professor.

Besides his studies, Zhang Yuhai excelled in basketball, swimming, violin—practically everything he undertook he mastered. Playing the tin whistle, in particular, he proved to be a remarkable talent—puckering his lips around the mouthpiece, he used every muscle in his cheeks to control the airflow, the long, long tune resonating out so smoothly, piercing heaven and earth. It was through his playing that I discovered Georges Bizet's "Pastorale." Whenever I hear that piece of music it still reminds me of his whistling.

Zhang Yuhai was the fourth child in his family, three elder brothers above him. His father had studied abroad in England and, not long after coming back to the motherland, died in a car accident. His mother worked in a university library and raised her children on her own.

The one thing Zhang Yuhai couldn't bear was mediocrity. Of an ambitious student who aspired to climb the social ladder: "He'll certainly be very successful, but by age forty he'll be bald." Yuhai asserted this while imitating the manners of a cadre officer, sinking lazily into a sofa, hands resting on his belly as his thumbs twiddled round and round.

Upper 2 Class 2 possessed enormous reserves of energy, and for a while even managed the publication of two papers. Mou Zhijing was the editor in chief of the *Secondary School Cultural Revolution News*, which published Yu Luoke's famous essay, "Family Background Doctrine"; Zhang Yuhai, along with other students, ran the *Harbinger of Spring News*. Yuhai chose the name of the paper, lifting it from a verse of Mao's to make a double-edged title. The second issue published his piece "Indoctrinating Family Background," which directly engaged with

Yu Luoke's article, echoing its arguments. Comparing the two papers, the influence of *Secondary School Cultural Revolution News* was much greater, copies circulating across the nation, while *Harbinger of Spring News* also basked in the other paper's light, benefiting from its popularity. I helped them sell copies on the street, hawking my wares. Once people heard Middle No. 4 was involved, and that the family background and class origin issues were being discussed, they fell over each other to purchase copies.

Upper 2 Class 2's paper operation took the city by storm, creating an enormous commotion; Upper 1 Class 1, unwilling to lag behind, followed Yifan's lead and decided to make a memorial badge. The proposed design displayed the busts of Marx, Engels, Lenin, Stalin, and Mao above the words "New Middle No. 4 Commune" in red characters. Making use of all our skills and resources, we went to the Seventh Ministry of Engineering, which previously headed the government's space program, to retrieve optimal-quality aluminum sheets; we enlisted artists from the Central Academy of Fine Arts to design it, and asked the Beijing Enamel Factory to manufacture the mold. While waiting for the mold, *an unexpected branch shot forth from a knot in the tree*: Orders from above decreed that Mao's image must not be placed side by side with the four other great leaders.

In the late autumn of 1967, around a dozen students from Upper 1 Class 5 and Upper 2 Class 2 convened at the enamel factory outside Yongding ("Eternally Fixed") Gate at the south entrance of the old city. Zhang Yuhai and Xu Jinbo, a student in my class, organized the operation. As history teaches us, when waging a battle, first position the troops—Shi Kangcheng, Lang

Fang, and Wu Weiguo kept watch by the factory gate, a bicycle at the ready; various nimble legs and feet were positioned along the way from the entrance gate to the machine room, each foot soldier pretending to be an anonymous loiterer. As Yifan appeared to be talking things over with management, Zhang Yuhai stuck as close to him as a shadow. Threats and inducements were all in vain; Yifan begged Boss Liu, the one in charge of the mold, to press just one sample for him as a memento. As Boss Liu handed over the sample, Zhang Yuhai snatched the mold and fled, the mold passing frantically between hands all the way to the main gate, where Shi Kangcheng and Lang Fang provided a screen for Wu Weiguo, who hopped on his bike and sped off into the sunset. The factory workers gave chase, wildly shouting, "Grab the tall, thin one! He's the leader—" Zhang Yuhai had long since vanished into the boundless sea of people. Management captured three hostages, but unable to get them to talk, ended up releasing them.

At our victory celebration in Study Six, everybody's lips flapped at the same time, each witness trying to retell the hair-raising scene from every angle. Zhang Yuhai seemed a little preoccupied, his mind elsewhere as he blew Bizet's "Toreador Song" on his tin whistle.

In the autumn of 1968, the workers' propaganda team wanted to take him into custody for questioning, apparently having something to do with "an incident involving a counter-revolutionary group." He made a precipitate decision, first holing up at a farm in Yunnan Province, then crossing the border and joining the People's Army in Burma. Before he left, he bid farewell to his friends, saying that, in the end, there wasn't enough room for him in the capital, and so why not go where *the sky's so high and the emperor far away*, to live a life boundless and free.

Yuhai crossed the Burmese border in the spring of 1969, and soon connected with the People's Army. That summer, at age twenty-one, he sacrificed himself on the field of battle. He had written numerous letters to friends from Burma, copies of which circulated among the Educated Youth after his death. Only days before he was killed, he wrote letters like this: "We're still young, the long road of our life still before us . . . not that there hasn't been the chance to throw ourselves into the current of history, we just weren't prepared, lacked the physical training, and when the moment came and we were swept into the current, it wasn't of our own free will, and on and on history slipped away...."

I wrote a poem called "Starlight" that opens this way:

> As our hands parted
> you said to me: *Don't be like this,*
> *we're still young*
> *the road before us still long.*
> You turned and walked away,
> leading astray a ray of starlight.
> The starlight accompanied you,
> fading away on the horizon line....

Over the years, a tall, beautiful woman, identifying herself as "Little Fourth Girlfriend," would visit the home of Zhang Yuhai's mother. She'd tell the elderly lady that she still awaited his return.

10

In 1965, I had just entered the gates of the school when Middle No. 4 became the experimental unit for the Education Bureau of Beijing's Socialist Education Movement, otherwise known as the Four Cleanups Movement; Upper 2 Class 2 quickly became the focus of the whole school, due to the public outing of a reactionary student, Mou Zhijing. This caused a deep psychological wound that spread like an immense shadow, forcing certain individuals into an early adulthood and isolating the class as a group.

Mou Zhijing, however, stepped out of this shadow before anyone. An optimist by nature, quick-witted and sharp, he stood out from the crowd. As a friend once said to me, "Mou Zhijing was never one for polite conversation or empty chitchat." He had high cheekbones, a wide nose bridge, and when others spoke, he listened intently. I had visited his home and found his family warm and harmonious: His father worked as a translator at the Railway Research Institute, his mother worked as a civil draftsman; he had one little sister, cute as a button.

Because he had exchanged diaries with other classmates, the words he wrote in it could be used as evidence against him and he was labeled a "filial son of the capitalist class." This actually didn't bother him in the least, although another matter infuriated him. "One day I returned to the classroom after kicking the ball around on the field," he later told us. "Several students were crowded around a small-character poster pasted on the wall. I also leaned in to take a look. Someone had written, 'Mou Zhijing is a "love-conquers-all idealist."'" For a second I wanted to kill myself—how could I let someone trample all over my emotions like this? I had two kuai in my pocket, and I decided to gorge myself with food and drink, then kill myself...."

Given Mou Zhijing's naturally upbeat disposition, it seemed unlikely he'd ever commit suicide, and plus, much more of greater consequence awaited him. When he first heard the couplet "If the father's a hero, the son's a worthy man / If the father's a reactionary, the son's a bad egg in a pan," he became so outraged that he immediately criticized the slogan in a big-character poster, which he pasted up at the affiliated secondary school at Qinghua University. Soon after that, at a debating session at the Central Conservatory of Music, he stormed up to the podium and attacked the couplet there, too. Several Red Guards rushed to grab the microphone, then spit in his face; a number of Middle No. 4 students in the audience clambered onto the stage and exposed him as a reactionary student. A criticism session was then organized at Middle No. 4, and not only did he refuse to bend, but he came to the aid of another unjustly accused student and ended up getting a front tooth knocked out by a murderous Liu Huixuan.

In the winter of the same year, Mou Zhijing saw a small-character poster on the street with the heading "Family Background Doctrine," and from the address listed on it tracked down Yu Luowen; the two talked animatedly, and, inspired, Mou Zhijing decided to letterpress a one fen per copy tabloid-format newspaper that could bring this article to more readers. On January 18, 1967, the *Secondary School Cultural Revolution News* launched; the text of "Family Background Doctrine" took up three printed sheets, and was signed "Beijing Family Background Problem Research Group"; its real author Yu Luoke, Yu Luowen's older brother, became the chief commentator for the paper.

At the time, though, even the eighteen-year-old editor in chief, Mou Zhijing, wasn't sure who had originally written the piece. He later recounted his impression of Yu Luoke upon first meeting him: "He looked a little peculiar—short with a prominent hunchback, pale face, his eyesight severely myopic, eyeglasses formed two perfectly round circles, and yet his gaze cut right through you, his voice sonorous, revealing a deeply intelligent and humorous individual.... It was the thick of winter. In the little hut he built beside his home and called the 'ice cellar,' I felt it to be exceptionally warm...."

The supply of *Secondary School Cultural Revolution News* couldn't meet demand, the print runs continuing uninterrupted. For a period of time, people from every part of the country poured through the gate of Middle No. 4, their anxious and expectant eyes like the bubbly foam on a vast ocean. Altogether six issues were published, until the Central Committee of the Cultural Revolution publicly criticized "Family Background Doctrine." Mou Zhijing convened an editorial meeting, saying that whoever wasn't prepared for the ultimate sacrifice must quit at once. No one flinched; everyone remained true to their task.

Yu Luoke was arrested near the end of 1968; under the ruling of the court of law, he was executed on March 5, 1970, at age twenty-seven. Before his arrest, he told Mou Zhijing, "I feel I must apologize to you—you're so young, and I've dragged you into this." Then he entrusted Mou with a "letter to be delivered to Chairman Mao." Unfortunately, this letter passed between many hands and secret hiding places, until at some point it was lost.

In the autumn of 1975, Liu Yu and I, while on a trip to Wutai Mountain, ran out of money. Passing through Datong on our way back to Beijing, I found Mou Zhijing, then working at the railway station, and borrowed five kuai from him. That night at his dormitory, Mou Zhijing played his accordion in a manic frenzy, eyes squinting, mouth stretched back in a grin, as if intoxicated, or possessed.

11

Zhao Jingxing was one grade below me, though intellectually quite above me. By the time he turned eighteen, he had already read the complete works of Marx, Engels, Lenin, and Stalin; *Das Kapital* he had read six times; Hegel, Kant, Feuerbach, among other giants of Western philosophy he knew intimately; plus, he had already finished writing his *Critique of Philosophy and Dialogic Outline on Political Economy*, among other book-length manuscripts. Following the frenetic ebb and flow of people's revolutionary reading habits, a group of students at the affiliated girls' secondary school at Beijing Normal University excerpted some of Zhao Jingxing's writings, printed a mimeographed booklet of them, and circulated copies among the student body. I still remember the first time I read it—though I could recognize every single character, to my complete astonishment, I couldn't grasp the main concepts, the lines of text a confusing jumble in my mind. Anger swelled within me, directed toward this young buck who shared my family name.

Zhao Jingxing was born into an impoverished family. His father worked as a tailor. He often went around shirtless wearing only Burma-crotch pants, revealing his dark complexion and rolls of fat. His family didn't have the slightest connection with any kind of literary culture, and yet he became a most formidable philosopher.

Zhao Jingxing openly fought against the Up the Mountains and Down to the Countryside Movement, writing big-character posters that were pasted onto the school bulletin boards. He thought that the average population increase per acre of land would inevitably be a more serious burden for peasants and farmers, as the crises cities faced would be passed on to them. Full of youthful vigor, he spoke his mind with no fear of repercussions, indifferent to his own personal safety.

At the second struggle session held in what was once the biology lab, the master of ceremonies thundered out, "Zhao Jingxing! You wolf with a savage heart, you go too far criticizing Chairman Mao! If this is tolerated, then what cannot be tolerated!" Zhao Jingxing first quoted the exact sentence from the exact paragraph on the exact page from the two-volume set of Marx and Engels: "To critique is to learn; to critique is precisely the making of revolution." He went on with the courage of his own convictions: "I've built on four aspects of Mao Zedong's thought," and then expanded on each point with perfect lucidity.

His speech could be said to have made *the stones shatter and heavens shake*. For instance, "The Great Proletarian Cultural Revolution is the eruption of social contradictions"; or, "The progression of socialism into the phase of the Great Proletarian Cultural Revolution is like the engine of a train wobbling left and right, unaware of where it's going." He wrote in his diary, "The emergence of a new stage of history will accompany the underground movement of the people." In *Dialogic Outline on Political Economy*, he wrote, "The commodity economy must be allowed to break open the planned economy." Such heretical ideas at the time were seen as a treasonous offense, and naturally incurred a range of punishments.

At Shi Kangcheng's house near the end of 1968, I ran into Zhao Jingxing's girlfriend, Tao Luosong, an Upper 2 student at the Normal University's secondary school. She wore a long, white dress totally out of place with the times. To this day I still remember her saying to me: "Zhao Jingxing isn't anti–Chairman Mao." Along with his abstruse notes on philosophy, some passages of love letters he wrote to Tao Luosong circulated: "Young girl, before you stands an eighteen-year-old philosopher."

Tao Luosong was quite a beautiful girl. One resident in the Baiwanzhuang ("Millions Village") district of Beijing, however, claiming to be a "handsome man and a beautiful-woman appraisal expert," gave her a score of only 79 percent. It eventually came out that this self-proclaimed expert's standard of beauty was the *Venus de Milo* and Michelangelo's *David*.

Yifan and I practiced shooting an air gun at my place, the targets discarded photographs that included head shots of ourselves, while a copy of *Red Flag* magazine served as a padded trap behind each target so that the ammo could be reused. Zhao Jingxing had recently asked us to take a portrait of Tao Luosong, and without thinking we used a discarded photo of her as a target. Who knew how this information leaked out. One day, Zhao Jingxing came over to borrow a book and said, "I wanted to talk to you about Tao Luosong—do you two hate her for some reason?"

The winter of 1968 passed with particular frigidness as one big snowstorm followed another. Study Six grew more and more cheerless and desolate; most of the boarders had left for the countryside to live and work with production teams. The campus showed few signs of life, students were sparse, and the big-character poster shed totally empty and deserted save for a few notices strewn here and there.

In one of the smaller courtyards, the workers' propaganda team brought four students into custody for questioning. Zhao Jingxing, one of the Ministry of Public Security's "most wanted criminals," was among them. He always seemed to be smiling, whether immersed in a book or soaking up the world around him with his musings. His interests eventually took a sharp turn from philosophy to political economy.

Apart from Zhao Jingxing, two other students from our class, Liu Huixuan and Shi Kangcheng, were bound next to him. For separate reasons, either publicizing or opposing the "theory of the bloodline," they were both detained, *two paths leading to the same destination*. Students guarded them, turning a blind eye. I often visited Shi Kangcheng, giving him books or delivering letters, and seeing Liu Huixuan I'd also say hello. The four of them got along well together, tending the fire from morning to night, passing the iron poker between them, exchanging updates on the case or knowledge discovered in a book.

In February 1970, Zhao Jingxing and Tao Luosong were both chained and thrown into prison.

12

Beginning around October 1966, the rebel factions in the Beijing secondary schools gradually supplanted the Cultural Revolution's early-stage Red Guards (now known as the Old Guards) and entered the mainstream; divisions within the factions, however, quickly became apparent. In the spring of 1967, two Central Committee senior official addresses on the third and fourth of April led to the formation of the two factions. The April Third Faction, also known as the April Three-and-a-Half Faction, was the more moderate of the two, and as mentioned before, the one to which the New Middle No. 4 Commune belonged.

August 11, 1967, a day the sun blazed down so bright. The Beijing Old Guard Chorus rehearsed the "Long March Song Cycle" in the Middle No. 4 cafeteria, conducted by Liu Huixuan, who would interrupt in a rage whenever the musical phrase rose to the climax: "Crow-black clouds that cover the sky won't last / The red sun will release its rays of light forever and ever." During breaks, the chorus of boys congregated outside the school gate to bask in the sun.

That day I gathered with other students at the main gate's reception office to copy big-character posters—as there was no need at the time to keep watch over the school's entrance, the reception office had been requisitioned for other uses. The sound of idle chatter trickled through the open window, followed by raucous jeering and booing, then a sudden exchange of shrill curses, a chase, and a fisticuffs. I watched them drag someone past the school gate as they punched and kicked him, but then, while hauling him up by his four limbs, his head accidentally thudded against a tree. Reportedly, two boys from another school were trying to catch up to a demonstration march and, passing by on their bikes, had a run-in with the chorus—one escaped and the other had been captured.

This stirred up a veritable hornet's nest. Their foes belonged to the Beijing Civil Engineering School's Flying Tigers Team, die-hard followers of the April Third Faction, their combination of fearlessness and fighting prowess known far and wide. As a life had been lost in the violence, they armed themselves to the teeth and marched to the Beijing Garrison Command with the corpse raised, and staged a protest. Word spread that the Flying Tigers Team were on their way with the intent to kill.

What happened next can only be described as the original blitzkrieg: First, a furious bombardment of stones and rocks descended on the campus with relentless force, thunderously pounding the earth, smashing the roof tiles and windows. Members of the Flying Tigers Team stormed through the school gate, soldiers splitting into two routes of attack, rapidly occupying the higher vantage points, three sentries posted every five paces on top of the courtyard wall, the campus sealed off. Wicker helmets protected their heads; their hands wielded spears fashioned out of steel pipe. After the vanguard troops cleared the way, their main forces rushed in, lining up row after row into a square phalanx, murderous cries shaking the skies, a coffin raised at the rear.

The Old Guard Chorus fled to the western end of the cafeteria. Fortunately, the New Middle No. 4 Commune and the Flying Tigers Team were part of the same big family, and through some persuasive pleading, we managed to slow down the advancement of their great army.

Then, suddenly, a figure dashed out from the side of the dorms' little courtyard, empty-handed and barefisted, hurling out a torrent of abuse and obstructing the path of the army. It was the conductor Liu Huixuan. Instantly, a dozen Flying Tigers surrounded him, spears pointed toward him *from four sides and eight directions*; under the rays of the sun, cold light glinted off the metal tips. Teacher Tian Yong, the head of our class, led some of us over to Liu Huixuan, whom we shielded with our bodies as we implored him to calm down, pulling him slowly back to the little courtyard, his verbal invective continuing on uninterrupted.

The army appeared to be an ascendant tide, the coffin a boat, circling around the vortex on its forward surge. Liu Huixuan appeared again, this time coming out from the cafeteria, leading a chorus of straggling troops shouting slogans, though once they caught sight of the great army pressing onward along the borders in a forest of spears, Liu Huixuan commanded the troops: "Lay down your weapons and retreat!" The chorus boys threw away their clubs and fled for their lives; schoolgirls shrieked in a confused mass. We tried our best to separate both sides, urging the chorus to take off their military uniforms, shed their obvious Old Guard appearance, and mix into the crowds. A few hid inside the cafeteria or along the narrow path by the courtyard wall, waiting for a chance to scale it and escape. Because of our attempts to intervene, the bloody battle only resulted in a few minor injuries. The greatest loss the Old Guards suffered involved their manganese bicycles parked outside the cafeteria, smashed to smithereens.

Recalling how he came to write his novella *When the Afterglow in the Clouds Fades*, the renowned author Liu Huixuan said, "At the time, there was an activist organization at our school called the New Middle No. 4 Commune, echoing the Paris Commune, that opposed our faction. A student in the Commune, Yang Xiaoqing, had accumulated many deep grievances against us, and whenever we saw him we'd exchange angry glares. Then violence invaded our school, a massive fight broke out, and in the middle of the melee, I found myself trapped in a tight encirclement. Yang Xiaoqing risked his life to rescue me. And although we still exchanged glares afterward, it was understood as 'sticking to principles.' In my heart, however, I respected him, and revered him...."

13

In the spring of 1968, some uninvited guests arrived at the school and went straight to the Revolutionary Committee Office for the Educational Revolution in the former principal's office at the southeast courtyard; a sign hanging above the doorway read "Secondary School Red Congress War-fighting Department Liaison Office," this committee also functioning as the April Third Faction's only standing body.

Because the guests, students from Beijing Normal University, carried with them a letter of introduction from the Central Cultural Revolution Group, they acted with arrogance, moving the tables and chairs around with a ruckus. The purpose of their visit was to investigate policies of revisionism relating to the college entrance exam system, namely, to figure out how the old exam system suppressed the children of workers and peasants and protected the children of the Five Black Categories, those classes of people whom Mao deemed enemies of the revolution.

A former student guidance counselor, Qu Datong, managed the college entrance exam and replied to their questions with fear and trepidation, knowing well in his heart that the revolution had been under way for almost two years and he had yet to face any serious combat. After reading the letter of introduction, he remained silent for a moment before letting out a long sigh, saying, "I fear I will disappoint all of you." The plain fact of the matter being that though the average score for Middle No. 4 students' college entrance exam hovered around 95 percent, those who did not come from a good family background and yet scored at that level or higher were filtered out. He said, "Let me tell you, a form is inserted in the front pocket of each student's file, and in the upper right corner of the form any secondary-school political leanings are indicated; if a rejection is recommended, your score can soar into the open skies and you still will not be admitted into the university."

Qu Datong himself was the son of a Kuomintang major general, and having persevered as a guidance counselor at an eminent school, knew its profoundest secrets. Upon seeing the look of astonishment on the faces of his guests, he became more complacent: "Let me give you an example: You know who Qian Weichang is, yes? The prominent scientist and professor who is also a big rightist. His son Qian Yuankai lacked the proper political credentials, and so even though he received high marks it made no difference, no university admitted him. This is the reality of the party's class line."

Qu Datong had been the Upper 3 head teacher for Qian Yuankai's class, and had once made a promise to Qian Yuankai that the family background problem would not influence his continuing education. And so Qian tried to test into Qinghua University and ended up receiving the second-highest score in the whole northern region—and indeed, not one university accepted him. In September 1958, Qian joined the Mt. Shijing Iron and Steel Works to serve as an unskilled laborer, two years later becoming a lathe operator, all the while continuing to study on his own through his toils. His passion for photography led him to build his own camera equipment, and in 1968 he transferred to the Beijing Camera Factory, where he worked his way up from technician to chief engineer, and eventually became a leading authority on camera technology and the practice and theory of photography.

After the calamity of his college exam rejection, Qian Yuankai's father said to him, "Opportunities to attend school are dependent upon others, but studying, reading books, putting what you learn into practice, together make up the principal classroom for gaining knowledge; the power to learn at this school can only be seized by your own hands, it is something no one else can ever deprive you of. Let learning become a kind of life habit, which compared to any badge bestowed by a prestigious university is of much greater importance!" These words he always kept close to his heart.

As for life's bitter wine, he initially brewed it with his teacher and couldn't share it with others. But many years later, for any school-related reunion, once word go out that Qian Yuankai would be attending, Qu Datong *beat a strategic retreat of many leagues.*

14

As summer turned to fall in 1968, a secret organization known as the Red Guard 6514 Unit emerged in Beijing, *stirring up trouble like a god or a ghost*, posting propaganda banners everywhere like: "Ferret Out and Suppress Beijing Secondary Schools' Cultural Revolutionary Little Reptile Li Zhongqi!"

"Those Who Suppress the Student Movement Will Come to a Bad End!" "The Principles of the Commune Will Last Forever!" Around the same time, the mimeographed tabloid newspaper *Principles* also circulated through the city.

In fact, this was all the work of five or six students from our class. The unit number, smacking of empty bravado, could be decoded with ease: Middle No. 4 Upper 1 Class 5 Study 6, reversed to make the 6514 Unit.

In the spring of 1968, because of ambiguous messages coming out of the Central Committee and the involvement of so many university factional organizations, conflicts escalated between the April Third Faction and the April Fourth Faction. The workers' propaganda team and the People's Liberation Army's thought-propaganda team delete entered the school gates together to contain the situation, setting up a Revolutionary Committee. The one in charge of implementing this secondary school martial law was the deputy commander of the Beijing Garrison, Li Zhongqi.

As the Cultural Revolution came to a swift and bewildering close, we all felt somewhat betrayed. In the meantime, from behind the fray of the two clashing factions, the Old Guard put forth the most eloquent challenge, having nothing to do with any "twenty years later we'll see who's won or lost": "Why don't you wield the brush and we wield the guns and then we'll see who owns this land under heaven in times to come?"

Whether along the campus's little paths or in the spaces between words, the committee cast its arrogant shadow everywhere. It originated from the elitism of the "blood lineage"—transgressing a history of arrogance, never mind youth and ignorance—the crux of the problem being their utter lack of self-reflection, never pausing to examine their own conscience (save for the few exceptions). This grew into a kind of self-inflicted wound, a wound that more than forty years later still festers—the line between "commoners" and "nobility" running like a scar across history, still visible to this day.

The Red Guard 6514 Unit marched on, not only making life difficult for a certain General Li Zhongqi but leaving unspoken meanings on the stage of official history, so that what originally seemed to be an inevitable, logical narrative progression became riddled with holes. By day we worked the wax-coated printing plates and brushed slogans, and at midnight dispatched our troops, even pasting up slogans on the wall that faced Garrison Headquarters.

One time we rode a flatbed tricycle in the middle of the night along West Chang'an Avenue and turned into the depths of an alley to Beijing Middle No. 6, not far from Tiananmen Gate. As we finished pasting up some slogans and an issue of *Principles* onto the brick wall outside the school's main entrance, ten or more boys suddenly rushed out from the campus with baseball bats and spring locks in their hands, while the only weapons we had consisted of a few brooms and metal buckets. Standing in a line face-to-face, bodies almost glued together, each side could hear the other side's breathing. My heartbeat accelerated, blood bubbled upward, brain blanked out; I could see my own bloodthirsty desire in the eyes I gazed into, a manifestation of man's primal instincts that could be traced back to our hunter-and-warrior ancestors and which in instances like this could take complete control over us.

We stood frozen in a deadlock; the seconds felt like the accumulation of a century. Then our side retreated a step, then another, insults traded as we stepped, the pace of our withdrawal needing proper assurance, neither too fast nor too slow, or face certain doom. We walked out of the alley onto Chang'an Avenue. The autumn wind picked up; I shuddered uncontrollably.

Principles lasted for three issues, then died of natural causes, hardly leaving a mark upon the world save in our hearts—we grew up overnight, daring to challenge the authoritarian powers. And then a moment later, just after the curtain had been raised, every principle, caught in the wave of the Down to the Countryside Movement, needed to be revised, changed, or stretched.

15

In the winter of 1968, a group of ten of us, including Teacher Tian Yong, made the trip to Baiyangdian in Anxin County, Hebei Province to participate in the Education Revolution Expedition. The fervor of the Down to the Countryside Movement engulfing the whole nation was simply unfathomable, each one of us caught in the middle of it as the target of revolutionary education. Our journey was infused with the epoch's madness, bearing its frenzied traces.

Soon we became embroiled in an epic struggle, as both factions—the provincial military command and the Thirty-Eighth Army Division—backed separate skirmishes *till the sky darkened and the land dimmed,* the conflagration spreading to Baiyangdian; indeed, this had been the base of operations for Japanese resistance and so the peasants possessed an abundance of real combat experience.

Just as we were settling into the county committee's hostel, we received notification that seven people involved in a battle to take control of the county seat had been killed, and a memorial service would be held. As we had no choice but to attend, we made a garland of flowers and brushed Lu Xun's elegiac couplet— "In enduring the sight of friends becoming new ghosts / Fury seeks a little verse in a thicket of swords"—onto an enormous banner and hung it horizontally across the main thoroughfare in town. A loudspeaker broadcast funeral music. We stopped by the tent where the corpses were being held and bowed three times to the dead. That was the first time I had seen a dead body in real life—the dead consisted of both males and females, their waxy yellow skin against the sunlight made them look almost translucent, reminding me of a shadow play. But the most terrifying thing was the stench, which forced each of us into a personal struggle for breath.

As representatives from Beijing, we were naturally accepted as elite members of "Chairman Mao's appointed family," the head of the rebel faction and the families of the deceased repeatedly imploring us to stay as special guests for the Flowing Water Banquet. We refused with diplomatic politeness and returned to the county committee hostel, where we succumbed to fits of vomiting, skipped dinner, and continued to heave and groan under the murky lamplight.

For safety reasons, our survey started with the middle schools outside the city gates. Those rural children who studied so hard seemed superhuman: rising early and working late, staying up all night by the burning light of an oil lamp, no downtime for play, no recreations, their food and shelter situation extremely impoverished. They dreamed of moving to the city to study at a university, thus altering their fate of being bound to the soil. Because of the limited number of spots for enrollment, however, these children had to exceed the standard Beijing student's exam score by a large margin to even have a chance at acceptance. This came as a huge shock to us—held to this standard, half of Beijing Middle No. 4 wouldn't test into college. Such societal injustices were far beyond anything we could imagine.

The fire signals appeared again, as the opposition began to attack the county seat. The sound of gunfire resumed mostly at night, the whistling of bullets making it difficult to sleep. At any moment, the county seat could fall, turning the hostel into a primary target. With a straw rope tied around his waist, Teacher Tianyong leaped up, determined to sneak over to the hostel gate and investigate the situation, see if the gunfire would soon be upon us. We watched him duck for cover, then slowly crawl forward. When he came back, he said that the elderly guard at the hostel gate had listened for gunfire, then yawned, saying that the enemy was still far away, best to go to sleep without delay.

Holed up in the county hostel for more than ten days, rumors swirled around us; we had no idea what was really happening in the world outside. Under military pressure, both sides finally sat down to negotiate. We took the first bus out to Baoding, fleeing the besieged city.

Not long after we returned to Beijing, Spring Festival was upon us. At a classmate's party, dishes and cups scattered about, we got drunk and raised our voices in song with bitter cries. We took turns writing fashionable old-style poems in antiphonal response, the passing moment steeped in our emotions, brimming over with the sorrow of parting! The Beijing train station served as our last classroom, for a new lesson in saying good-bye.

Mother at the Henan May Seventh Cadre School, 1971

*Father reading Lu Xun at the May Seventh Cadre
School dormitory in Hubei, 1971*

*With Father at the May Seventh
Cadre School in Hubei, 1970*

*Cultural Revolution struggle
session at Beijing Middle No. 4*

Family photo at the Temple of Heaven, 1972

Father with relatives after returning to the capital from the May Seventh Cadre School (from the left: Uncle Han Yaohui, Uncle Zhao Yinian, Uncle Zhao Yannian, Father)

The Great Linkup

1

I N THE MIDDLE of September 1966, six of us students—
Zhang Qian, Pan Zongfu, Yang Xiaoyun, Zhang Youzhu,
Xu Jinbo, and myself—stepped onto a southbound train.

A few weeks before, beginning on August 18, Chairman Mao
had granted the Red Guards eight consecutive audiences at Tiananmen Gate, leading to the Cultural Revolution's new tidal
wave—the Great Linkup. The CPC Central Committee directive
supported students from all parts of the country to come to Beijing, while also encouraging Beijing students to travel all over
China, in order to exchange revolutionary experiences—transportation and living expenses would be subsidized by the state.
Trains and public transit throughout the country became free for
secondary school and university students, and reception tables
were quickly set up at each station to handle the logistics of food
and shelter. While the Old Red Guards were given priority, political records needed to be checked (i.e., family background) in

order to leave. But Chairman Mao *pushed the waves and aided the ripples*, and the sluice gate swiftly opened.

Xu Jinbo procured a standard, blank letter of introduction from such and such Red Guard organization, and summoned us children of ordinary civilians to fill in our names, intending to use the blanks on the page as proof of our own blank innocence. With the letter in hand, we lined up at the Dongdan Railway Station ticket office and ended up receiving six free tickets.

It was my first journey far from home, away from my parents. Baggage was simple—besides a small schoolbag stuffed with extra clothes, just the little wooden case I had made with Mao's words brushed on it in red paint and the four volumes of his writings packed inside it.

We transferred at Baoji City in Shaanxi. Chilly night; thick billows of smoke puffed out of the locomotive, blocking the platform lights. By the time we reached Chengdu it was already past midnight. The warm, moist southern air washed over our faces, flowing slowly on as the train gently rocked forward to a stop. The Red Guards working the reception table in the railway station plaza assigned us to Middle No. 14. Upon learning that we were coming from Beijing, the teachers and students in charge of reception were particularly hospitable, and even prepared a midnight snack for us—sautéed shredded bamboo shoots with a huge vat of rice. Males and females slept in separate classrooms; we arranged our beds on the floor, desks and chairs piled up to the side. Jittery with excitement, we whispered secretly to each other in the darkness, until complaints silenced us and we put our heads down to sleep.

The next morning, we checked in at the Sichuan Provincial Party Committee Headquarters. Big-character posters everywhere, *shaking heaven and earth*, pointed accusingly at the southwest region's first in command, Li Jingquan, who was still the party committee secretary of Sichuan. We acted like students studying abroad, looking around and copying down every line we saw. Big-character posters divulged all sorts of astonishing insider information. For example, in this heavenly prefecture of the nation, several million people had starved to death during the Difficult Period of the three-year famine, and Li Jingquan's infamous remarks about it had spread to households near and far: "China is so vast—what dynasty, what epoch, has there ever been in which people haven't died from hunger?" There were also those cases of corruption that, like pornographic novels, made faces heat up and hearts leap.

About one hundred li (fifty kilometers) from Chengdu, Anren Ancient Town in Dayi County became a hot spot during the Great Linkup, due to the landlord Liu Wencai's infamous feudal manor and Rent-Collection Courtyard, where he had supposedly exploited peasant farmers during the Republican period. In 1965, teachers and students from the sculpture department at the Sichuan Fine Art Institute teamed up with local artisans to create a series of life-size clay sculptures in the Rent-Collection Courtyard, depicting the plight of the peasants in the hands of the landlord. The exhibit became a nationwide sensation, and even traveled to the Beijing Art Museum where schools from all over the area organized field trips to see it. I still remember writing about it for a class assignment at the time.

There were actually a number of grand residences with connecting courtyards hidden behind walls in Anren Ancient Town, the Liu Wencai Feudal Manor merely one of them. We slogged our way through a constant swarm of people—no will of our own, no place to rest. Shadows stretched west to the sun, the crowds gradually thinned; then a sudden whiff of a rare fragrance we traced to a deep-fried duck stall by the roadside, one mao five for a piece. After we each bought a portion, we stored it carefully in the plastic bag where we kept our steamed rolls, gnawing small bits of it over time, until only the fragments of duck bone remained. On the way back to the railway station, Pan Zongfu and I each took a steamed roll and dipped it into the residual oily duck juice, savoring each bite with prodigal praise, reaching for the most superlative adjective under heaven, "Oh, so *motherfucking good*!" Even if it was pestilent duck, it left a rich, lingering aftertaste for the rest of our lives.

Zhang Youzhu—tall, strong as a horse—played center on our basketball team. Whenever anyone brought up his family's brand of sesame-paste sweet cakes, his eyebrows danced with delight. I actually called him Sesame-Paste Sweet Cake. From the moment we arrived in Chengdu, he contracted diarrhea and couldn't get out of bed; he soon returned to Beijing, *exiting in the middle of the show*. I changed his nickname to Ah Li Li ("Ah Dysentery"), not only because it sounded good but for its piercingly exotic yet familiar ring.

Arriving in Chongqing, we stayed at the Southwest University of Political Science and Law at the foot of Gele ("Clarion") Mountain, the Revolutionary Martyrs' Cemetery only a short walk away. The compound once served as the headquarters of the Kuomintang Military Bureau and Sino-American Special Technical Cooperative Organization, a jointly run intelligence agency that operated against Japan. All of us had read Luo Guangbin and Yang Yiyan's coauthored novel *Red Crag* early on in elementary school: That gruesome tale of prison torture and espionage, so terrifyingly vivid, was set here in the cooperative's prisons, where the two writers had been held as underground communists. The ancient trees of Gele Mountain still towered to the skies, clouds and mist floating by—just another ordinary, immortal paradise.

2

Chongqing, Chaotianmen ("Gate to Heaven") Dock. The horn blared three times; the ship unmoored and set off; the deck quaked. We were put in a third-class berth with six bunks. Tickets were difficult to obtain and the number of passengers far exceeded the number of bunks, so we slept two per bed, a much more comfortable setup, nevertheless, than sitting on a train—the ride smooth and silent, air fresh as can be. Gazing at the steep cliffs from the deck, I couldn't help but recall a Li Bai poem I had read in school: "Apes on both shores howl without end / The boat glides lightly by ten thousand hills." Any apes had long vanished, and the overloaded boat seemed in danger of capsizing at any moment. The little speaker in each cabin broadcast quotations and revolutionary songs interspersed with a reminder repeated over and over again for passengers not to all crowd onto one side of the boat when admiring the scenery. It must've been past midnight when we passed the Three Gorges, our sleep so deep that the mythic beauty of the landscape didn't leave a single trace behind in our dreams.

Some students from the Beijing University of Technology shared the cabin with us—one guy and three girls. The guy, Xu Rongzheng, was nicknamed Old "Pia"; I couldn't verify the word for "Pia" but I thought it had something to with his enlarged lower jaw (scientifically known as "cherubism"), while also suggesting the smack of falling flat on the face: from "pia" to "pia," the latter onomatopoetic and the former homographic (for his condition). Our company also included three male students from the Fisheries College at Jimei University in Xiamen, one of them, Weng Qihui, guileless and taciturn, I connected with straightaway.

Three days aboard ship and my two new friends and I mingled easily, getting to know one another well—we decided to stick together for the rest of our travels. Old Pia—intelligent, capable, always putting service before self—became our natural leader. He spread out a map and marked the trail we would blaze: landfall at Wuhan, and after a few days there of rest and recuperation, pass through Zhuzhou to Shaoshan, and onward to Guangzhou.

We stayed at a school in the Hankou section of Wuhan, where the mouth of the Han River opens into the Yangzi. I went to visit Uncle Da Jiu, my mother's eldest brother. He was born in the Huangpu district of Guangzhou, and graduated from Jinling University; after the July Seventh Incident in 1937 that sparked another war with Japan, he joined the guerrilla fighters in Hubei, and eventually was appointed the county magistrate of Yingcheng, while still serving as a commanding officer in the guerrilla movement. By the time the Cultural Revolution launched, he had become the deputy mayor of Wuhan. As an activist for democracy, however, he didn't wield any real power, and so after the first big, surging wave of the revolution, he emerged as a survivor.

Da Jiu lived on Tianjin Road in a small building with a

guard at the front gate. The sitting room was spacious and bright. I feared being sucked into their enormous sofa and sat stiffly on a corner of it, in a rabbit-on-alert position. Doors opened and closed as my two older cousins, male and female, kept coming in and out, as if waiting for a most honorable visitor—the Breaking Storm. The normally cheerful and chatty Da Jiu seemed distracted, *his spirit not guarding his dwelling*, his mind wandering, his laughter empty, floating up to the ceiling with the smoke. Only my aunt Da Jiu-Ma asked me how I was doing, and made me a big bowl of hot soup noodles. Though I may have been young, I understood enough, and after quickly finishing my noodles, I said my good-byes.

On the leg from Wuhan to Zhuzhou, the passenger cars were full so we had to ride in a freight car. The car rocked constantly back and forth, on and on, halting for a moment then starting again, the landscape outside glimpsed through a crack in the door. The bathroom situation proved to be the most annoying inconvenience; whenever the train stopped, no one dared to go far from the car, and so boys and girls divided left and right to settle their business nearby. If the train was moving, the boys who couldn't hold it any longer turned around to pee and the girls helped each other by holding up a blanket as a screen. The acrid smell assailed us until we could barely gasp for another breath.

At Zhushou, we transferred to a truck heading for Shaoshan. All along the road red flags were raised by processions of people journeying from great distances, some having walked for more than a month already, their hair matted, faces filthy, clothes ragged—once they caught sight of our spirited presence, they sang quotations back to us.

Our pilgrimage destination consisted of nothing more than

a number of hollow, totally emptied brick-and-tile houses surrounded by semi-barren hillsides. This was the place where the red sun rose. I took out the four Mao volumes from my wooden case, and standing before his former residence with my comrades, we swore an oath, raising our right arms high: To carry the revolution to the end.

3

As the train journeyed farther south, the air temperature abruptly shot up and the parching heat became difficult to bear; one by one, everyone removed their outer clothing, until the boys went skins versus the girls' tight undershirts.

Arriving in Guangzhou in the middle of the night, palm trees gently swayed here and there, their huge fanlike leaves swept along the moist wind. We were divided up at the South China Agricultural University. All of us boys charged into the water taps with only our underpants on and rinsed off with uninhibited delight.

Aunt Da Yi (my mother's eldest sister) lived in Guangzhou— she and my uncle both worked as high-school teachers. They had suffered a lot, but their plight wasn't as bad as many of those who lived in the interior. Because of its unique geographic location, Guangzhou's degree of openness far surpassed that of the inland regions. We visited Chrysanthemum Hill, Yuexiu ("Luxuriant Blooms") Park, Baiyun ("White Clouds") Mountain, and the Canton Fair—for us, the Great Linkup really did bring about an understated change: In the name of the revolution, take a tour of the world.

Old Pia carried around a Kiev 135mm camera, and captured

some unforgettable moments. I still have in my possession a few group shots of us. The frame cuts out each external scene, removing the wild clamor and turning an electrifying world into a fuzzy image. Our expressions, too, were stiff; our eyes were glazed, like the gaze of the terra-cotta warriors; it looks as if we awaited some secret sound to rouse us awake.

Guangzhou seemed like a totally different world to us. The tropical air emanated exoticism, adding to the feeling of being in a foreign country—plus, we couldn't understand the language. Trying to find a bathroom and unable to make sense of any replies, we had an epiphany and wrote our question down with a successful result. And the girls on the street with their ultra-sultry airs, sporting their blue coats and dark green military uniforms as well as a glimpse here and there of a lotus-red or apricot-yellow undergarment peaking out.

4

At our final stop, Shanghai, we stayed at the State Cotton Factory No. 11. I was eight when I last visited the city, accompanying my mother to see Waigong. Being back with my comrades, I found it difficult to pierce through the aloofness of its floating world. I brought the group to Waitan to see the huge ships on the Huangpu River and the bustling ten-li foreign settlement zone, which felt closest to being back home. In contrast with the glittery night-scape, the daily lives of the common people shone forth—the open skies above the lanes bloomed with colorful clothes, as if flying ten thousand flags; a bus turned a corner, pulled up to its stop, the ticket seller poked his head out the window, sang out his hawking cry, and banged his plank of wood against the bus's side, echoes rippling out to the hills; everywhere, old people raised little flags, less for safety reasons than to prove they were still alive; then, one day rising early to wait in line for train tickets, we saw from household to household in the faint dawn light, a figure outside each front gate, pouring out the chamber pot with the solemnity of a morning prayer ceremony.

I went to the Shanghai Hôpital Sainte-Marie on Ruijin Road to visit Second Aunt Eryi. Big-character posters had been pasted up everywhere, but the hospital continued its normal operations. I found Eryi at the nurses' station. As the chief nursing officer, she was busy designating various assignments and tasks. Things finally settled down around noon, so she took me to a nearby restaurant for lunch.

There was hardly another soul in the restaurant. Eryi ordered some fish and meat dishes especially for me—a boost of nourishment. We sat across from each other, sunlight slanting across our table. I told her everything I had seen and heard on my journey; Eryi occasionally interrupted to ask a question, her eyes blank, and offered a few bureaucratic words of encouragement. That was the last time we saw each other before her persecution and death two years later.

A quiet afternoon, the clock on the wall ticked on *di da di da di da*. My neck started to itch; I rubbed my hand to scratch it and unexpectedly picked off a louse. During the Great Linkup, everyone called the louse the "revolutionary bug," their collective life force extremely tenacious—poison spray, burning flames, boiling water, freezing cold all useless—they persevered on their human prey to the far corners of the sea and sky.

Pinching the louse between my fingers, I placed it onto the

table, then squeezed it to death with my fingernail. Eryi didn't notice, or at least didn't complain; she only insisted on dragging me back to the hospital to be thoroughly disinfected. That squeezing sound, so infinitesimal yet sharp and clear, if amplified through a loudspeaker would certainly reverberate like a thunderclap.

5

On November 10, 1966, thousands of members of the recently established Shanghai Workers Revolutionary Rebel General Headquarters (or, "Workers General") decided to make their way to Beijing to present their grievances in person. Activists lay across the railroad tracks some thirty kilometers from the northwest outskirts of Shanghai at the Anting Station in Jiading County, intercepting a Beijing-bound express train, and then holding up the Beijing–Shanghai rail line for more than twenty hours as the authorities refused to allow the train to run with the activists on board. And so unfolded the momentous Anting Incident.

As luck would have it, on the second day of the incident, we went to the Shanghai Railway Station with our return tickets to Beijing in hand and a spectacular scene awaited us: the waiting rooms and platforms jam-packed with people, not a trickle could pass, crowds even sitting on the tracks themselves, the riotous and chaotic atmosphere like a thick fog enveloping the earth.

From morning to afternoon we scrambled around at a loss, finally accepting the fact that no train would be entering or leaving the station. With Old Pia as our leader, we decided to take immediate action—the Shanghai Special Patrol Team met its historic destiny. First, Old Pia stepped forth to consult with other students from Beijing, and the Patrol Team swiftly expanded into the dozens; then we began to initiate talks with the rebel faction of the Shanghai Railway Administration.

Old Pia deployed me on a mission, namely to establish contact with officials at the East China Bureau and the Shanghai Municipal Committee, the leaders of which we long ago discovered from big-character posters, so-and-so Chen Pixian and Cao Diqiu. As a member of the Patrol Team, I took over a phone in the dispatch office, first obtaining the number for the Shanghai Municipal Committee through the switchboard directory, then dialing Cao Diqiu's office, but no one picked up. I tried Chen Pixian's office at the East China Bureau, finally reaching someone who claimed to be a clerk; I made a show of force by insisting on speaking to Chen Pixian himself. The voice claimed ignorance of any Shanghai Special Patrol Team, and added that they were simply overwhelmed with requests. I flew into a thunderous rage, telling him to tell Chen Pixian that as the first secretary of the East China Bureau he must take charge of the unprecedented fracas at the Shanghai Station. The clerk mumbled yes, yes, of course, and he promised to pass on the message.

Once the Central Cultural Revolution Group intervened, the Anting Incident crisis dwindled. The Patrol Team cleaned up the station the same night, clearing off the crowds from the tracks, as well as those holed up in the cars, and checked each person's ticket. Our voices grew hoarse from yelling as we battled the multitudes, subduing certain troublesome elements. The following morning, at long last, the first train to Beijing ever-so-slowly rumbled to life. Fleet-footed, we boarded immediately, shutting the doors and windows of our car, the Shanghai Special Patrol Team concluding its almost two-day historic mission.

The train, however, far exceeded its normal capacity, each car's safety limit of 108 passengers had roughly tripled. People lay on the luggage racks and sat on the back of seats, squatted on the floor and packed into the bathrooms, which of course couldn't be used anymore. The train trundled along, stopping occasionally for a few hours, whereupon everyone would take turns to get off to eat and drink and relieve themselves. Often, without any warning whistle, the train would suddenly start, and the people below would make a mad dash to overtake the slowly moving cars, crawling in through the windows, while those moving too slow would be left behind forever.

My "seat" was perched atop the back of a real seat, and as I couldn't help myself any longer, I wedged my head between two clothes hangers and fell asleep, keeping my balance like this through my dreams. I dreamed about returning home and about running away from home.

Three days three nights. The train pulled into Beijing.

Father

You summoned me to become a son
I followed you by becoming a father

—"For Father"

1

Among Father's earliest memories arises an old photograph: With the Temple of Heaven's Hall of Prayer for Good Harvest in the background, Father smiles jubilantly, one arm overlaps the other in front of him as he leans forward on a white marble balustrade. He asked the photo studio that developed the picture to trim part of the white balustrade at the bottom as it wasn't light-sensitive, and so at first glance, there's the illusion of the sleeve of his coat slipping out beyond the photo's frame. This portrait had been taken before I was born. The reason why I'm so fond of it is because I never saw my father smile like this, brimming with the self-confidence of spring youth. I like to believe this could be the starting point of my memories of him.

October 1949, we chose a pet name for our son: Qing Qing ("double celebration"). Having our first child now, the two of us are very busy. Mei Li made some little clothes for him, and bathes him often; as she hasn't been producing enough breast milk, she gives him some *nai gao*, rice-flour mush, each day. I frequently walk around the room with him in my arms, patting him asleep, and take photos of him in all sorts of positions, from different angles. Our little family now has this little treasure, everything has come alive. (*From my father's notebook*)

Not long after my birth, we moved from Duofu Alley to Fuqian Street, very close to Tiananmen Gate Tower. National Day. Father carries me as he crowds around the courtyard gate with the neighbors, everyone watching the military parade march by in formation. The fireworks are even more marvelous to behold. The next morning in the courtyard, one can pick up all the unburned seeds of the fire-blooms and string them together into a fuse that, once ignited, releases a rainbow of sparks, and with a fleeting spin, a flash, a wink, disappears.

Chang'an Avenue's wide thoroughfare slants across to Zhongshan Park. My father used to take me there for some sun and air. *Ding ding dong dong* the streetcar trundled along the avenue, making a stop right in front of Fuqian Street. Father liked to ride it with me to the end of the line at Xidan, then ride it straight back again. During off-peak times it was often empty, the hand rings shaking in the open air. The sheer delight I felt standing behind the driver, watching him maneuver the nickel-plated lever. My father and I called it the "ding dong car."

Summertime in Zhongshan Park—almost every weekend an outdoor movie would be screened there. Nearby residents arrived early to reserve their seat with a stool, while others sat scattered around the grass or stone steps, waiting for the day to darken. Whenever a reel needed to be switched or if the film-strip snapped, a square of light filled the blank screen while the machinery whirred on monotonously.

The Soviet animated film *The Scarlet Flower* made the deep-est impression on me—details of the plot I've forgotten, but I remember the young daughter as the lead, longing for that most beautiful little scarlet flower, meeting the mythical beast by chance (who was really the incarnation of a prince). Toward the end of the film, her calling out on the journey with such forlorn melancholy "Brother Kai" seeped deep into my dreams.

The most wondrous thing I observed occurred as the movie started, the moment behind the screen when the green titles above the palace walls of the Forbidden City faded away. I asked my father about this phenomenon but didn't get a sat-isfactory answer; actually, he just ignored me. Eventually, the two worlds became wholly distinct, the world on the screen temporarily blocking out the real world.

One Sunday, I heard that *The Scarlet Flower* would be screened again at Zhongshan Park. Too jubilant with excite-ment, I couldn't settle down for my afternoon nap, so Father lost it and threw me out, locking the door behind him. My feet were bare; I cried and wailed, pounding on the door, the ice-cold steps intensifying my indignation. I don't know how but I fell asleep. I woke up to a circle of shadowed light on the ceiling, socks on my feet bringing a feeling of tranquillity. Mother's face neared mine with a look of concern. I asked her about *The Scarlet Flower*; she replied that it was nighttime already, we had missed the movie.

2

Qing Qing really doesn't want to go to the nursery; each Saturday when we pick him up he's always so happy, and then the problem of sending him back repeats all over again Monday morning. On one of these Monday mornings, nothing we said could persuade him, his reply only one sentence: "I won't go to the nursery." We needed to get to work, and with no other option, we tricked him, saying that instead we were going to the zoo; he believed us. On the way, his expression grew anxious, then realizing we were going to the nursery, he broke into a fit of screaming and crying. I held him tightly, afraid he'd leap out of the trolleybus. At last we reached the gate of the nursery; he collapsed to the ground and rolled around. I could only hold him stiffly and carry him inside. Upon seeing the kind Ayi there, he calmed down a little, and with tears in his eyes, blurted out, "Good-bye Baba!" (*From my father's notebook*)

I had a fairly weak immune system as a child and I didn't escape a single contagious bug in the nursery. The hundred-day cough, or whooping cough, proved particularly troublesome—I hacked up a storm deep into the sleepless night; my parents took turns holding me. A doctor said only chloramphenicol would be effective. This imported medicine's cost was exorbitant, but bit by bit Father saved and bought a bunch of pills for a tael of gold. Following the doctor's prescription, the outer capsule of each pill was discarded and the powder inside divided in half, one dose taken in the morning and one in the evening. The harsh, acrid taste made me spit it out the first time. My father looked at me hard and told me how much the medicine cost, that if I spit it out they wouldn't have enough money to buy more so I must swallow it, no matter what. I nodded my head, clenched my teeth, and with tears flowing down, swallowed the dose.

Later on, as I grew older, my parents often liked to tell this story, as if I had performed a heroic feat. But really, lore of this sort makes up a part of every family tradition, and discloses formidable psychological implications, backed, moreover, by the will of the ancestors—succeed at any cost, failure is not an option.

Qing Qing got the measles and they had to put him in an isolated room at the nursery. We could only see him through the glass partition, but he still looked very happy, using hand gestures to converse with us. The next time we came, Ayi told us that after we had left the other day, he stood on his bed all night and wouldn't sleep. When she asked him why he wouldn't sleep, he said he needed to wait up for Baba and Mama. (*From my father's notebook*)

My little brother differed from me by a hundred and eighty de-grees—he loved the nursery with matchless ardor. When Father came to pick him up each Saturday, he'd turn his head with disdain and say, "I'm not going to your house."

From a very young age, Zhenkai and Zhenxian had very different temperaments. If you gave them each a mooncake, the two utilized entirely disparate eating methods—Zhenkai first ate the filling and then the outer crust; Zhenxian does the opposite, first nibbling the outer crust away before wrapping the filling back up and putting it in his pocket to savor slowly, making one mooncake last for many days. (*From my father's notebook*)

My father was normally quite patient with us as children; he'd often play with me, tell me stories. On a little notepad he would draw a small figure on different pages, each in a slightly different position, and upon flipping the pad from beginning to end, the figure would move about, as if in an animated film. My younger brother and sister gradually replaced me; I felt a slight sense of loss, tasted the slight vinegar tinge of jealousy, though I felt a little proud, too—I had grown up.

From Fuwai Street we moved to the single-family apartment in Three Never Old Hutong No. 1. Ordinarily, Mother and Father would leave early and return late, and under Qian Ayi's supervision, we'd go to sleep, get out of bed, do homework according to our routine schedule—Sunday the only exception. On those days, Mama would rise early to help Qian Ayi prepare breakfast; we'd linger on our parents' bed and play with Father. For a spell we became enraptured with language games, like the one based on colors where we named father "Red Baba," "Blue Baba," "Green Baba" at whim, rolling with laughter.

Father really did display a range of colors.

Our earliest clash occurred when I was around seven. At the time, we resided in the Fuwai Insurance Company Apartments, living with Uncle Yu Biaowen's family in a four-room unit, two rooms for each household, shared kitchen and bathroom. That was the summer when Uncle Yu Biaowen was labeled a "rightist," then leaped to his death, leaving his wife and two sons alone and heartbroken.

The storm swiftly picked up and squeezed through the cracks of our house—my parents started to argue more, as if it were the only way they could release the strain that had reached capacity overload within them. In an instant, Father assumed the nature of the storm, sick with madness, a malevolent expression spreading across his face, his actions frenzied, unhinged, his person totally changed. I stood firmly at Mother's side, as she was defenseless against him.

The causes were *chicken-feather-and-garlic-peel* trivial matters, nor, it must be noted, did the fault always lie entirely with Father. For instance, he took pleasure in buying books, and once purchased a huge brick of a Russian-Chinese dictionary—nothing wholly inexcusable as he was teaching himself Russian at the time. I still remember its twenty-nine kuai nine price tag to this day, it being the most expensive book I had ever seen. To the lady of the house with five mouths to feed, however, it was a little hard to accept. This turned into the darkest stretch of domestic politics in our household.

Another scene: Father gripped the bedroom door with a huge roar and a shout; Mother, enraged, grabbed a flower vase on the dresser and hurled it at him; he dodged it, the vase sailing past him, shattering to the ground. I happened to be present, sole eyewitness who observed everything; my whole body trembled, and yet I managed to bolt over and stand between them, while glaring at my father with intense hostility. He didn't anticipate this, and raised his palm with a halt in midair.

Mother's illnesses always seemed to coincide with their quarrels; whenever she lay in bed, too sick to rise, I'd go to a bakery nearby and buy her a fluffy piece of egg-and-cream cake roll, as if it could be the elixir of immortality. On the way back I'd open the paper bag, see how much extra snowy-white cream had spilled out, drool dribbling down my mouth, though not once did I dip a finger in.

One evening, Father convinced himself that I had pilfered snacks from the cabinet. Though I had before, this time I was innocent, his accusations totally unjust. I refused to own up to his allegation, saying that I would die first, and so he forced me to kneel on the floor and endure his palm-of-the-hand blows. What wounded me most was the shock of seeing Mother standing by Father's side, although she secretly had protected me, preventing his violent lashes with the feather duster.

Red Baba Blue Baba Green Baba transformed into Black Monster Baba.

By the time we moved to Sanbulao Hutong No. 1, my parents fought almost continuously. I resembled an injured animal, nerves taut, senses acute, waiting for disaster to drop each second. My premonitions often came true. I hated myself, hated my small, weak, powerless self, unable to do anything to protect my mother.

Father's authoritarian behavior spread beyond our household. Preparing to go to bed one night, I found him in one of his dark moods, pacing back and forth as he smoked. I pretended to read, taking note of his each and every movement. He hurried out and rapped loudly on Uncle Zheng Fanglong's door next to ours. I couldn't make out their conversation, but my father's voice grew louder and louder, interspersed with slaps on the table. I covered my head with my quilt, listening to the *dong-dong dong-dong* of my heart beating faster and faster. I felt ashamed. Father didn't return until the middle of the night; he whispered privately with Mother in their bedroom. A nightmare engulfed me.

I bumped into Uncle Zheng in the corridor the next day; he retracted his neck and chuckled weirdly; gazing up at him, it was as if the real meaning of life had revealed itself. I pieced together as much as I could from snippets between my parents I overheard: Uncle Zheng had made a serious mistake of some sort, and on behalf of the Central Committee, Father had spoken to him. Many years later Father told me that if the situation had taken place a few months earlier, he would have stumbled first and fate would have switched their situations.

Zhenkai only wants to have fun, his school grades very mediocre, though his compositions for Chinese class frequently earn the praise of his teacher. Zhenkai's faults raised in parent-teacher conferences are always "not paying attention in class," "loves to play little tricks," and so on. Once, checking over his grade book, a mark for what looked like a midterm mathematics test was noted as 4.5. I thought this very strange, how could a score like this exist? I asked Zhenkai about it, and he said: "5 is a perfect mark; I made one mistake and so got a 4.5." His explanation seemed somewhat reasonable, but I still wasn't convinced. I visited the school to ask the teacher and learned that Zhenkai had actually received a 45 percent on the test. He had added the decimal point himself to make it 4.5. I reprimanded him for his behavior and he expressed his remorse. (*From my father's notebook*)

With time my parents gradually reconciled. In their later years, they never ran out of conversation, causing one to ponder deeply the full import of that name for a spouse, *lao ban* ("old other half"). Three years after my father passed away, my mother told the interviewer working on an oral history project on women in China:

> Our whole life living together as a married couple was harmonious, comforting, even when the winds raged and the rains poured down....

4

At the start of the summer in 1960, my father temporarily transferred from the CAPD to the Central Institute of Socialism, working in the office of academic affairs. The institution was part of the CPC's United Front Work Department initiative, and all the students there belonged to families connected to the upper echelon of the democratic parties.

Every weekend I took my younger siblings out to play. The Central Institute of Socialism lay just north of Purple Bamboo Park—we rode the No. 11 trolleybus to the last stop, crossed the White Stone Bridge five or six hundred meters northward to deserted wilderness, trickling water, the chattering of frogs and insects. The institute consisted of a white cluster of six-story buildings, the fountain in front perennially dry. Army soldiers guarded the front gate, and upon entering, one needed to register at the reception desk, though we quickly became familiar faces and could skip this formality.

Father borrowed a room for us next to his interim living quarters. We basked in the beneficial rays of the United Front, the meals there decent, movies shown on weekends, and the facilities top-notch, like the Ping-Pong room. Father had received certification to be a level-three Ping-Pong referee, the lowest level of national officiating for amateur competitions, though these matches maintained the intense atmosphere of a professional tournament. He sat upright and rigid, like a stiff robot, lenses gleaming, each word and numeral of the score announced with emphatic enunciation, "*Three to four*, switch serve," and crossing his arms when declaring a change of sides.

At the institute, Father was so busy he usually only appeared in the cafeteria for meals. I liked to wander around alone, lost in the crowded maze of the buildings. I got to know the elevator operator, Uncle Wang, and would help him run it. When he told me that he used to be a soldier in the military, my esteem for him ballooned; I pestered him about the kinds of guns he used. Much later I would learn that he killed himself during the Cultural Revolution.

One day, Father told me that a student's dorm room had been broken into, everything cleaned out, the loss totaling more than one hundred thousand yuan, an astronomical figure indeed. But then my father furtively added, "It wasn't a problem; the student flew back to Shanghai the same day and repurchased a whole new set of household items. He's the country's famous 'little red master'...." Father whispered the wealthy son's name as if it were a state secret.

Bored to the stars with nothing to do, I lay on the bed with my brother and sister singing "We Are the Heirs of Communism," the two of them deliberately veering off-key at the end, infuriating me—this wasn't just a matter of respect for the eldest sibling but respect for our reputable surroundings. I lodged a complaint to Father, who rubbed my head and said, "They're smaller than you, you should be more patient with them."

During those difficult times, the children came to the institute where they could eat much better. We felt so bad for them we sometimes bought them a few pieces of Gaoji candy. Seeing the kids so happy as they sucked on those sweets gave us some measure of consolation. Having to endure such straitened circumstances for so long, we tried hard to think of ways to improve our children's diets, afraid the undernourishment would affect their normal growth development. The institute allocated a plot of land on campus for a collective farm, dividing up the land between the staff. I planted mung beans and white yams on the third of a mu of land given to me; I had little time to tend it, though come autumn, lo and behold, the harvest wasn't meager. Zhenkai and I loaded the mung beans and white yams into burlap bags and brought our bounty home, adding to our rations. (*From my father's notebook*)

That was my first run-in with physical labor. Under the cruel sun, I used a spade to dig up the yams, then shook out the lumps of earth and bundled them into the burlap bags. Father pedaled the flatbed tricycle; I sat on the lumpy burlap, swelling with pride at the fruits of our toil, prouder still for rising to an equal footing with my father.

The white yams stored in a heap on the balcony through the winter started to rot; I sat on a little stool gnawing on a mushy tuber. Father had just bought his Peony radio–record player. The radio broadcast the "Spring Festival Overture" over and over, soaking into memory's abyss, along with the taste of mushy white yam.

5

In the summer of 1974, my father bought Zhonghua Book Company's newly published forty-eight volume *Draft History of the Qing*; the whole set wouldn't fit on our bookshelf so a tall stack formed on the floor beside his bed. I noticed that he always flipped through the same volume. Evidently, many accounts of our ancestors filled the pages in that one tome.

Our family genealogy could only be traced as far back as the period of Kangxi, the second Qing emperor, our ancestral home in Huizhou, Xiuning County, Anhui Province; in the twenty-seventh year of his reign, Zhao Chengheng moved to An County in Zhejiang Province, today's Huzhou. Our ancestors' residence, Qing Lan ("Surging Waters of the Qing") Hall, used to be located on Huzhou's Zhu An Lane, its earliest master, Zhao Bingyan, held the position of provincial governor of Hunan, deputy minister of justice. From a young age, his third son, Zhao Jingxian, studied under Yu Hongjian, the father of the prominent Qing dynasty scholar Yu Yue; and with Yu Yue, he successfully passed the triennial provincial imperial exam. Yu Yue observed, "As a child, unrestrained, though with the graces of a feudal son, as well as chivalric airs, Zhao gambled and reveled in drink, his spirit one of abundant integrity." Later, Zhao Jingxian donated vast sums to acquire the title of prefectural magistrate, but he never took office.

The Taiping Army sprang into being; Zhao Jingxian organized the training of a local militia in Huzhou and plated the west city gate in bronze (the names Bronze Gate and Bronze Bridge are still used in Huzhou to this day). In February 1860, Li Xiucheng's mighty army descended on Huzhou. Zhao Jingxian and the militia forces tenaciously guarded their city for more than two years. In the annals of Qing history, this is known as the Battle to Defend Huzhou. The Qing government wanted to save this talented commanding officer and appointed him to a different post as the leader of a "lightly armed division," but Zhao Jingxian was determined to defend the city to his death, remaining there as the food supplies emptied and the ammunition ran out; in May 1862, the city walls fell and he was taken prisoner.

As recorded in the *Draft History of the Qing*: "Jingxian, wearing the imperial crest, spoke to the traitors, 'Kill me swiftly, do not hurt the people.' The chief traitor Tan Shaoguang spoke: 'No, you won't be killed.' As Jingxian drew a blade to cut his own throat, Shaoguang seized him and took him to Suzhou, pleading with him a hundred times to join him, but Jingxian remained unbending. Half a year passed, Li Xiucheng surrendered, sent a letter of exhortation.... Xiucheng went on to Jiangbei north of the river, warned Shaoguang not to kill Jingxian, although Jingxian had been waiting for a chance to stab Xiucheng, Xiucheng had already gone, not knowing the danger he was in, spent the days resting, imbibing wine. In the third month of the following year, Shaoguang heard from the traitors in Taicang that Jingxian had corresponded with the imperial army and planned to attack Suzhou; Shaoguang confronted Jingxian with these accusations; Jingxian grew incensed, unleashed a string of curses, and so perished by a gunshot."

After the walls fell in Huzhou, the members of the Zhao clan either fled if they could flee, or died an early death. Jingxian's firstborn son, Zhao Shenyan, was in Hunan when he heard the calamitous news; he immediately drank some poisoned wine and killed himself, age twelve. When the Xianfeng ("United Prosperity") emperor was informed of Zhao Jingxian's death, he issued an imperial edict calling him "Loyal Upright Solitary Stalwart, Most Exemplary and Most Exalted" and, according the highest honors of reparations to the grieving family, established an ancestral hall in Huzhou, their deeds recorded in the Official Archive of National History.

Many years later, Yu Yue became a generation's Great Master of the Classics. One day, while sitting silently in Zigzag Garden at his home in Suzhou, someone came looking for him—the visitor none other than Zhao Jingxian's grandson, Zhao Hong. He brought with him some of the calligraphy and writings his grandfather had left behind, including some confidential letters that were smuggled out of Huzhou during the siege. Yu Yue spread out some of Zhao Xingjian's five-character regulated verse to read, sighing endlessly with admiration; among his calligraphy were these quoted lines of the Qing army general Li Hongzhang's celebrated memorial to the emperor: "Where disorder reigns swords cross and wave, solitary the crown sits when in danger."

Xingjian's second son, Zhao Binyan, my paternal great-grandfather, was given an official appointment because his father had died in battle; Zhang Zhidong, the viceroy of Huguang (now Hubei and Hunan Provinces) had the deepest confidence in him and made him the director of the Guangdong Manufacturing Bureau; Zhang Zhidong eventually became the viceroy of the Liangjiang territories and appointed Binyan as the head of the Shanghai Manufacturing Bureau, and later moved on to become the salt commissioner for the Lianghuai district and the judicial commissioner for Guangdong, among other posts. Because of troubles arising out of the nation's turmoil, he fell out of favor with his superiors and resigned for reasons of old age and recurrent illness, settling in Suzhou. Several months passed and the Wuchang Uprising broke out—among the revolutionary heroes who abetted the overthrow of the Great Empire of the Qing was my maternal grandfather, Sun Haixia.

The Zhao family, once worth a fortune, with wives and concubines in abundance, branched out wildly. But as the saying goes, *Prosperity never lasts more than three generations*; by my grandfather Zhao Zhiliu's lifetime, the family had declined, and he eked out his days selling scrolls of calligraphy and paintings, and other antique curios.

Turning now to my father, I fear he never experienced a shadow of his ancestors' former splendor. His mother died of an illness when he was four or five; by the time he was twelve, his father departed this world, too, and a maternal uncle took him in. He had no choice but to break off his studies, and from age fifteen helped his new family scrape by as a copyist of official documents, while also taking care of his little brother and sister. Father brushed Chinese characters with a natural grace. A former colleague who worked under him at the insurance company, Mr. Xu Fulin, recalled that when Father saw his awful penmanship, he made him copy, over and over again, a stone-inscription rubbing of Song Lian's Yuan dynasty composition "Parting Words for Ma Sheng on His Return to Dongyang."

Swallowed by the galloping turmoil of war, my father joined the growing stream of refugees ceaselessly moving across southern China. In Guilin, a Japanese fighter plane once swooped down with machine-gun fire and, in his confusion, my father opened up his umbrella to block the bullets. In those days a life wasn't worth so much; people around him fell, one after another, yet by some miracle he survived. He took up various temporary jobs while continuing to study on his own, and eventually passed the test to work at the Chongqing Central Trust Bureau. Then came his fated encounter with my mother in early 1946, at Chongqing's Coral Dam Airport.

The two of us first met at the time of the 1946 victory of the war of resistance; because of the war, my parents had been forced to live apart from each other for seven or eight years; I accompanied Mother on a flight to Chongqing to visit Father. At Coral Dam Airport, we wished to make a phone call but didn't know how to dial through; by chance, an attractive young man there was about to make a call, and my mother told me to ask him for assistance—this person turned out to be Zhao Jinian.(*From my mother's interview*)

In Beijing on the eve of liberation, my father used his position of power to help his older cousin in the underground party gather intelligence throughout the whole city, such as the locations of food stores, and so on. One night, the Kuomintang military police were carrying out house-to-house searches and a confrontation with the police captain resulted in his arrest and overnight confinement. At the time, my mother was pregnant with me. As my father related the story, he couldn't sleep in the prison cell and spent the whole night awake, longing for the birth of his child, as well as the birth of a new China.

6

Father loved to read, but at most he could be regarded as maybe half an intellectual. He had mixed literary tastes, claiming to be a "fan" of Lu Xun, Mao Dun, Zhang Henshui, Ai Wu, and Ru Zhijuan. And then the assorted magazines he subscribed to over the years, from *Red Flag*, *Harvest*, *People's Literature*, to *Cinematic Arts*, *Study Russian*, *Folk Arts*, and *Wireless*—it was very difficult to discern the direction and depths of his interests.

What my father was, however, down to the marrow of his bones, was a technology fetishist. Thus the Peony combination radio and four-speed record player he bought during the Great Famine, bringing *The Blue Danube* into our depressing lives. Then the Cultural Revolution sparked his new passion, diverting his struggles toeing the political line to a connecting wire: the transistor radio.

From the winter of 1967, he rushed between a variety of equipment shops, buying piles of electronic components. Our home became a workshop, expanding from desk to dining table, spots to eat quickly disappearing. Consulting a stack of reference books he had borrowed, he soldered red and green wires onto an electrical board. Jabbing the tip of the soldering iron into the rosin released a faint *zhi zhi* along with thick wisps of smoke. Whenever I woke up in the middle of the night, the lamp would be on, his crooked shadow hunched on the wall, clouds and mist swirling in the air. After repeated tests, grumblings and mutterings transformed into an opera's orchestral interlude— the whole house sighed with relief.

At long last the project entered its final phase: Father took three-layer plywood boards and constructed a wooden box, fixed a little speaker into it, stuffed the rat-stomach-chicken-intestine jumble of wires inside it, added a lid, and, with much solemnity, handed it to me as if it were a family heirloom. I packed the transistor radio into my book bag, and on the way to school it broadcast the model opera *Red Detachment of Women*; but because of a loose or defective wire, or because of a bad connection or problem with the angle of the antenna, the transmission started and stopped, on then off again, and only incessant slapping could carry the revolution through to the end. By the time I arrived at school there was no chance to show it off before the whole thing fell apart.

It was in the summer of 1975 that our family bought the nine-inch black-and-white Red Lantern television set, which caused such a sensation in our building, our family the first to have one save for the one in the home of Min Jin's Secretary-General Ge Zhicheng. The flood of neighbors into our house after dinner each day, the cheerful laughter and chatting. It was as if everyone were reading the same illustrated storybook. When a climactic moment coincided with signal interference, Father would promptly rescue the show, swiveling the antenna around, determined to restore the picture to normal, mission accomplished, but the enemy had already been shot and killed. To aid the audience in the back row, he put a magnifier window in front of the screen, deforming the picture and distorting the figures.

Reform and opening up came at an opportune moment, as Father's passion for technology pointed the way. From old-style turntables and tape recorders to mono sound and answering machines, then on to the four box-type stereo-sound speakers—the audio revolution advanced us into a state of semi-deafness. At the same time, Father spared little energy for the color television and video recorder. Once the computer age dawned, however, his soul got sucked up and absorbed. His fingers tapped the keys in time with each upgrade, walking straight ahead as a faithful consumer on the front lines. Trying to catch the last train of the new age in his old age, he still harbored some regrets, telling me that if he were twenty years younger, he'd certainly switch to the computer trade. Clearly he overestimated himself—that world simply cannot be soldered together with an electric iron.

7

After liberation, my father worked at the main branch of the People's Bank, and in 1952, by helping to establish the People's Insurance Company, became one of the founders of new China's fledgling insurance industry. As summer turned to autumn in 1957, he moved to the CAPD, serving as the deputy secretary in the central propaganda department, a completely hollow and thankless position. The true heart and soul of the organization lay with the party branch secretary. Its former incumbent was one Wang Susheng, an extremely bookish man who treated others with sincere enthusiasm; he visited our house frequently, where he talked about everything under the sun. Toward the end of 1950, Wang Susheng was demoted for his "rightist" inclinations and transferred to Harbin; at some point during the Cultural Revolution he committed suicide.

Wang's successor, Xu Shixin was the archetypal smiling tiger. Still, his exceptional Ping-Pong skills were undeniable, his ferocious smashes, his swift and stinging attacks no opponent could withstand. Though not an upper-echelon party official, he effectively controlled this small, small kingdom, everyone respecting him from a distance, guarding their words and acting prudently.

One summer day, while we were playing Ping-Pong at the CAPD, Xu Shixin challenged a few of us to a competition. With his vertical paddle grip, he'd slice a low backspin shot, then smack a quick loop drive, chameleon-like, defending then attacking. He crushed each one of us in rapid succession, our heads hanging down with funereal airs.

Xu Shixin brought the crestfallen troops into the conference room and closed the door, saying he just wanted to have a casual chat with us. We exchanged a few pleasantries and then he quickly got to the point, asking us what our fathers did at home, what our fathers talked to us about. We may have been young, but we were fully aware of his viciousness and played the fool. As I didn't get along with my father, I voiced a few complaints about, for instance, his strict educational methods. Xu Shixin encouraged me to continue, but the words faded from my lips and I couldn't think of anything else to say. Xu Shixin concluded by saying, "Your parents' generation belonged to the old society; it's hard for them not to bring over old thoughts and old habits, and in order to help them reform their ideology, we need the co-operation of you Young Pioneers." He ended by warning us three times that his meeting with us must remain confidential, that we shouldn't tell our parents about it and from now on we should keep in close contact with him about matters. Finally, he left us with, "This is the trust the party has in you."

After the meeting, Xu Shixin asked me to stay behind. He mumbled something to himself, then inquired if I had in my possession a fountain-pen pistol. I stared at him totally stupe-fied. He said that the local police had been investigating the whereabouts of an alleged fountain-pen pistol. Two or three months ago, to frighten my little brother, I claimed that my fountain pen was actually a silent pen pistol, and with a wave, shot a bullet into the wall above his bed (I had surreptitiously put a hole there beforehand). This really spooked my brother, which made me feel one hundred percent pleased with myself. Obviously, my actions amounted to nothing more than a prank, a case of turning the not-real into the real. As far as the local police stepping in, a likely deception, too, though Xu Shixin obviously nosed his way into a hodgepodge of information channels. After I explained myself, Xu Shixin tousled my hair and said, "I'm convinced you're telling the truth," and added, "You did well today."

At home I felt like a traitor and couldn't look my father in the face. When he asked me what was wrong, I told him we had played Ping-Pong with Xu Shixin, and each one of us had lost.

8

My parents visited me in America in the fall of 1999; I often drove them around on outings. One day, on our way back to my place, my father mentioned something in passing that felt like a punch in the face. Both my parents sat in the backseat while I drove, and I tried to see my father's expression in the rearview mirror. After dinner that evening, Mother went to bed first while my father and I sat facing each other across the dining table. I picked up the thread we had left in the car; it seemed as if he had been waiting for this moment, too, to clear the air.

As the titular head of the CAPD's propaganda department, the widely renowned, pioneering writer Xie Bingxin (popularly known as Bing Xin)* hardly listened or bothered to inquire about anything when Father, as deputy secretary, gave her regular work updates. Basic bureaucratic protocol required these updates from my father, though he actually had another task, too: writing reports about the details of his conversations with her to pass on to the organization. Every two or three weeks he'd call on her, first making an appointment over the phone, usually for an afternoon to converse over tea. Afterward at home, he'd recollect the details of their discussion in a written report.

As my father remembered it, most of the intelligentsia actively accepted "ideological thought reform" to be carried out in two basic ways: a small study group or a private talk. An individual of Xie Bingxin's character naturally became a primary

---

* Bing Xin (1900–1999): May Fourth poet and writer also known for her war memoirs as a soldier, as well as her essays, fiction, translations, and, most popular today, her children's books. In 1997, the Bing Xin Literature Museum opened in the coastal city of Fuzhou.—Tr.

target for "ideological thought reform," the content of her private discussions with others relayed to the organization, a practice as inalienable as the principles of heaven and earth.

This made me wonder: What sort of heartfelt truths could my father have actually drawn out? Father shook his head and said, "Xie Bingxin wasn't so pure in deed as in her earlier days. As her name suggests, her heart, *xin*, had already turned to ice, *bing*." Each time they spoke, stride by stride, she fortified her camp, always on the alert, nothing leaking out. Only once did she reveal anything significant in front of my father: "Those of us who have been overtaken by the wind rustling the grass blades are like snails, first stretching out our feelers to test the air." In her heart she seemed to know what this meant, and tried to persuade my father to send a message to the organization that they needn't bother about these trivial thoughts.

It was a late-autumn night, a night like chilled water, insects chirped in the backyard, the refrigerator hummed. I urged Father to write everything down, to give an account for himself and for history—this wasn't just a typical individual's experience; it touched on an extraordinary historical moment, it touched on the complicated and tangled relationship between the intelligentsia and the revolution. He nodded his head and said he'd think about it some more. The matter was thus set aside, and never mentioned again.

I started to write poems in the early 1970s. Father returned to the capital on his days off from the cadre school in Hubei. Xie Bingxin came up in one of our conversations and he told me she was still living in Beijing, in the residential housing for the Central Institute for Nationalities. After he returned to the cadre school, I went to call on her.

A small, slight grandmotherly figure opened the door and asked who I was; I said I was Zhao Jinian's son, and that I had come to ask her advice about something. Bing Xin led me into the sitting room and steeped a pot of tea. Her husband, Wu Wenzao, appeared; he stopped for a moment to greet me and then went out. She had rolled up her smoothly combed gray hair into a bun, her face full of wrinkles, her eyes unusually bright; she wore a blue padded ao jacket with buttons down the front, black cloth shoes, her appearance clean and neat. I sat down and took out my poetry manuscripts, including my first efforts *Because We're Still Young* and *Songs of Fire*, and a few other drafts of poems. Her overall assessment was positive, and she suggested revisions to specific words and phrases. As her enthusiasm grew, she brought me into her study, sat down at her desk, and from the bookcase behind her extracted the *Grand Dictionary of Chinese Characters*, using a magnifying glass to lock down the precise meanings of each word.

For a short while after that we met up every now and then. Bing Xin even wrote a poem in reply to *Because We're Still Young*, subtitled "For a Young Friend." Perhaps poetry and youthfulness allowed her to be completely unguarded with me. Perhaps this, too, along with my father's antagonizing role, let me draw her into a widening vortex so many years after her encounter with my father. From link to interrelated link, who can clearly discern the world's karmic chain?**

Father ... your spirit in the sky ... would surely understand me ... to say the things you want to say. That night we arrived

---

* Oblique reference to an "open letter" student protestors addressed to Deng Xiaoping during the Tiananmen protests in 1989. Bei Dao initiated the letter, which was signed by thirty-three intellectuals, including Bing Xin.—Tr.

at a silent understanding: To speak the truth openly, no matter if the truth might wound us.

9

Father said, "Life is a continuous picking up and dropping off."

Nineteen sixty-nine, no doubt a year of transformation. I was assigned to work at the Beijing No. 6 Construction Company in early spring; I picked up my little brother and dropped him off at the production and construction corps on the Mongolian border; Mother was sent to the cadre school in Xinyang prefecture in Henan; one of her colleagues brought my little sister to another cadre school that autumn; Father stayed behind to tend to things, until the end of the year when he was sent to the cadre school in Shayang County in Hubei. Not a year had passed and, *the dear ones gone, the chambers empty*, the five members of our family had been split up and scattered to five different places, carbon paper a necessity for writing letters in quadruplicate.

Zhenkai was assigned to the Beijing No. 6 Construction Company to work as a manual laborer. His first time leaving home and his parents were naturally very anxious. The evening before his departure, our family of five went to a dairy shop in Xinjiekou for a little send-off party with some milk and dessert. As Zhenkai packed his things, we were afraid he'd be too cold and let him take our family's only sheepskin overcoat. The next morning, the day of his departure, we all sent him off at the front gate. I wanted to see him one more time, to make sure he would get on the bus at Chong Yuan Temple, and so not long after he left, I quickly hopped onto a trolleybus; I saw him waiting at the bus stop but didn't approach him, just watched from afar as he boarded, and afterward returned home, tears in my eyes. (*From my father's notebook*)

At the construction site in Hebei's Yu County, I set off explosives to blast open a mountain, making way for a new power plant. That summer I received a telegram from Father: "Shan Shan's sick return quickly"; I asked for leave, bought some fresh eggs from a local villager, and returned to Beijing in one of the construction transport trucks. Shan Shan had been running a persistent high fever, her diagnosis juvenile rheumatoid arthritis; by the time I got home her fever had subsided.

That single week passed like a stolen moment. Beijing City, a vast emptiness, deserted, hardly a single visitor in Beihai Park. We rowed a boat, snapped photos, ate lunch at the Hall of Rippling Water. Father ordered crispy fried meatballs for me, and for Shan Shan braised fish in brown sauce. He drank a bottle of beer and, a little tipsy, said to the waitress, "This is my son and daughter ... as you can see my good fortune overflows."

Each year we were given twelve days of home leave, plus holidays, which gave me something to look forward to during the misery of my daily life. My first days off I went to visit family in Henan and Hubei Provinces, then traveled around a bit, *wandering through mountains, playing in waters*. Later the same year I set out from Mother's cadre school in Henan, and together with Shan Shan, went to visit Father in Shayang. The second year I journeyed alone from Henan to Hubei; at the time, Father had been transferred from the cadre school to work in the fields, and was living with a family in a local village.

I had been living on the Five-Stars Farm No. 3 Production Team in Gaoqiao Village. One day I was working in the fields and someone came to tell me that Zhenkai had arrived. I hurried back to the residence, and from a distance I could see him squatting by the pond, washing my clothes. He had taken my bedsheets, clothes, everything to wash, and had even swept up my pigsty of a room. That evening, my landlord asked his son to go buy some tofu, treating Zhenkai like a guest of honor. For three meals a day the local peasants only ate pickled leeks—tofu was very precious indeed. Zhenkai had brought three cans of meat. The next day, we walked together to town and ate at a tiny restaurant there; I alone inhaled the three cans of meat. Zhenkai watched me devour my food wolf-and-tiger style, and felt pity for me; although he didn't say anything, I could see it in his expression. (*From my father's notebook*)

At the end of autumn in 1971, Father came back to the capital for a few days. On the eve of his return, I cooked up a few small dishes, father and son drinking and chatting. I brought up the recent September 13 Incident, the questionable circumstances of Vice Chairman Lin Biao's plane crash in Mongolia, the more I spoke the more emotional I became. Father simply parroted assent. Intoxicated, we passed out across the desk from each other. Early the next morning, I woke up and discovered my father staring blankly at the ceiling; a long duration passing before he opened his mouth, repeating the same warning over and over to me—to avoid provoking a fatal disaster, I mustn't speak carelessly beyond the walls of the house. For the first time ever, out of an alcoholic stupor, father and son formed a political alliance.

Spring Festival 1972, our whole family reunited in Beijing. I gave a draft of my poem "Hello, One Hundred Flowers Mountain" to my father to read. I didn't foresee that he'd order me to burn it immediately, the line "Green sunbeams scatter and flee through the seams" really terrifying him. I could see the fear in his eyes, and with no other recourse, I obeyed his command. I decided right then to never show him another poem of mine again.

10

In 1972, my parents returned home from distant climes and transferred to the cadre school in Shahe, in Hebei, just outside of Beijing, where my mother worked in the infirmary; Shan Shan remained in the Xiangfan district in Hubei, working as a technician in a munitions factory.

Father turned fifty that year, still full of youthful vigor, each day toiling away in the fields. My parents would come home to rest on the weekends; my little brother malingered around Beijing; our empty void of an abode suddenly seemed crowded again. My friends of the three religions and nine schools, a motley crew, shuttled in and out of our place, bewildering my father with their riot of flowers, particularly Peng Gang, Jiang Shiwei (the poet Mang Ke), and others of the avant-garde, who could be compared, more or less, to space aliens. Apart from

Shi Kangcheng and Liu Yudeng, the others suffered the cold shoulder of a shut door. One mention of my father and their conditioned reflex would be to stick out their tongue.

Peng Gang forged me a canvas of Isaac Levitan's oil painting *Lake* and fixed it above my bed. Peng Gang's interpretation of Levitan had no relation to the styles of nineteenth-century Russian painting, its *accordatura* transformed into burnt-ocher ash-grays, reminiscent of the half-crazed expression in his eyes. Indeed, his version served as an archetypal work of expressionism.

In the small space of our house, Father paced back and forth like a lion in a cage, casting a sidelong glance at the painting each time he passed it; one could feel the trembling within him, caused by fear and anger, Peng Gang's Levitan apparently distressing him deeply—plain proof that modernist aesthetics chafes against the patterns of the real world, creating friction. One night, Father finally exploded, and with a roar ordered me to take down the painting. I refused. He pulled it down from the wall and tore it with one stroke in half. By chance, right beside it hung an ink-and-wash portrait of my father that his younger brother Zhao Yannian had painted for him, and *as courtesy demands reciprocity*, I handily grabbed it and hurled it to the floor with feral ferocity, the picture frame shattering to pieces.

Each time we fought, it usually ended the same way—him opening the door and shouting, "This is not your house, get out of my sight!" If I couldn't get back to the construction site, I'd go to Shi Kangcheng's or Liu Yu's place and sleep on the floor; ultimately, my mother would appear as peacemaker, soothing me to come back home.

Summer 1975: In a spasm of rage after another big fight

with my father, I took a trip with Liu Yu to climb Wutai Mountain. Returning home ten days later, I found Shan Shan had come back, too, to mind some business in the city. Our brother-and-sister bond ran quite deep, and not wanting to worry her about any family dispute, I tried my best to conceal the situation. But during her stay, Father and I had another infuriating row. Deep in the night, while waiting for things to simmer down, Shan Shan and I stared at each other silently in the kitchen. She mournfully leaned against the wall; I stood over the sink, the faucet *di di da da* dripping, dripping.

Life is a continuous picking up and dropping off—and inevitably a last time will come. The last time we dropped Shan Shan off, the trolleybus was so crowded and slow we only had ten minutes to spare by the time we reached the Beijing railway station. We charged onto the platform, somehow stuffed her luggage atop a crammed rack, the cars clanged, began to rock, and steadily, little by little, pushed forward as she waved from the train window—we had barely exchanged three sentences. Who could have known that it would be our final parting.

On the night of July 27, 1976, at the reception office at the main gate, I received a long-distance call. Shan Shan had disappeared while swimming to someone's rescue. I rode my bike immediately to the telegraph building and cabled my father and little brother at the outskirts of the city with the news. In the zero-dark hours of the morning, the mountains shook and the earth trembled—what would become known as the Great Tangshan earthquake struck, killing hundreds of thousands of people. My father and brother returned home around midday; all the residents had gathered in the courtyard, including my mother, who stood in a stupor, already half crazed.

My father and I decided to leave right away for Xiangfan. We hurried upstairs to pack. I followed closely behind him as he stumbled up, staggering, practically scrambling and tumbling all the way up to the fourth floor. His old tears fell freely as he murmured to himself. I impulsively embraced him and bitterly wept with him, promising from then on to never fight with him again.

Too excruciating to recollect, the trip to Xiangfan passed like a journey to hell.

During the two years that followed, *troubled clouds and wretched mists* hung over our family. I asked a fellow brother from the construction site, Chen Quanqing, to come perform some *kuaibanshu* ("quick clapper talks"), witty storytelling with bamboo-clapper accompaniment, for my parents, and won some laughs from them.

But after two years of chronic depression, my mother developed an acute psychogenic psychosis. Each of us took turns caring for her.

A mother, suffering the pain and sorrow of losing a daughter, reaches the edge of a complete psychological collapse; but then to reach further, to prevail over the illness, so much strength needed, so much willpower—Jinian took me hand in hand, picked me up, supported me so I could stand strong to face this test of life or death. Jinian often consoled me by saying that our daughter sacrificed herself to save someone else, one life saving another life. The root of life is impermanence, and life itself so precious, one must live on with steadfast tenacity, for one's own life and the lives of others. (*From my mother's interview*)

11

In 1979 the People's Insurance Company of China opened for business again. My father transferred back from Min Jin, returning as the director of the domestic sales department. All day he flitted to and fro, tending to meetings, researching markets, the joys of being excessively busy. When I got married in the fall of 1980 and moved out of the house, my relationship with him noticeably improved.

Ordinarily, with others so busy as well, we'd try to get together on certain weekends or over New Year's and other holidays to eat, play mahjong, ramble on about this or that, yakking east to west. The decade of the 1980s was *a white corridor connecting two nights*—danger signs lurked here and there, shadows emerging from shadows, yet everyone seemed so full of hope, until we entered a night of even greater loss, of the people wholly lost.

I left China in the spring of 1989. Two years later, my parents brought my daughter, Tiantian, to see me in Denmark. Mother broke her leg and could only walk with great difficulty, so my father and I took turns pushing her in a wheelchair. Father had retired the previous year and he looked old, his body shrunken, mouth full of false teeth; I imagine we both couldn't stand the sight of each other. I still bickered with my father, but rarely fought, a state of affairs equivalent to a cold war. Whenever we went out on foot, I'd deliberately push my mother at a trot, leaving him far, far behind, then turning around I'd see his wisp of a figure *too weak to stand up to a gust of wind*, pity once again rising in my heart, and I'd slow my pace back down.

Father became embroiled in a number of humorous situations abroad that made for amusing stories to tell friend and relatives back home. While in Denmark, Tian Tian's pair of little parrots died, so Father took her to the pet shop to fill the vacancy. With the few words in English he could manage, he said to the shopkeeper, "One bird dead," and nothing more, causing the shopkeeper to rub his head in perplexity. When I came home after teaching my class, I discovered three parrots in the cage.

One Sunday morning in Paris, Father went out alone with his video camera. A young lad approached him with generous cordiality, gesturing animatedly that he could take some footage of my father. Once the video camera landed in his hands, however, he took to his heels and ran off. Father pursued him closely, various passersby tried to cut him off and encircle him, the thief panicked and scurried into his own home. Some people called the police, who quickly arrived, found the perpetrator, and recovered the stolen item. The most interesting part of the story was that my father went to the police station to file a statement, not knowing a word of French, and yet miraculously a detailed, thorough account was successfully transcribed. It turned out that the video camera had been running the whole time, recording the entire course of events, from the wobbling earth to the thief's gasps for breath. That year my father turned seventy-three.

After I had settled for a while in California, my parents came to stay with me on two separate visits. Life in rural America was boring to the extreme. Being so busy with work, I could only take them out on the occasional excursion, giving them intermittent relief from the tedium. At some point in the 1980s, my status and role in relation to my father reversed—from that point on he listened to my advice and almost always followed it, or at least *his mouth said yes even if his heart rebuffed*. We had never been equals, and from time to time I've felt a deep desire to be his friend, to express the true feelings in my heart, and so on, but have found it impossible to do so.

In truth, within the heart of many Chinese-blooded men resides a little tyrant who plays a complicated role: In society, the little tyrant is essentially a magistrate's servant, a docile subject, true to the menial tasks at hand and *never crosses Lei Chi River for the capital*, taking not one pace over the fixed boundary; but then, *once rich his face changes*, and he treats rivals and commoners with vicious cruelty, something particularly apparent with each successive generation of political rebels, the key being to switch smoothly, no need for a period of transition. In the family, the little tyrant rules by force, with no equals to speak of, neither wife nor child, to the degree that the master of the house has everyone in the palm of his hand.

Until I became a father, I didn't realize that this tyrant consciousness arose from the bloodline, from the depths of civilization, deep-rooted, ingrained; it would be difficult for even a renegade outlaw like me to escape it. Looking back on the paternal life-road my father walked, I can recognize my own footprints, *step by step blindly following*, crisscrossing, coinciding—this discovery shocked me to the core.

The end of 1999 neared, the arrival of the rumored apocalypse at hand. Driving back home from San Francisco, night deepening, moon gigantic and round, glowing with golden light, surely a sign of the end of days. Father sat in the back, blabbering to himself, "How did I live to such a great age ... each life has its fated span, right?"

I remember a spring day when I was nine and Father took me to Beihai Park to play. On the road home the gloaming surrounded us, a slight chill in the air of the seasonal thaw. We strolled along the edge of the lake and exited through the back gate. After two or three hundred meters, my father's steps slowed, he scanned the people drifting by, and suddenly turned to me and said, "All the people around us here, a hundred years from now, everyone will be gone, us included." I froze, then raised my head to look at my father; his glasses glinted and a hint of a jeering grin exposed itself.

12

On December 2, 2001, I took an American Airlines flight from San Francisco to Beijing and experienced the pleasures of special treatment upon my arrival—the welcoming committee, the sleek black sedan.

When my father saw me from his sickbed, he burst into tears like a child. I sat beside him and held his hand firmly, not knowing how to console him. With quick-witted resourcefulness, I whipped out the new digital camera I had bought for him, ready to let technological fetishism work its comforting, calming magic. But his left hand could no longer obey his commands, and the camera sat idle.

Father had kidney cancer and hepatitis B, plus suffered paralysis of the left side of his body. He could only shuffle along with excruciating effort, while his mind remained sharp. He needed a walker to use the bathroom. I encouraged him, trying to convince him that persevering with his physical therapy would lead to his recovery.

Each day I'd visit relatives, meet up with friends, come home in the evening to be with my father, sit by his bedside, pour some red wine into a glass that he'd sip with a straw, reveling a bit in this drunken world. When he took out his false teeth, his cheeks sank into two pits, gaze vacant. He told me that he had asked the doctor if being cremated hurts or not. His attempt at confronting death with humor.

Before my father died I was able to obtain official permission for three visits from the state, each visit lasting no longer than a month. Owing to the fierce tenaciousness of his conscious will to survive, he crossed one critical pass to the next, until half a year later he experienced a total breakdown and needed heavy medication to keep going. The second blood clot in his brain destroyed his verbal abilities, an unimaginable torment for a person like him with the gift of the gab. His voice couldn't come out, so he used his finger to write on my hand while making otherworldly *yi yi yi ya ya ya* chirping sounds.

Every morning during my time with him I'd cook a few dishes and pack them into insulated containers to bring to room 304 at the hospital, where I'd spoon-feed him each bite. I wanted to speak to him so much, but it would only stir up his emotions, make him agitated not being able to reply, cause him even more pain. Every time I returned and saw the helpless expression in his eyes and his stiff, rigid tongue, it felt as if a knife pierced my heart.

On January 11, 2003, a Saturday, I arrived at room 304 around ten in the morning as usual. I was supposed to fly back to the States the next day. Around midday, I finished feeding him lunch and helped him shave with an electric razor. We all knew the final moment had arrived. His tongue flopped frantically in his mouth, until suddenly, a few distinct words spilled out: "I love you." I embraced him: "Baba, I love you too." As far back as my memory allows, this was the first and last time we ever spoke to each other in this way.

Early the next morning, on my way to the airport, I had originally intended to stop by to say good-bye once more, but there wasn't enough time. I sat in my seat in the cabin, the velvety soft voice of the stewardess came over the intercom, soon the plane would take off. I turned toward Beijing City, toward the place where Father would be, and offered a silent prayer.

Father on the San Francisco Bay, 1997

Translator's acknowledgments

My eternal thanks and gratitude to Maria Lauper at the Foundation OMINA–Freundeshilfe for an initial grant in support of this translation. And to Amy Stolls and the National Endowment for the Arts for their vital, incredible backing of this project. Their generosity translated into free time to translate this book. For a translator to receive such a gift is equivalent to living a dream—a dream of the humanities.

Thanks to Bei Dao for entrusting me with the keys to his beautiful city, and to Eliot Weinberger for his encouraging feedback on an early sample of the work. Gan Qi's assistance on many fronts, along with her good humor and patience, guided this book to completion. Discussions of various questions and passages with Zhang Yanping were invaluable—thank you! And a deep thanks to Barbara Epler, president of New Directions, who believed in this project from the start and made it shine, and to the rest of the ND staff, particularly Erik Rieselbach for designing the beautiful cover. Thanks also to Eileen Baumgartner for tending to the interior design with such care, and to Karla Eoff for her meticulous reading of the proof. Lastly, my thanks to Yunte Huang for including a chapter of *City Gate* in his anthology *The Big Red Book of Modern Chinese Literature* (W. W. Norton & Company, 2016) and to Chloe Garcia Roberts and the editors at the *Harvard Review* for publishing a chapter in their journal.

About the author

Bei Dao, the pen name of Zhao Zhenkai, was born in Beijing in 1949. He is one of contemporary China's most distinguished poets and the cofounder of the pivotal underground literary journal *Today*. He has received numerous international awards for his work, including the Cikada Prize in Sweden, the Golden Wreath Award in Macedonia, the Aragana Poetry Prize in Morocco, the Jeanette Schocken Literary Prize in Germany, and the PEN/Barbara Goldsmith Freedom to Write Award; he is also an honorary member of the American Academy of Arts and Letters. In 2009 Bei Dao attained U.S. citizenship, and he is currently Professor of Humanities in the Centre for East Asian Studies at the Chinese University of Hong Kong.

In addition to *City Gate, Open Up*, New Directions publishes eight books by Bei Dao: *At The Sky's Edge: Poems 1991– 1996, The August Sleepwalker, Forms of Distance, Midnight's Gate, Old Snow, The Rose of Time: New and Selected Poems, Unlock*, and *Waves*.

New Directions Paperbooks—a partial listing

Martín Adán, The Cardboard House
Ah Cheng, The King of Trees
César Aira, Ema, the Captive
An Episode in the Life of a Landscape Painter
Ghosts
Will Alexander, The Sri Lankan Loxodrome
Gennady Aygi, Field-Russia
Paul Auster, The Red Notebook
Honoré de Balzac, Colonel Chabert
Djuna Barnes, Nightwood
Charles Baudelaire, The Flowers of Evil*
Bei Dao, The Rose of Time*
Nina Berberova, The Ladies From St. Petersburg
Max Blecher, Adventures in Immediate Irreality
Roberto Bolaño, By Night in Chile
Distant Star
Last Evenings on Earth
Nazi Literature in the Americas
Jorge Luis Borges, Labyrinths
Professor Borges
Seven Nights
Coral Bracho, Firefly Under the Tongue*
Kamau Brathwaite, Ancestors
Basil Bunting, Complete Poems
Anne Carson, Antigonick
Glass, Irony & God
Horacio Castellanos Moya, Senselessness
Louis-Ferdinand Céline
Death on the Installment Plan
Journey to the End of the Night
Rafael Chirbes, On the Edge
Inger Christensen, alphabet
Jean Cocteau, The Holy Terrors
Peter Cole, The Invention of Influence
Julio Cortázar, Cronopios & Famas
Albert Cossery, The Colors of Infamy
Robert Creeley, If I Were Writing This
Guy Davenport, 7 Greeks
Osamu Dazai, No Longer Human
H.D., Tribute to Freud
Trilogy
Helen DeWitt, The Last Samurai
Robert Duncan, Selected Poems
Eça de Queirós, The Maias
William Empson, 7 Types of Ambiguity
Shusaku Endo, Deep River
Jenny Erpenbeck, The End of Days
Visitation

Lawrence Ferlinghetti
A Coney Island of the Mind
F. Scott Fitzgerald, The Crack-Up
On Booze
Forrest Gander, The Trace
Henry Green, Pack My Bag
Allen Grossman, Descartes' Loneliness
John Hawkes, Travesty
Felisberto Hernández, Piano Stories
Hermann Hesse, Siddhartha
Takashi Hiraide, The Guest Cat
Yoel Hoffman, Moods
Susan Howe, My Emily Dickinson
That This
Bohumil Hrabal, I Served the King of England
Sonallah Ibrahim, That Smell
Christopher Isherwood, The Berlin Stories
Fleur Jaeggy, Sweet Days of Discipline
Alfred Jarry, Ubu Roi
B.S. Johnson, House Mother Normal
James Joyce, Stephen Hero
Franz Kafka, Amerika: The Man Who Disappeared
John Keene, Counternarratives
Laszlo Krasznahorkai, Satantango
The Melancholy of Resistance
Seiobo There Below
Eka Kurniawan, Beauty Is a Wound
Rachel Kushner, The Strange Case of Rachel K
Mme. de Lafayette, The Princess of Clèves
Lautréamont, Maldoror
Sylvia Legris, The Hideous Hidden
Denise Levertov, Selected Poems
Li Po, Selected Poems
Clarice Lispector, The Hour of the Star
Near to the Wild Heart
The Passion According to G. H.
Federico García Lorca, Selected Poems*
Three Tragedies
Nathaniel Mackey, Splay Anthem
Stéphane Mallarmé, Selected Poetry and Prose*
Norman Manea, Captives
Javier Marías, Your Face Tomorrow (3 volumes)
Bernadette Mayer, Works & Days
Thomas Merton, New Seeds of Contemplation
The Way of Chuang Tzu
Henri Michaux, Selected Writings
Dunya Mikhail, The War Works Hard

*BILINGUAL EDITION

For a complete listing, request a free catalog from New Directions, 80 8th Avenue, New York, NY 10011
or visit us online at ndbooks.com